bbni for a

EDWARD
·VII·

EDWARD VII

·VII·

GEORGE PLUMPTRE

PAVILION

First published in Great Britain in 1995 by
PAVILION BOOKS LIMITED
26 Upper Ground, London SE1 9PD
Text copyright © George Plumptre 1995

The moral right of the author has been asserted.

Designed by Nigel Partridge

A CIP catalogue record for this book
is available from the British Library.

ISBN 1 85793 0762

Printed and bound in Great Britain by
Butler & Tanner Ltd, Frome and London

2 4 6 8 10 9 7 5 3 1

Typeset in Ehrhardt by Dorchester Typesetting Ltd

This book may be ordered by post
direct from the publisher. Please contact
the Marketing Department.
But try your bookshop first.

—— ∽ ——

M.J.G.
1913–1993
In Fond Memory

Contents

THE FAMILY OF EDWARD VII

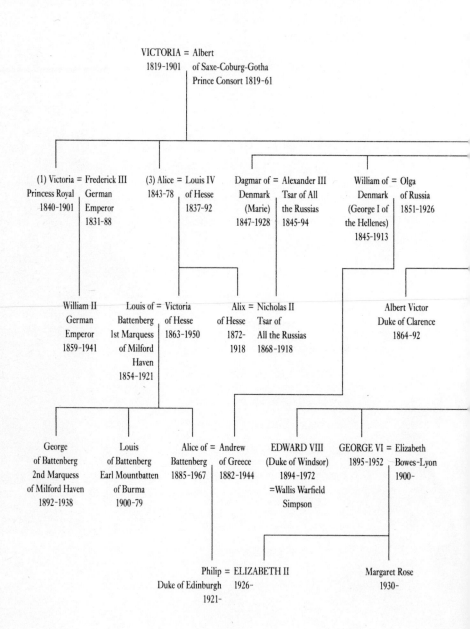

VICTORIA = Albert
1819-1901   of Saxe-Coburg-Gotha
Prince Consort 1819-61

(1) Victoria = Frederick III   (3) Alice = Louis IV   Dagmar of = Alexander III   William of = Olga
Princess Royal   German   1843-78   of Hesse   Denmark   Tsar of All   Denmark   of Russia
1840-1901   Emperor   1837-92   (Marie)   the Russias   (George I of   1851-1926
1831-88   1847-1928   1845-94   the Hellenes)
1845-1913

William II   Louis of = Victoria   Alix = Nicholas II   Albert Victor
German   Battenberg   of Hesse   of Hesse   Tsar of   Duke of Clarence
Emperor   1st Marquess   1863-1950   1872-   All the Russias   1864-92
1859-1941   of Milford   1918   1868-1918
Haven
1854-1921

George   Louis   Alice of = Andrew   EDWARD VIII   GEORGE VI = Elizabeth
of Battenberg   of Battenberg   Battenberg   of Greece   (Duke of Windsor)   1895-1952   Bowes-Lyon
2nd Marquess   Earl Mountbatten   1885-1967   1882-1944   1894-1972   1900-
of Milford Haven   of Burma   =Wallis Warfield
1892-1938   1900-79   Simpson

Philip = ELIZABETH II   Margaret Rose
Duke of Edinburgh   1926-   1930-
1921-

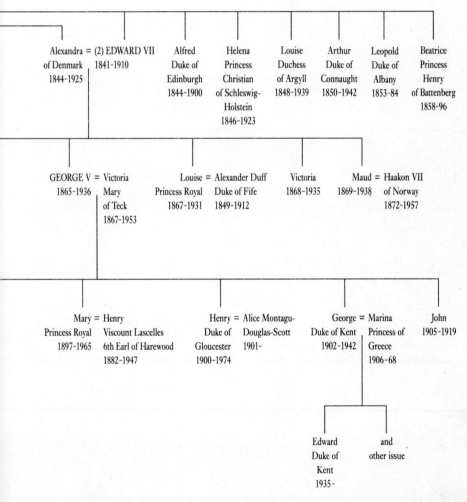

Alexandra = (2) EDWARD VII
of Denmark   1841-1910
1844-1925

Alfred
Duke of
Edinburgh
1844-1900

Helena
Princess
Christian
of Schleswig-
Holstein
1846-1923

Louise
Duchess
of Argyll
1848-1939

Arthur
Duke of
Connaught
1850-1942

Leopold
Duke of
Albany
1853-84

Beatrice
Princess
Henry
of Battenberg
1858-96

GEORGE V = Victoria
1865-1936   Mary
of Teck
1867-1953

Louise = Alexander Duff
Princess Royal   Duke of Fife
1867-1931   1849-1912

Victoria
1868-1935

Maud = Haakon VII
1869-1938   of Norway
1872-1957

Mary = Henry
Princess Royal   Viscount Lascelles
1897-1965   6th Earl of Harewood
1882-1947

Henry = Alice Montagu-
Duke of   Douglas-Scott
Gloucester   1901-
1900-1974

George = Marina
Duke of Kent   Princess of
1902-1942   Greece
1906-68

John
1905-1919

Edward
Duke of
Kent
1935-

and
other issue

Chronology of
Major Events

1841
9 NOVEMBER Albert Edward born

1842
DECEMBER Queen Victoria bestows title
of Prince of Wales
25 JANUARY Prince of Wales christened

1852
SEPTEMBER Duke of Wellington dies

1854
FEBRUARY Outbreak of Crimean War
JULY Meets Charles Carrington

1856
AUGUST Visit to Paris with parents

1857
FEBRUARY Outbreak of Indian Mutiny
JULY Expedition with friends to
Königswinter, Germany

1858
1 APRIL Prince of Wales confirmed
SUMMER Residence at White Lodge,
Richmond

1859
JANUARY Visit to Rome
OCTOBER Begins study at Oxford

1860
JULY–NOVEMBER Official visit to Canada
and the United States

1861
JANUARY Begins study at Cambridge
MARCH Duchess of Kent (Queen
Victoria's mother) dies
JULY Joins army camp at the Curragh
SEPTEMBER Meets Alexandra for first
time
14 DECEMBER Prince Albert dies

1862
FEBRUARY Tour of Middle East begins
SUMMER Sandringham purchased
9 SEPTEMBER Proposes to Alexandra

1863
10 MARCH Wedding to Alexandra

1864
JANUARY Prince Albert Victor born

February Schleswig-Holstein crisis

1865
June Prince George born

1866
Christmas Alexandra contracts
rheumatic fever

1867
February Princess Louise born
Summer Alterations to Sandringham
begun

1868
April First official visit to Ireland, with
Alexandra
July Princess Victoria born

1869
November Princess Maud born

1870
February Gives evidence in Mordaunt
trial
June Francis Knollys appointed private
secretary
July Franco-Prussian war begins

1871
April Prince Alexander born and dies
the following day
October Contracts typhoid

1872
27 February Service of Thanksgiving at
St Paul's
Autumn End of Gladstone's plans for
employment in Ireland

1875
Summer Registers his racing colours
October Departs for tour of India

1876
February Returns from India

1881
April Death of Disraeli

1882
May Lord Frederick Cavendish
murdered in Phoenix Park

1884
February Joins royal commission on
housing of working classes
March Prince Leopold dies

1885
January General Gordon killed at
Kartoum
April Visits Ireland with Alexandra

1888
June Emperor Frederick of Prussia dies

1889
July Princess Louise marries Earl of Fife

1890
September Stays at Tranby Croft for
St Leger

1891
May First grandchild, Princess
Alexandra of Fife, born
June Appears in court in Gordon
Cumming slander case
November Fire at Sandringham
December Prince Albert Victor engaged
to Princess May of Teck

1892
January Prince Albert Victor dies at
Sandringham
December Joins royal commission on
the aged poor

1893
JANUARY Death of Oliver Montagu
JULY Prince George marries Princess
May of Teck

1894
FEBRUARY Final resignation of
Gladstone
JUNE Prince Edward (Edward VIII) born
NOVEMBER Visits Russia with Alexandra
for funeral of Tsar Alexander III

1895
DECEMBER Prince Albert (George VI)
born

1896
JANUARY Jameson Raid fails
JUNE Persimmon wins the Derby
JULY Princess Maud marries Prince
Christian of Denmark
JULY Yacht *Britannia* races for last time
at Cowes

1897
JUNE Queen Victoria's Diamond Jubilee

1898
FEBRUARY Meets Alice Keppel
MAY Death of Gladstone

1899
OCTOBER Outbreak of Boer War

1900
JUNE Diamond Jubilee wins the Derby

1901
JANUARY Death of Queen Victoria
AUGUST Death of Vicky, Empress
Frederick of Prussia
AUGUST Visit to Kaiser at
Wilhelmshöhe

1902
JANUARY Anglo-Japanese treaty signed
JUNE End of Boer War
JUNE Order of Merit instituted
JUNE Operation for acute appendicitis;
coronation postponed
JULY Balfour succeeds Salisbury as
Prime Minister
AUGUST Coronation

1903
MAY State visit to Paris
JULY State visit with Alexandra to
Ireland

1904
APRIL Anglo-French Entente signed
OCTOBER Russian ships fire on British
fishing boats in North Sea

1905
MARCH The Kaiser visits Tangiers
AUGUST Curzon's resignation as Viceroy
of India
DECEMBER Resignation of Balfour's
government. Campbell-Bannerman
forms Liberal government

1906
JUNE King Edward VII sanatorium
opened at Midhurst
OCTOBER First Dreadnought enters
service with Royal Navy

1907
SEPTEMBER Anglo-Russian agreement
signed

1908
APRIL Resignation of Campbell-
Bannerman due to ill health. Asquith
becomes Prime Minister
JUNE Meeting with Tsar Nicholas II at
Reval

October Bosnia-Herzegovina crisis

1909
April People's Budget presented to parliament by Lloyd George
June Minoru wins Derby

November Budget rejected by House of Lords

1910
January Asquith's Liberal government win election with reduced majority
March Last visit to Paris and Biarritz
6 May Death of King Edward VII

1925
20 November Death of Queen Alexandra

INTRODUCTION

In recent discussions about the monarchy Edward VII has rarely been credited with a significant role. Instead his reign is often dismissed as a brief interlude between the great Victorian era of his mother and the twenty-five years of his serious son George V, whose reign had hardly begun when Europe was plunged into the First World War. There is tangible continuity with George V in that he was the present Queen's grandfather and his upstanding, dutiful kingship, which many people can remember, presents his reign in a more favourable light than the image of his father.

The monarchy's debt to Edward VII is, however, considerable. During the nine short years of his reign between 1901 and 1910, Queen Victoria's long-established but inflexible style was moulded into an institution that could survive in a modern, democratic society. Much of the change was enforced by Britain's changing political and social make-up. Much of it was achieved thanks to Edward's personal character.

He ascended the throne after the longest period as Prince of Wales in history. Waiting, whether for his beautiful but unpunctual wife Alexandra, or to succeed his mother, was never something that Edward was good at. Restless and easily bored, for successive decades he was forced to fill his time while Queen Victoria denied him any

involvement in affairs of state. And yet, as Prince of Wales he regularly demonstrated where his strengths would lie. Edward enjoyed people, and it would be as a human king that the foundations of his reign were to be laid.

Throughout most of his adult life he willingly carried out the ceremonial duties of royalty without the authority of the crown and at the same time attracted regular censorious criticism for his comfortable, social way of life.

Queen's Victoria death came at a time when Britain was on the brink of momentous change. For many people the continuity of the Queen's reign, as she sailed from Silver to Diamond Jubilee and on, was the most powerful single factor for stability. As Edward inherited his birthright, at his mother's bedside in Osborne House, some onlookers were appalled. Even ardent admirers were apprehensive. But he had been born and brought up to reign and when this came he assumed the position of monarch with zest and commitment. By the time of his own death, less than a decade later, Edward had won over his critics.

The greatest challenge of his reign was steering a course for the monarchy which preserved its integrity and dignity. Assaults on the royal prerogative began immediately; on the constitutional powers large and small which Queen Victoria had clung to tenaciously. They continued unabated until his death when, with the reform of parliament in progress, the old constitutional order was doomed. The events of Edward's reign confirmed that government ministers would increasingly regard the activities of the monarchy with suspicion. In response he revealed how the monarch could act effectively without causing alarm.

Short-tempered he may have been, but Edward could not understand jealousy and did not bear grudges. Even when provoked to the extent of enforcing social ostracism – as he did to Lord Randolf Churchill and wife for a period of years – Edward always relented. More often his feelings subsided far more swiftly. Once he became King, bad-mannered assaults were less frequent. Nonetheless, they occurred. Ministerial arrogance or impertinence often aroused a furious private response. But the retention of courtesy in the face of provocation became Edward's most winning political asset. But courtesy was an issue over which he was never afraid to confront his ministers. He was expected to uphold the dignity of the crown and in return he demanded that they uphold the dignity of their office. He hated the prospect of politics descending into the realms of personal antipathy and insult.

In his constitutional role Edward proved himself reliable to a degree that at first surprised some observers. A faultless speech-maker, he was equally impressive abroad speaking in French or German. State papers did not dominate his life in the way they had his mother's, but there were many weekend parties when he would retire to the boxes when his guests had retired to bed. His method of kingship was more personal. His private secretary Francis Knollys was the linchpin of a small informal group of friends and advisers who included Lord Carrington, Lord Esher and Sir Charles Hardinge. Beyond them was the far wider network of friends and acquaintances, their names and faces etched into his infallible memory, who either regularly or on occasion, appeared to play a part in his wide-ranging role as King.

The breadth of his activities was another cornerstone of the monarchy for the future. Edward perfected the job of royal ambassador and the prestige abroad which he brought to Britain and the crown were enormous. His enjoyment of people was undiminished and he never lost the slightly raffish touch which social leadership of the Marlborough House set during the 1870s and 80s had imbued. Towards the end of his life, in 1908, Lord Esher recalled a visit the King made to have tea with a dancing girl. 'The King saw her dance at the Pagets and was enchanted. He insisted in going to tea with her and toiled up all the stairs – a good height – and stayed two hours!' Afterwards Edward said to Esher with a chuckle; 'You know, I have always been a bit of a Bohemian myself'.

Throughout his life Edward wanted to be liked, not least because of parental criticism during his youth. Self-indulgent rather than selfish, he gained enormous pleasure from making those around him enjoy themselves. The role of host was one to which he was well-suited and which he used to good effect. His sociability was not limited to those immediately around him, for he held a strong conviction that to survive, the monarchy's appeal must be broad-based. Sir Edward Grey recognized this when he wrote: 'He had a capacity for enjoying life, which is always attractive, but which is peculiarly so when it is combined with a positive and strong desire that everyone else should enjoy life too. These, it may be thought, are not very uncommon qualities, but King Edward had a particular power of making them felt . . . There was, in fact, real sympathy of feeling between himself and his people'.

Edward presented a monarchy that was both personal and symbolic. The two together made for an aura of goodwill which was to prove of lasting value. During the last years of his life he was often weighed down by the political problems at home, the instability of Europe and Britain's position in the world. And yet if traditionalist in his outlook he was never reactionary and he saw that change had to be accommodated not ignored. His lack of intellectual depth was counteracted by more tangible personal qualities which he brought to the monarchy and which enabled Lord Esher, writing after his death, and comparing him to the other great figures of the age, to call him: 'The most kingly of them all'.

CHAPTER ONE

A STIFLING CHILDHOOD

Albert Edward, the future Prince of Wales and King Edward VII, was born at Buckingham Palace on the morning of 9 November 1841. His arrival came less than two years after the marriage of his parents, Queen Victoria and Prince Albert of Saxe-Coburg-Gotha, and only a year after the birth of their first child, Princess Victoria 'Vicky', the Princess Royal. The weeks before and immediately after the birth of Bertie, as he was called by his family, were marred by domestic turbulence and acrimony in the royal household.

Ever since his marriage the studious but determined Prince Albert had been engaged in a struggle for authority against Baroness Lehzen, his wife's childhood governess and life-long companion. The Baroness had a number of foibles, not least her writing paper headed with a gold railway engine and the inscription 'I am coming'. According to Prince Albert's biographer, Robert Rhodes, she also delighted in 'malicious gossip'.[1] It was a struggle destined to come to its climax following Bertie's birth. As well as a battle of wills the conflict was closely tied to the political situation during Queen Victoria's early reign and its impact upon her household. Lehzen was an unashamed and at times unprincipled supporter of the Whigs, not above diverting royal funds towards the party.

Lord Melbourne, the Whig leader and Prime Minister at the beginning of Victoria's reign until his resignation in 1841, had assumed the official position of political adviser to the young Queen, which he carried out in intimate, avuncular style. She viewed with dismay any prospect of his removal by political events. Neither Melbourne's manner nor his humour appealed to Prince Albert, however, who was more drawn to Sir Robert Peel, the leader of the Tories. Victoria, who throughout her life either abhorred or adored her successive prime ministers, could hardly abide him. In 1839 the Queen's prejudice caused the 'Ladies of the Bedchamber' crisis. Following the defeat of Lord Melbourne's government, she refused to accept the replacement of the Whig ladies holding official positions in her household by Tory nominees. As a result, Peel refused to take office.

Throughout her life political trouble often combined with her personal situation to affect Queen Victoria's mood. In this case the problem added to depression brought on by her acute distaste for childbearing which she bleakly referred to as 'this occupation'. Despite the size of her family Queen Victoria's lack of enthusiasm for small children was regularly repeated, most frequently in later years in correspondence with her eldest daughter. On one occasion she wrote: 'What you say of the pride of giving life to an immortal soul is very fine, dear, but I own I cannot enter into that; I think much more of us being like a cow or dog at such moments; when our poor nature becomes so very animal and unecstatic.'[2] She was horrified to discover within weeks of Vicky's birth that she was pregnant again – feelings greatly understated by Prince Albert when he wrote to his brother Ernest with the news in January 1841, 'Victoria is not very happy about it.'[3] She was, at the same time, weighed down by the domestic wrangling in which her loyalties were divided between Lehzen and her husband, and by early summer 1841 was faced with the defeat of Melbourne's Whigs and their replacement by Peel and his Tories. Little wonder that Queen Victoria regarded her pregnancy with no enthusiasm; it was her 'severe trial'.

Whatever her feelings, it appeared her physical health was unimpaired. One witness was Sarah Lady Lyttelton, at the time a Lady of the Bedchamber. A daughter of the second Earl Spencer, her husband died in 1837. In 1842 she would be appointed governess for Vicky and Bertie. A few weeks before the birth she wrote to her daughter: 'I believe she could run round the Great Park, and she is in such almost crowing spirits at having done the doctors and stayed here, and how they are ever to move her I don't know.'[4]

When the infant Prince did appear it was with a punctuality that later characterized his adult life. The constitutional arrangements for a royal birth were thrown into comic disarray. Charles Cavendish Fulke Greville, secretary to the Privy Council from 1821-59, whose waspish and revealing diary covers the years 1817-60, recorded with amusement: 'From some crochet of Prince Albert's they put off sending intelligence of Her Majesty's being in labour till so late that several of the Dignitaries, whose duty it was to assist at the birth, arrived after the event had occurred, particularly the Archbishop of Canterbury and the Lord President of the Council.'[5]

Queen Victoria was relieved that the baby's arrival released her from entertaining Peel to dinner that evening. Instead, the Prime Minister attended the Lord Mayor's Banquet in the City of London, a climax for the national celebrations at the first birth of an heir to a reigning monarch since that of George III's eldest son nearly eighty years previously. Even the Queen herself recorded with some satisfaction in her diary that he was 'a fine large boy',[6] and a month later she bestowed upon the child the traditional title of Prince of Wales.

Initial euphoria within the family circle was rapidly dispelled. Queen Victoria declined into severe post-natal depression which brought about the final row between Prince Albert and Lehzen. A sudden illness suffered by Vicky, for which her adoring father blamed her mother and Lehzen in equal portion, prompted the fiercest of matrimonial rows. Albert furiously reproached his wife: 'Dr Clark has mismanaged the child and poisoned her with calomel and you have starved her. I shall have nothing more to do with it; take the child away and do as you like and if she dies you will have it on your conscience'. Beside herself with rage, the Queen replied that Albert could: 'murder the child if he wanted to.'[7] On the same day, Albert fired off a broadside to his trusted adviser, Baron Stockmar, who by this time had played a central role in the fortunes of Albert's family for two decades. It demonstrated the strength of feeling Lehzen had succeeded in arousing in him. She was 'a crazy, stupid intriguer, obsessed with the lust for power, who regards herself as a demi-God, and anyone who refuses to recognise her as such is a criminal. The welfare of my children and Victoria's existence as sovereign are too sacred for me not to die fighting rather than yield them as prey to Lehzen.'[8] In such confrontation something had to give. At last Victoria realized that there could be no peace in the household while Lehzen remained. The Baroness herself had to accept that without Victoria's partisan support she could no longer compete against Albert. Within a matter of weeks she had capitulated and left England for her native Germany.

The row removed the cloud that had blighted the royal household and served to strengthen the bonds of a marriage that thereafter became increasingly close. Robert Rhodes James has written: 'Both became more cautious and sensitive to each other's feelings, and out of near-disaster there came a greater strength, a deeper mutual understanding and an increased love.'[9]

In an atmosphere of new-found harmony they were able to enjoy Bertie's christening on 25 January 1842 at St George's Chapel, Windsor, performed by the Archbishop of Canterbury and organized by Prince Albert to ensure efficiency if not universal comfort. Poor Sarah Lyttelton wrote afterwards: 'My "personal memories" of the christening consisted of being squeezed very close between the Duke of Wellington and the Sword of State and a somebody with an enormous silver mace . . . Before me were numberless "broad backs" and occasionally I could just see half the Queen's head through a crevice between elbows.'[10]

Prince Albert's hard-won supremacy within the royal household and Queen Victoria's increasing desire to accommodate his wishes were confirmed by events during the early weeks of Bertie's life. Loyalty to her husband's Germanic origins prompted her determination that the new Prince's coat of arms should be the royal arms of England quartered with those of Saxony, to which Albert, and hence his son, were entitled. She had her way, but not without some fierce and understandable opposition from the political and heraldic establishment who felt, as Greville, that 'the Saxon arms ought not to be foisted upon the Royal arms of England. It is Her Majesty's predilection for everything German which makes her insist on this being done . . .'.[11] Furthermore, Frederick William, King of Prussia and as such the most important ruler in Germany, was the senior royal among the exclusively German godparents at Bertie's christening. The King, who was, according to Sarah Lyttelton, 'fat and tall, like a good-looking farmer'[12] recited the baptismal vows and named the child Albert after his father and Edward after his maternal grandfather the Duke of Kent. His christening gift, a circular shield of gold, studded with precious stones and depicting the principle mysteries of the Christian religion, arrived a few days after the ceremony. Most Englishmen agreed with Lord Melbourne that the order of the names should have been reversed, but even he failed to influence Queen Victoria for whom the name Albert had now assumed almost saintly significance.

His domestic battles won, Prince Albert's most pressing task became the planning of his infant son's education. In this he was assisted by Stockmar. Having been Prince Albert's companion and mentor for some years before his marriage, Stockmar concentrated on moulding the young Queen and her consort into an ideal of constitutional monarchy. Citing the conduct of Victoria's Hanoverian forebears as the depths to which monarchy could sink, and equally aware of the shortcomings of Albert's own parental background – a womanizing father who divorced his wife only for her to marry her lover – Stockmar stressed that the sole guarantee of success for the monarchy was through unimpeachable and enlightened personal example. The message had the desired effect; by 1846 Prince Albert was writing to him that 'the exaltation of Royalty is possible only through the personal character of the Sovereign. When a person enjoys complete confidence, we desire for him more power and influence in the conduct of affairs. But confidence is of slow growth.'[13]

Against this background and confident in the possibilities of education – 'a man's education begins the first day of his life'[14] – Stockmar set about the planning of Bertie's training. He produced ponderous documents, of which one of the earliest and longest, dated March 1842, gives an indication of his message:

Good Education is very rare, because it is difficult, and the higher the Rank of the Parents the more difficult it is. Notwithstanding, good Education may be accomplished, and to be deferred from attempting it, merely because it difficult, would be a dereliction of the most sacred Duties . . . The first truth by which the Queen and Prince ought to be thoroughly penetrated is that their position is a much more difficult one than that of any other Parents in the Kingdom. Because the Royal

Children ought not only to be brought up to the moral character, but also fitted to discharge successfully the arduous duties which may eventually devolve upon them as future Sovereigns.[15]

Opinions of Bertie's upbringing have been divided about the degree to which its demands were unacceptable and over who was most at fault, Queen Victoria, Prince Albert, or Stockmar. Of the three, Queen Victoria's position was the clearest, for throughout she was guided by characteristically unshakeable sentiments – if scarcely reasonable. As she made clear in an often-quoted letter to King Leopold of the Belgians, uncle to both Victoria and Albert, she had only one ambition for her son and heir: 'You will understand how fervent my prayers and I am sure everybody's must be, to see him resemble his angelic father in every, every respect, both in body and mind.'[16] Such strongly voiced ambition was tempered by her lack of interest in, at times dislike of, small children – especially her own. Much later in her life she claimed it was a reaction to her own mother's sentiments, saying: 'I know dear Grandmama went into such ecstacies over them [babies], so that I felt the reverse'[17]. More relevant to her own family was an earlier letter, written in 1856 when Bertie was fifteen: 'Even here, when Albert is often away all day long, I find no especial pleasure or compensation in the company of the elder children . . . and only occasionally do I find the rather intimate intercourse with them either easy or agreeable'.[18]

It was not surprising, with such an unenthusiastic approach, that Queen Victoria became increasingly vexed by Bertie's apparent shortcomings. She compared him to his father and his quick-witted sister Vicky. By the time Bertie was seven, Greville had gleaned that: 'The Queen says he is a stupid boy; but the hereditary and unfailing antipathy of our Sovereign to the Heir Apparent seems thus early to be taking root, and the Queen does not much like the child.'[19] The situation was more serious and sad than Greville's comments suggest. Given his mother's lack of enthusiasm, his father's dogged ambition and their joint endorsement of Stockmar's rigid programme, he was condemned to a childhood of suffocating control, discipline and work. No wonder that shortly after his accession in 1901, he was to remark with uncharacteristic candour to his adviser and confident, Reginald Brett, second Viscount Esher: 'But then I had no boyhood.'[20]

Initially the rigours to come were clouds on the horizon as Bertie grew up in the nurseries of the royal homes; most often Windsor Castle – which both Victoria and Albert favoured – and Buckingham Palace, with visits to Osborne House on the Isle of Wight. Queen Victoria and her husband bought Osborne in 1843 which, once Albert had rebuilt the house, became the latter's special pride. Presided over by Sarah Lyttelton, the royal nursery steadily expanded with the arrival of new babies: Princess Alice in 1843; Prince Alfred in 1844; Princess Helena in 1846; Princess Louise in 1848; Prince Arthur in 1850; Prince Leopold in 1853; and finally Princess Beatrice in 1857.

There seems no doubt that the happiest and most relaxed occasions for the royal children were when they were together. Their strength of numbers made it impossible to maintain the same strict decorum enforced when they were alone. Such family occasions were when Queen Victoria and her husband appear in their best light as parents, putting on shows or parties for the children. Sarah Lyttelton's granddaughter Lucy, who was the same age as Bertie, described in her diary a dance given in 1855 at Buckingham Palace to celebrate Prince Arthur's fourth birthday.

> With the Queen were the Prince of Wales, Prince Alfred, the Princess Royal, Princess Alice, Princess Helena, and Princess Louise, the latter pretty and one of their Royal Highnesses very like the Queen. Besides these there were the Duchess of Kent and a number of more fat duchesses . . . Then the dance began, the Royalties dancing with the rest. But the whole was a sort of romp, the little ones not knowing exactly what to do, and an unfortunate dancing master in vain trying to establish order.[21]

While the children were still infants their security was a constant source of worry to their parents, in particular Prince Albert. Elaborate precautions were necessary, as Sarah Lyttelton described in confidence to her daughter:

> The last thing we did before bedtime was to visit the access to the children's apartments, and to satisfy ourselves that all was safe. And the intricate turns and locks and guardrooms, and the various intense precautions, suggesting the most hideous dangers, which I

fear are not altogether imaginary, made one shudder! The most important key is never out of Prince Albert's own keeping; and the very thought must be enough to cloud his brow with anxiety. Threatening letters of the most horrid kind (probably written by mad people) aimed directly at the children, are frequently received. I had rather no one but our own family knew about this. It had better not be talked about; and hitherto it has been kept from me and all of us here.[22]

Despite unstinting attention to the children's health, safety and general welfare, things occasionally went awry. Shortly after Bertie's sixth birthday Sarah Lyttelton wrote to her daughter in breathless tones describing how the royal ponies had bolted:

I suppose you will see something in the newspapers of the great escape for which we all, beginning at the top of the tree, have to thank God. The Princess Royal was quietly thrown off after a few yards of canter; and not hurt. The Prince of Wales was run away with at the fleetest gallop his pony could go at, all round the lawns. He was strapped into his Spanish saddle . . . but had the pony gone against a tree . . . we should now be thinking of him in happiness such as I trust in mercy he may live to inherit some more distant day. He did not cry, showed no signs of fear after one loud cry for help at first.[23]

Fears for the royal children's safety reinforced Queen Victoria and Prince Albert's belief that Bertie was best brought up in a strictly regulated society, only meeting people who had their prior approval. The inevitable result was that he grew up surrounded by adults; members of the court and royal servants, and the succession of foreign relations entertained by his parents during the early years of his life. He was confronted with the curious mix of deference and discipline which was the only way that members of the household and his teachers were allowed to treat him. Beyond this limited circle he aroused universal curiosity as to how the heir to the throne was developing.

He was forever reminded of his destiny, surrounded by distinguished elderly men who bowed to him and called him 'Sir', and taken at intervals on a series of cruises by his parents to be shown to his future subjects – Cornwall and the Channel Islands in 1846, the Welsh coast and Scotland in 1847, Scotland again in 1848 (the visit which prompted the purchase of Balmoral) and Ireland in 1849 (when Queen Victoria appointed him Earl of Dublin, a title last held by her father).

The cruises took place during the late-summer in an annual calendar which had assumed regularity from one year to the next. Christmas was always celebrated at Windsor and the early months of the year spent between the castle and Buckingham Palace in London, with occasional visits to Osborne, which was used more extensively during July and August. Queen Victoria and her husband usually made a point of being at Osborne for his birthday on 25 August. Osborne was the setting-off point for cruises in the royal yachts. After the acquisition of Balmoral in 1848, a month during September and October at the Scottish castle became an annual event. The paraphernalia of Bertie's schoolroom moved from residence to residence and only the occasional relaxing of the timetable – for instance at Osborne during the summer, when various drives and excursions took the place of some lessons – gave a suggestion of holiday.

The child that emerged from this oppressive environment showed conflicting traits that remained throughout his life. Sarah Lyttelton, who saw him daily, and other observers confirmed that his natural character was one of impeccable politeness, honesty, bravery and affection. The circumstances of his upbringing, however, prompted ill-temper and intolerance, an over-anxious desire to please, a tendency to gaucheness with children of his own age (on the rare occasions when he was allowed to see them) and a lack of appetite for education. His parents enjoyed his natural qualities but never ceased to remind themselves – and those charged with his upbringing – that these qualities alone fell far short of the necessary requirements for his future station and their fiercely held aspirations.

There is evidence of the demands imposed from an extraordinarily early age, as demonstrated by the daily programme noted down by his governess, Miss Hildyard, early in 1848 only a few weeks after Bertie's sixth birthday and a year before the appointment of his first tutor.

From 20 minutes after 8 until 9 – Arithmetic, Dictation, Writing
¼ past 11 to ¼ past 12 – French
1 to 5 minutes before 2 – German
4 to 5 – Reading, Geography, Writing on the Slate
5 to 6 Dancing
On other days Chronology & History, read aloud Poetry
After 6 read some story book
Play with the map of History or some counters.[24]

This programme was only an introduction to Bertie's formal education, which began with the appointment of Henry Birch as his first tutor in April 1849. Birch oversaw a regime of lessons for six days a week, taught by himself and a group of assistants. Three years later, when Birch departed, there was little sign of the desired results. The tutor's daily reports on Bertie's academic progress filled his parents with gloom and angry frustration. They increased the pressure on their eldest son by responding to his supposed stupidity with unpleasant sarcasm. Their search for results was exhaustive; in 1850 Dr George Combe, a leading exponent of the then highly regarded practice of phrenology, who had first been consulted some three years earlier, was called in to inspect the young Prince's skull and give his diagnosis. His analysis was dominated by comments such as: 'Intellectual organs are only moderately well developed. The result will be strong self-will, at times obstinacy . . .'[25], which only served to alarm the parents.

To his parents Bertie seemed to be emerging as a failure despite all their best efforts. Yet his inherent qualities – which went largely unnoticed by them – were proving remarkably tenacious. If anything, the period of Birch's tutelage saw Bertie grow steadily more fond of him and this capacity for affection was noticed by others. When the time came for Birch's departure one of Victoria's ladies-in-waiting, Lady Canning wrote to a friend: 'It has been a trouble and sorrow to the Prince of Wales, who has done no end of touching things since he heard that he was to lose him, three weeks ago. He is such an affectionate dear little fellow; his notes and presents which Mr Birch used to find on his pillow were really too moving.'[26] Birch himself remembered: 'I saw numerous traits of a very amiable and affectionate disposition' and went on to say in conclusion that he would 'eventually turn out a good and in my humble opinion a great man.'[27]

Birch's resignation was brought about by his decision to take Holy Orders. This had always been his intention, but Prince Albert made it clear that it would be unacceptable for the Prince of Wales's tutor to be a clergyman. Neither he nor Victoria ever fully suppressed their suspicion of Birch's religious enthusiasms. At one time he was driven to offer his resignation when Albert told him he did not approve of their son being taught the catechism. This accounted for Victoria's verdict: 'I never felt at my ease with Birch. There always seemed to be something between us.'[28]

The clergyman was replaced by a barrister, Frederick Weymouth Gibbs, appointed through Prince Albert's connections as Chancellor of Cambridge University, where Gibbs had been a fellow of Trinity College. Birch's priggish but essentially kindly control of the royal pupil was replaced with something far more draconian, as Gibbs, with confident relish, set about the task of reversing the failures of the educational system to date and moulding his charge to the satisfaction of his parents. The degree to which he was unsuccessful was illustrated by Queen Victoria's vexed comment on his eventual resignation in November 1858: 'Poor Mr Gibbs certainly failed during the last two years entirely, incredibly, and did Bertie no good.'[29]

With the approval of Queen Victoria and Prince Albert, Gibbs's remedy for Bertie was to increase both attendance at lessons and discipline. Queen Victoria decreed that 'the temper of the Prince of Wales should be put down very decidedly'[30] and Gibbs duly complied. Not long after he took up his post, one or two others who taught Bertie, in particular Dr Becker who taught him German, attempted to point out that what Queen Victoria and Prince Albert all too easily considered to be symptoms of deliberate laziness were, in fact, brought on by mental and physical exhaustion. Becker wrote to Prince Albert: 'To anyone who knows the functions performed by the nerves in the human body, it is quite superfluous to demonstrate that these outbreaks of passion, especially with so tender a child as the Prince of Wales in his moments of greatest exhaustion, must be destructive to the child.' It is equally revealing that Becker wrote in the same message that Bertie possessed 'a sense of truth to such an extent as I scarcely ever witnessed in a child of his age.[31]

29

It was to no avail. The curriculum taught to Bertie, as well as to his younger brother Alfred who joined the royal classroom, steadily expanded. A the same time, as part of his preparation for the high office that lay ahead, Bertie was expected to converse knowledgeably with the high-minded scholars and experts whom Prince Albert summoned to Windsor Castle and Buckingham Palace. Little wonder Sir Sydney Lee wrote in the 1920s, with the understatement of the official biographer, that Charles Tarver, who joined the team under Gibbs, 'painfully sought to initiate the Prince in the classics and in theology' and that William Ellis, who was brought in to teach political economy noted 'his failure to move much interest in the boy'.[32]

Prince Albert tended to blame Queen Victoria for excessive strictness or intolerance thereby disguising his own paternal shortcomings. In 1856 he wrote to her with extraordinary bluntness:

> It is indeed a pity that you find no consolation in the company of your children. The root of the trouble lies in the mistaken notion that the function of a mother is to be always correcting, scolding, ordering them about and organizing their activities. It is not possible to be on happy friendly terms with people you have just been scolding.[33]

Prince Albert had a point. The manner in which Queen Victoria treated all her children hardly altered as they grew up and among those who commented on various occasions was Henry Ponsonby. Ponsonby began his royal service as an equerry to Prince Albert in 1857 and went on to become Queen Victoria's private secretary in 1870. For the next twenty-five years he had closer involvement in the Queen's relations with all her children than any other person. Ponsonby's combination of common sense and strong conviction – enlivened by a droll wit – enabled him to forge the position of private secretary into the integral link between the monarchy and all aspects of official life be it politicians, the army, or foreign affairs.

Ponsonby regularly recorded his disapproval of Queen Victoria's treatment of her children, as illustrated in two telling instances. The first concerned Prince Arthur (Duke of Connaught) the

Queen's third and favourite son, who in 1867 and aged seventeen was visiting his mother at Osborne, not having seen her for some months: 'The Queen is an odd woman. I believe she is as fond of her children as anyone. Yet she was going out driving and started at 3.25. Just as she was getting in up comes the advance Groom to say Arthur had arrived and was following. Yet she wouldn't wait for one minute to receive him and drove off'. The second concerned the youngest son, Prince Leopold (Duke of Albany), who suffered from haemophilia and died prematurely in 1884, at the age of thirty-one. Throughout his life Queen Victoria maintained close control of his activities. In 1878, when she had attempted to use Ponsonby to impress her will on Leopold, the exasperated private secretary wrote in his diary: 'Will the Queen never find out that she will have ten times more influence on her children by treating them with kindness and not trying to rule them like a despot.'[34]

Nonetheless, observers also confirmed that the fault did not all lie with the Queen. Greville recorded a conversation he had in 1858 with the Earl of Clarendon, at the time Foreign Secretary and held in considerable respect by both Queen Victoria and Prince Albert. Clarendon followed up his doubts about the Queen's treatment of her children by telling Greville 'that the Prince himself, in spite of his natural good sense, has been very injudicious in his way of treating his children and that the Prince of Wales resented very much the severity with which he had been treated.'[35]

If the Prince of Wales was resentful he was certainly not in a position to give vent to such feelings at the time. To his eternal credit, throughout his life he never made a remotely disloyal or critical remark about his father. Loyalty was a quality that he displayed transparently as a child and continued to demonstrate as an adult. Once someone had earned either his affection or respect he abandoned them only in extreme circumstances.

Determined as he was that his son could be moulded into a Victorian equivalent of the Renaissance *uomo universale* Prince Albert extended Bertie's 'education' beyond the classroom, albeit within strict limits. He was introduced to outdoor activities considered suitable for a gentleman. Shooting was to become one of the great enjoyments of his life, despite a discouraging introduction.

Sarah Lyttelton described the occasion at Windsor in 1849 when Prince Albert was shooting watched by the eight-year-old Bertie:

> A pheasant having fallen, the Prince desired it might be picked up, and Colonel Grey and the Prince of Wales, close to him, went to find it. Just then a shot was fired by Lord Canning. It rattled straight at Colonel Grey, shot him in the face and all down one side and leg, very slightly, all but one face wound is quite insignificant, but gave pain and drew blood. The Prince of Wales was close by – not hurt.[36]

Canning collapsed on the spot believing he had shot the Prince.

Equally important to Prince Albert was his son's role in his far-sighted vision of the monarchy as an institution in touch with the nation both politically and at the apex of society. He felt that royal contact should extend beyond the traditional links with the aristocracy immediately below. There should be empathy with the broadening cross-section of the emerging middle classes, and an interest – however formalized – in the economic and artistic achievements of that society. To this end Bertie regularly accompanied his parents in public, going to the Great Exhibition, watching naval reviews at Spithead and witnessing the presentation of medals to heroes of the Crimean War.

On these occasions the ever-curious and highly enthusiastic public glimpsed only a façade of their young Prince's personality. They were able to conclude that he was good-looking if pale and rather slight, unfailingly well-mannered and interested in a naive, childish way. What they could have no knowledge of was the fierce pressures of which the childishness was a rare visible result. Even as late as a few months before his eighteenth birthday he wrote to his father in tones that poignantly reflected his early life:

> My Dear Papa, I hope you will accept my best wishes for many happy returns of your birthday. May you live you see me grow up a good son, and very grateful for all your kindness. I will try to be a better boy, and not to give Mama and you so much trouble. Very many happy returns of the day. I am, my dear Papa, Your most affectionate son, Albert.[37]

CHAPTER TWO

A NEW WORLD, FRIENDS AND PLACES

'His peculiarities arise from want of contact with boys of his own age, and from being continually in the society of older persons, and from finding himself the centre round which everything seems to move . . . He has no standard by which to measure his own powers.'[1] Birch's comment in his farewell report on the ten-year-old Prince raised a theme taken up by Gibbs. Throughout Bertie's youth the idea of companions met with strong opposition from his parents. Despite Prince Albert's belief that the monarchy should be accessible, this did not extend to support for personal friendships for the heir to the throne. Companionship of the kind the tutors were suggesting would, they thought, lead to familiarity; unacceptable and possibly compromising. Later some of Bertie's mature friendships would vindicate their fears, but by then the structure of his personal relations, and his unfailing appetite for people would be the essence of his success as heir and subsequently as King.

His ability to form friendships was hindered by the formalities of the royal household. In July 1854 Lady Carrington, mother of the nine-year-old Charles Carrington, received a letter from Gibbs: 'Mr Gibbs is commanded by HRH Prince Albert to ask Lady Carrington to allow her son to come and play in the palace gardens this afternoon at five till a quarter before eight with the Princes.'[2]

Carrington was one of a select group of boys deemed suitable for brief and irregular social intercourse with the Prince of Wales; he was also the most important, becoming Bertie's closest lifelong friend. He was the first person outside the immediate family – and one of the very few – to whom the Prince ever broke the code of addressing people in letters by their surname. By the mid-1860s 'my dear Carrington' had become 'my dear Charlie'.[3] In 1905, when the new Liberal Prime Minister, Sir Henry Campbell-Bannerman, consulted the King about his Cabinet and said that he would like Carrington as President of the Board of Agriculture, the King replied, 'I look upon Charlie as a brother and I would like him as Lord Chamberlain again, which is now a most important office.'[4] (Carrington, in something of a quandry, discussed the matter with the King's private secretary Francis Knollys, who said, 'the King and Queen both want you but he does not wish to stand in your way.'[5] Carrington joined the Cabinet).

As a young boy Carrington immediately took to Bertie liking his 'open, generous disposition and the kindest heart imaginable'.[6] But the progress of these early friendships was difficult. Bertie's isolated childhood had given him no insight into striking up normal relations within the confines of his protected royal status. Lacking in self-assurance he often resorted to haughtiness which put those around him at a distance. Yet he soon showed what became one of his most likeable qualities, the ability to see fault in himself and to apologize.

In July 1857 he left England to study at Königswinter in Germany; among his party were four young Etonians, including George Cadogan (whose mother, Countess Cadogan was the sister of Gerald Wellesley, Dean of Windsor). In September the quartet returned to school. Bertie set off on expeditions into Switzerland and France. From Lausanne he wrote to Cadogan describing the scenery and towns he had visited and finished the letter:

> I have missed you very much all the way and I hope that the row we had will be quite forgotten; I have nothing to forgive you, as all you did served me quite well as I provoked you, but I hope that all will be forgotten and that we are as good friends as we ever have been. Hoping soon to hear from you, I remain, your sincere friend, Albert Edward.[7]

The expedition to Königswinter was an indirect result of Gibbs's arguments against the isolation imposed by Bertie's parents. In making his case for contact with his contemporaries he stressed that 'travel would remedy in some degree the disadvantages he labours under from a want of companions. He is behind his contemporaries in those qualities which are brought out by intercourse with other boys, and in the self-reliance resulting from being thrown on one's own resources. The latter cannot in any case be acquired at home.'[8] On none of his future travels abroad was Bertie ever thrown on his own resources; but pioneering was not for royal princes and his spirit of adventure never outweighed his enjoyment of well-ordered comfort.

Nonetheless, travel became one of his most enjoyable pastimes. The definitive style of the royal tour which he mapped out as Prince of Wales and continued as King was tailor-made for his energetic, restless character. Equally, he never forgot a face or a name, however brief the encounter. Enthusiasm was only rarely, but very obviously, interrupted by outbreaks of irascible boredom. His travel broke new ground both geographically and in its purpose: he used it to change the monarchy from being primarily impersonal and revolving mystically around the British trilogy of court, parliament and empire, to being a personalized institution, with which thousands enjoyed visual if not personal contact.

Inevitably his first expeditions abroad were with his parents. In 1852 the family visited King Leopold of the Belgians, uncle to both Queen Victoria and Prince Albert. Far more momentous was a state visit to Paris which the Queen and her husband undertook in August 1856, accompanied by Bertie.

After Louis Napoleon's grasping of the French presidency during the year of revolutions in 1848, followed by the coup d'état at the end of 1852 which enabled him to assume the position of Emperor Napoleon III, he was regarded with suspicion by most people in England, including Queen Victoria and her husband. But French support in the Crimean War and Napoleon III's aspirations for recognition raised the possibility of more cordial personal relations and in April 1855 the Emperor and his wife Eugenie, whom he had married in 1853, were invited to stay with Queen Victoria at Windsor. The following August the Queen agreed to make a return visit to Paris.

Napoleon III's popularity in France rested upon nostalgic hopes that he would revive the glory and prestige of his uncle's empire. The rebuilding of Paris initiated by the Emperor and carried out by Baron Haussmann, giving the city its broad avenues and boulevards, and his revival of a glittering court life were both seen as evidence of a resurgence in French self-esteem. His royal English guests were entertained in splendour at the palace of St Cloud and Queen Victoria greatly enjoyed the enthusiasm of French crowds, the splendour of St Cloud and the other royal palaces, and the flattery of the Emperor whom H. A. L. Fisher described as 'at once mystic and Lothario'.[9] Shortly after their arrival she wrote in her journal, 'Imagine this beautiful city, with its broad streets and lofty houses, decorated in the most tasteful manner possible, with banners, flags, arches, flowers, inscriptions, and, finally, illuminations; full of people, lined with troops – National Guards and troops of the line and Chasseurs de' Afrique – beautiful kept and most enthusiastic!'[10] Her husband, guided more by his pro-Germanic sentiments and suspicions of someone he regarded as at heart a mountebank, remained more circumspect.

For the young Prince of Wales the visit was a revelation. Attired in Highland dress he was a figure of fascination and generated immediate affection from the Emperor and his wife, their court and the Parisian crowds. On one excursion through Paris he had the excitement of sitting alone beside the Emperor in an open carriage, his genial host waving to the crowds and puffing a huge cigar in a manner that Bertie himself would later do. He accompanied Queen Victoria to the Invalides where he knelt beside the tomb of Napoleon I and his mother was moved to record, 'The coffin is not yet in the vault, but in a small side chapel of St Jerome. Into this the Emperor led me, and there I stood, on the arm of Napoleon III, his nephew, beside the coffin of England's bitterest foe; I the grand-daughter of that king who hated him most and who most vigorously opposed him, and this very nephew, who bears his name, being my nearest and dearest ally!'[11]

The visit ended with a ball at Versailles, the like of which had not been seen since the reign of Louis XVI before the revolution, and the programme for which was taken from the print of a fête held there by Louis XV. Paris itself and the people Bertie met left their mark on the impressionable fourteen-year-old boy and introduced him to an environment quite different from that of England. For the first time he experienced the effect that a brief personal appearance could evoke; something that he was not to forget.

For the next few years his life was organized so that occasional, minutely planned expeditions provided short bouts of relief from long periods of intensive, solitary study. Returning from Paris he was sent to Osborne with Gibbs and the rest of his tutors where he remained until the autumn when he set off on a walking tour of Dorset with Gibbs and one of his father's grooms-in-waiting. As Sir Sidney Lee described, the tour was not a success: 'Public curiosity led to inconvenient demonstrations of loyalty, and within a week the tour was brought to an abrupt close at Honiton. The experiment was too short to be serviceable.'[12] In May of the following year a second tour was attempted in the Lake District, this time with the four Etonians who later in the year would accompany him to Germany: William Gladstone, son of the politician, Frederick Stanley late Earl of Derby, Charles Wood later Viscount Halifax, and George Cadogan later Earl Cadogan. As they were in somewhat less accessible country the trip was relatively undisturbed and for Bertie, the presence of his contemporaries made the atmosphere far more congenial.

On his visit to the continent that year Königswinter was the base for a stay of some four months in all. In August he dined with the venerable survivor from post-Napoleonic Europe, the 84-year-old Prince Metternich. The impression that the young Prince and the elderly statesman made on each other provide insights both poignant and telling. The old man wrote to a friend that 'Le jeune prince . . . avait l'air embarrassé et très triste',[13] while Bertie's child-like comment which, like the rest of his diary for the trip, fell far short of his father's expectations, was 'He is a very nice old gentleman and very like the late Duke of Wellington.'[14]

In 1858 the Queen and Prince Albert announced that Bertie would have his own residence at White Lodge, Richmond. To them it was a great step forward and a significant concession, but for Bertie it was merely a relentless continuation of the same regime but in different surroundings. Coming a few months after the marriage of his sister Vicky to Prince Frederick William (Fritz) of Prussia, whose father was heir to the Prussian throne, he was glumly aware of the contrast. She, aged seventeen, was embarking on an independent adult life while he remained a schoolboy. Nothing emphasized this more than the gruelling hour-long oral examination which he was given by Gerald Wellesley, Dean of Windsor, not in private but in front of Queen Victoria, Prince Albert and the Archbishop of Canterbury, before his confirmation in April. At the same time his contact with the young Etonians had brought home to him how little he led the life of the average schoolboy. His letters to them make it clear how closely he watched their progress and how much he would have liked to join them. In October 1858 he wrote to George Cadogan from White Lodge, thanking him for sending a picture, 'a most excellent likeness' and congratulating him on 'having won the Second French prize at Eton, which I am sure must be most satisfactory to you; I see van der Weyen won the first.'[15] His enthusiasm might have been more subdued if he had been privy to Charles Carrington's later opinion of Eton, 'We were badly housed and fed, and neglected . . . I was taught absolutely nothing during the five years I was there.'[16]

From his parents' point of view the time at White Lodge was designed to provide Bertie with an education in etiquette and behaviour that would complement his academic training. If successful he would positively glow with the sheen of the perfect gentleman and ideal prince. To this end, Prince Albert selected in his opinion three exemplary young men in addition to Gibbs: Lord Valletort (later Earl of Mount Edgcumbe and Major Christopher Teesdale and Major Robert Loyd-Lindsay (two heroes of the Crimea, both awarded the Victoria Cross). They were to act in rotation as companions or unofficial equerries and were armed with a lengthy directive from him on what they should be instilling into his son.

Other than these, Bertie was to see only the politicians and important men whom Prince Albert considered the company the Prince of Wales should keep. But while his parents persevered grimly in their plans, Bertie was doing no more than going through the motions. The months at White Lodge were among the worst of his life, dominated by appalling boredom as he was force-fed his father's code of behaviour by well-meaning companions and tested on his reading by Gibbs and Tarver.

His parents came as close as they ever did to admitting failure when Gibbs was replaced as governor in November 1858. The post was taken on by a soldier, Colonel The Hon. Robert Bruce (his sister, Lady Augusta Bruce, was one of Victoria's favourite court ladies). For the next four years Bruce's progress repeated precisely what had happened with both Birch and Gibbs. He embarked with a fistful of instructions from Prince Albert as to his priorities and how he should proceed, and reported punctiliously. At first he was uncompromisingly critical of his pupil's ability and attitude. Only after some time was he able to concede: 'With a considerable share of wilfulness and constitutional irritability the Prince combines a fund of natural good sense and feeling . . . The Prince is really anxious to improve himself, although the progress is but slow and uncertain.'[17] How often it had all been said before. No less part of the pattern were the regular broadsides of parental written advice which Bertie received throughout his upbringing, none more powerful than that which marked his seventeenth birthday. Its general tone was embodied in one passage beginning: 'Life is composed of duties.'

So the programme continued inexorably. Prince Albert hoped that a visit towards the end of 1858 by Bertie to his married sister in Prussia would provide an opportunity for her to be seen as an example and her advice to prove beneficial. Instead Bertie enjoyed it more for the parties and the chance it gave him to cement his friendship with his new brother-in-law Fritz. A few weeks later, in January 1859, came another educational expedition, this time to Rome. Mid-Victorian enthusiasm for classical sculpture and archaeology, and the continuing presence of a strong community of English artists and writers (both Keats and Shelley who died in 1821 and 1822 respectively were buried in Rome's Protestant cemetery), made the city an important destination for those seeking an education in the arts such as Prince Albert intended his son would receive. Bertie, however, wished only to join the army. But his father, encouraged by Colonel Bruce's warning of, 'the temptation and unprofitable companionship of military life,'[18] and ponderous advice gleaned from leading churchmen, Cabinet ministers and academics, as well as the President of the Royal Academy, Sir Charles Eastlake, planned the trip to Rome as a prelude to Bertie's educational finale, successive periods at the universities of Oxford and Cambridge.

The objectives in Rome were to broaden Bertie's appreciation of art, to stimulate an interest in archaeology, to enable him to study the current affairs of Italy and its neighbours and to enjoy conversation with eminent men. Before departure from England his chaplin, Mr

Chambers, consulted John Ruskin on how best to foster his charge's artistic sensibility. Ruskin's reply urged that Bertie should be made aware that, 'One of the main duties of Princes was to provide for the preservation of perishing frescoes and monuments.'[19] He would not have been much impressed by Bertie's doleful comment at one point during the visit: 'You look at two mouldering stones and are told its [sic] the temple of something.'[20]

Bertie preferred the paintings of beautiful women that he saw in the studio of the young English artist Frederic (later Lord) Leighton, and he proudly bought one before leaving Rome. Would-be guests at the Prince's dinner table were closely vetted by Bruce and Odo Russell – a diplomat resident in Rome – and the succession of brilliant minds was continuous. The poet Robert Browning was warned by Bruce to 'eschew compliments and keep to Italian politics',[21] and left with the impression of 'a gentle, refined boy'.[22] The artist Edward Lear's opinion was similar; 'Nobody could have nicer or better manners'.[23] Such comments confirm how Prince Albert's earnest desire for his son's intellectual stimulation was instead suppressing Bertie's natural personality. Bertie's show of politeness combined with his boyish good looks to give a favourable impression and to disguise the immaturity that lay below.

Amidst the intensive art history and archaeology Bertie had an audience with the Pope. Pope Pius IX had recently ruffled some Protestant feathers in England by announcing his intention to revive Episcopal titles for Roman Catholic clergymen in England but Queen Victoria was unperturbed by anti-Catholic sentiment and was adamant that a visit by her son to Rome's spiritual, if no longer political, ruler was demanded by courtesy. At the end of April the outbreak of war between Piedmont and Austria which heralded the Unification of Italy, prevented the planned journey to the north of the country. With his visit thus brought to a premature end after three months, Bertie made his way home via Gibraltar, the Spanish coast and Lisbon. Only days after his return to England he was sent to Edinburgh for three months, specifically to study applied science under Dr Lyon Playfair (a professor of chemistry held in high esteem by Prince Albert, having helped him with the 1851 exhibition).

Bertie was now able to regurgitate enough of his ceaseless intake of knowledge to give Prince Albert occasional optimism that progress was being made. More often, however, he took refuge within the shell of apologetic politeness which he had built for his own protection. When in Italy he knew that his diary was for inspection by his father so on departure he dutifully noted: 'I left Rome with very great regret, as I had spent three months most agreeably there, and I think most instructively.'[24] The same diary brought a volley of paternal criticism to which he replied, 'I am sorry you were not pleased with my Journal as I took pains with it, but I see the justice of your remarks and will try to profit by them'.[25] But his lack of interest was hinted at by his comment about mouldering stones and the things that he enjoyed were inevitably light-hearted: parties in Berlin or some 'larking' in Gibraltar. As far as Queen Victoria was concerned, she could hardly see or think about him without irritation and despair, as she revealed in her copious correspondence with her now absent eldest daughter.

During Bertie's absence in Italy she had written, in April 1859:

Bertie continues such an anxiety. I tremble at the thought of only three years and a half before us – when he will be of age and we can't hold him except by moral power! I try to shut my eyes to that terrible moment! He is improving very decidedly – but Oh! it is the improvement of such a poor or still more idle intellect. Oh! dear, what would happen if I were to die next winter. It is too awful a contemplation.[26]

To the casual observer many of Victoria and Albert's comments appear damning and dismissive – as indeed they were. But, however distasteful a verdict of two parents on their child, the comments should be seen in the context of their parental hopes. Having set out with ambitions of unattainable loftiness they were forced to concede that their son's ability was not going to bring about the desired result. So they convinced themselves that perseverance would make up the shortfall. The result was years of self-inflicted frustration that manifested itself in these critical outbursts. Dashed hopes caused sourness and blame to be heaped upon the Prince, with one of the most constant sources of provocation being his supposed laziness.

Other people were able to enjoy his qualities. The future Lady Frederick Cavendish remembered with excitement attending her first

Queen's Ball at Buckingham Palace on 29 June 1859: 'The Pr[ince] of Wales was there, just back from abroad, decidedly grown, tanned and more manly looking, with all the royal courtesy and grace of manners. Pr[incess] Alice quite pretty, so very improved in looks. The brother and sister valsed together with marvellous charm and dignity, considering that neither is tall.'[27]

Despite often being at odds with the upbringing they formulated for him, Bertie did not respond to his parents with open rebellion. The first signs of change appeared when he went up to Oxford in October 1859; where he was to remain for four terms. Conflict preceded his arrival because his father insisted that he should live in suitable isolation. To Dr Henry Lidell, the Dean of Christ Church and Albert's own domestic chaplain he wrote: 'The more I think of it the more I see the difficulties of the Prince being thrown together with other young men and having to make his selection of acquaintances when so thrown together with them.'[28] The university was not to be browbeaten even by so considerable a figure and, despite repeated protests, Albert had to accept the Vice Chancellor's decision that the Prince of Wales could not attend without formal attachment to one college. In return they agreed that he should have his own residence and Frewin Hall, a house near the centre of the town, was rented for the purpose.

The Prince's earlier contact with his contemporaries had shown him the marked differences between his situation and theirs, which he was powerless to change. Now he felt frustrated and resentful that barriers were being raised which would greatly impair his enjoyment of Oxford. He never lost the unpleasant memory. A year before the end of his life he told Lord Esher that he 'hated being given a house apart at Oxford and thinks it injured his education'.[29] However difficult it would have been for the Prince of Wales to live on equal terms with other undergraduates, it should have been attempted. The result was the first of what became regular confrontations, in which Bertie showed signs of holding his own.

Despite the efforts of Bruce, who remained in attendance, Bertie made new friends. They were high-spirited young sportsmen with whom he played tennis and hunted: Sir Frederick Johnstone, a baronet and later a notorious womanizer who remained unmarried until aged nearly sixty; and Harry Chaplin, the son of a clergyman

who later held government office and was a created a viscount in 1916, but earned far greater renown as the epitome of the English sporting squire. They were to share Bertie's later passion for racing and were both, by reputation, the kind of people his parents dreaded him meeting let alone befriending. Another small success, taking on his first private chef, was provoked by Prince Albert's insistence that he hold regular dinner parties at Frewin Hall for Oxford dignitaries. If the conversation with dons and deans was hard work, the food offered some respite.

More important than the learning – or lack of it, the new friends, or the differences with his parents during his time at Oxford was the trip he made between July and November 1860 to Canada and the United States. It proved a turning point in his life and a landmark in royal tours. Originally the Canadians had invited Queen Victoria to cross the Atlantic, following their involvement in the Crimean War. The prospect of such a long and strenuous journey did not appeal to her. The refusal was sweetened, however, by the assurance that the Prince of Wales would go in her place at a convenient date. When the plans for Canada were finalized, James Buchanan, the President of the United States, who had previously served as the minister in London, extended an invitation for the Prince to visit him in Washington. This was accepted on the understanding that Bertie's time in the United States would be spent 'anonymously', as a private individual. To that end, he would travel under his title of Baron Renfrew. From the moment he set foot in the United States, however, any attempt at maintaining such anonymity became quite laughable.

Alone among the colonies, Canada had shown loyalty by sending a regiment to fight in the Crimea, but as the Prince's official biographer, Sir Sidney Lee wrote of the imperialist ideal: '. . . in 1860 that sentiment was a sensitive plant of precarious life. Neither of the two great political parties yet fully identified themselves with the principle of imperial solidarity.'[30] At the same time British and French Canada were still divided; one of Bertie's official engagements, laying the foundation stone of a new federal parliament building at Ottawa was aimed at speeding integration. There was also danger of tension between the partisan Protestant and Catholic inhabitants of the two communities. As for the United States, the prevalent feeling on both sides of the Atlantic was mistrust perpetuated by memories of the War of Independence and later hostilities in 1812. In Britain there was condemnation of slavery and suspicion that the Americans harboured territorial ambitions towards Canada. In return American indignation at the treatment of the Irish, thousands of whom had fled across the Atlantic from the famine of the 1840s fuelled the emerging republicanism. So the royal tour was planned in the hope of improving relations and strengthening ties. Both were achieved. Most important for Bertie, it was a personal success, ensured by his enthusiasm and energy which delighted his hosts and surprised even the most cynical observers at home. Away from his parents, for the first time he was able to appreciate the significance of his royal position and the benefits that derived from his appearances in public. Suddenly his life was given purpose in a manner both useful and enjoyable, and a potential for fulfilment which had been previously lacking.

When, on 9 July 1860, he left Portsmouth in the battleship *Hero*, the inclusion in his party of the Duke of Newcastle, the Colonial Secretary, and Lord St Germains, the Lord Steward of his mother's household confirmed the official importance of his visit to Canada. In addition there was the ever-present Bruce (since 1859 a Major-General), two equerries and a doctor. During the two weeks spent crossing the Atlantic the need to study Canada's history and geography was impressed upon Bertie, but from the day he landed in Newfoundland it soon became clear that it was not knowledge that mattered, but the appearance of the young Prince himself and demonstrations of his engaging personality. The key to his success – as it was to be on all future tours – was his ability to demonstrate the same good manners and interest on countless stops and to leave those who were granted fleeting contact an agreeable impression to remember. On a more prosaic level, nothing was too ordinary to be without interest: he dutifully informed his parents that St John's, Newfoundland, was: 'a very picturesque seaport town, and its cod fisheries are its staple produce'.[31] Describing his first visit to an Indian encampment he wrote: 'They received us very civilly and they wore more modified Indian costumes than those that are generally represented in pictures.'[32]

Neither the incessant rain in the first few weeks nor the unremitting programme of travel, public welcomes, speeches of thanks and introductions to local worthies dampened Bertie's evident enjoyment.

He progressed through Canada's towns and cities to tumultuous receptions. In Sidney's Lees words, '. . . although the accommodation was often rough, the Prince's zest was unabated.'[33] It was, as the Duke of Newcastle reported, his ability to 'enter into the spirit of the thing'[34] which at times astonished and always delighted people who were entertaining him. His enthusiasm at the successive balls which were held in his honour was at times in contrast to the less active involvement of members of his party. While he danced the night away, the special correspondent of the *Illustrated London News* noted: 'the nobles who attended His Royal Highness did not mingle in the festivities of the dance.'[35] At another, in Montreal, Bruce and Lord St Germains fell asleep.

After Bertie had conferred knighthoods in Quebec, opened the new Victoria rail bridge across the St Lawrence River in Montreal and laid the foundation stone of the future parliament building in Ottawa, all in his mother's name, the only crisis on the tour arose. Predictably, it was a result of the fierce rivalry between the French Catholic community and the Protestants of Irish descent whose strongholds were in Toronto and Kingston. The latter, resentful at the Prince's reported overindulgence of the Catholics in Quebec, determined to demonstrate their disapproval. Bertie's polite refusal to be drawn into the dispute or to take sides, combined with a strong feeling among the Canadians that on no account should the generally friendly welcome to the Prince be marred, ensured a peaceful outcome to the latter stages of the tour.

One of the last excitements in Canada came at the Niagara Falls where the famous French acrobat Blondin crossed on a tightrope pushing a man in a wheelbarrow. Bertie was all for taking up Blondin's offer that he should be the acrobat's passenger on the return journey, but Bertie's fearful guardians intervened and Blondin returned alone – on stilts.

After just over two months in Canada, on 20 September, he crossed Detroit River between Lake Erie and Lake Huron and entered the United States. Once across the border the itinerary was organized by Lord Lyons, the British minister in Washington who had joined the party in Quebec. It was immediately clear that public curiosity would overwhelm any hopes of privacy. In a special train provided by the American government he travelled from Detroit to Chicago, broke off for two days' shooting quail in Illinois, continued to St Louis in the still embryonic Midwest and then returned eastward through Cincinatti, Pittsburg, Harrisburg, and Baltimore. At times the programme's lack of ceremony must have been a startling contrast to royal life in England. The Duke of Newcastle certainly found many Americans unbearably basic and devoid of any sense of protocol, but apart from the monotony of some of the journeys, Bertie found the unravelling spectacle fascinating.

In Washington he spent three days at the White House as the guest of President Buchanan whose niece, Harriet Lane 'a particularly nice person and very pretty' acted as hostess. The most significant episode of the stay for his American hosts was the visit to George Washington's home at Mount Vernon, overlooking the Potomac River. Here the Prince planted a chestnut tree, a simple act that was applauded as one of remembrance for America's most revered national hero. From Washington the journey continued to Richmond, where Bertie noted that 'every fourth person one meets is black'[36] and then to Philadelphia where he visited a penitentiary and a lunatic asylum, went racing (which was 'not particularly good') and to the opera, where the audience burst into 'God Save the Queen' on his arrival. He heard Adeline Patti who had performed for him in Montreal and whose voice he considered, 'though not strong, a pretty one.'[37]

The most frenzied welcome of the whole tour came in New York where Bertie stayed at the Fifth Avenue Hotel. Newcastle warmed to his subject when he wrote to Queen Victoria:

> The enthusiasm of much more than half a million of people was worked up almost to madness and yet self-restrained within the bounds of the most perfect courtesy, by the passage through their streets of a foreign Prince not coming to celebrate a new-born Alliance or to share in the glories of a joint campaign, but solely as a private visitor and as exhibiting indirectly only the friendly feelings of the country to which he belongs.[38]

Precious little self-restraint was evident at a ball at the Academy of Music where a guest list of 3,000 swelled uncontrollably to 5,000 and the floor gave way under the crush.

It was something of a relief to move onto the subdued atmosphere of Boston. There was a literary emphasis among the visitors whom he received in his rooms at the Revere Hotel, who included the writers Ralph Waldo Emerson, Oliver Wendell Holmes and Henry Wadsworth Longfellow. Longfellow considered that the Prince 'looked remarkably well on horseback'. The party finally reached Portland, Maine and on 22 October once again boarded the *Hero* and set off across the Atlantic. Bertie celebrated his nineteenth birthday in a gale and continued storms delayed his return to Plymouth until 15 November. Immediately reports of the tour were universally complimentary, whether from the members of his party or others such as Lord Lyons, President Buchanan or less elevated figures. For the young Prince the tour had been a revelation in its combination of independence for him, the excitement of travel, and his emerging enjoyment of public appearances.

The time for eulogies and congratulations was kept brief. Bertie was back in England and therefore once more the child of his education. The delay in the sea journey had already made him late for his last term at Oxford, so after only three days at Windsor he returned to the university. Considering the Prince's achievements and exertions his parents' decision was ungrateful. The return also proved no more than a gesture on Bertie's part as he saw out the few weeks with a lack of enthusiasm only partially dispelled in the new year when he moved on to Cambridge. Here his circumstances were much the same. He matriculated at Trinity College under the supervision of Dr William Whewell the Master and again lived in isolation – this time actually outside the city, at Madingley Hall. Whenever he could he hunted with the university's pack of 'drag' hounds run by Charles Carrington and Natty Rothschild (later the first Lord Rothschild, the eldest of three brothers all of whom became friends of Bertie). With them and other similar types he joined the Athenaeum, one of Cambridge's more raffish clubs. He discovered one of the rare sources of inspiration offered by his education, the lectures by Charles Kingsley, who was Professor of Modern History. As at Oxford, his interest and involvement in the university's Volunteer Corps – of which he became Honorary Colonel – reflected his frustrated ambition to join the army, while his enjoyment of the Amateur Dramatic Club heralded his later love of the theatre.

As the Prince of Wales grew older it became clear that his parents' obsession with his future position had prevented them from planning for an interim period as heir to the throne. Both Victoria and Albert felt it quite possible that he would suddenly be called to succeed. Albert exclaimed angrily in a letter to his daughter Vicky, written while Bertie was at Oxford, that he had never 'met such a thorough and cunning lazybones . . . it does grieve me when it is my own son and when one considers he might be called upon at any moment to take over the reins of government.'[39] In the event the interim period was to last four decades.

Most frustrating for Bertie was the fact that his often stated preference to join the army, to him a sensible way for the heir to gain experience, was rejected out of court. As if to emphasize that there was no possibility of a military career, on his eighteenth birthday he was elevated straight to the rank of lieutenant-colonel with no attachment to an individual regiment; to Bertie it was an embarrassing and meaningless appointment which showed scant regard for military protocol. He was therefore surprised when it was decided that he would spend the long vacation of 1861 training with the infantry at Curragh Camp in Ireland and that, although officially a staff colonel, he would be attached to the Grenadier Guards.

Much of the impetus for the military training came from Queen Victoria. Following the death of her mother the Duchess of Kent in March 1861 she had collapsed into a state of inconsolable grief from which she showed no intention of recovering. Bertie had caused great offence by giving the impression of not being sufficiently heartbroken at the death of his grandmother, although Lord Clarendon remarked knowingly after spending Easter with the royal family: 'The poor P. of Wales who can never do any thing right gave great offence by not crying when he arrived from Cambridge – if he had cried he wd [sic] probably have been rebuked for increasing his Mother's grief.'[40] Victoria only wished for him to be away from her. As to be expected, every detail of his programme at the camp was drawn up by Prince Albert. It was predictably over-ambitious so that again Bertie appeared to fail expectations.

Bertie's shortcomings as a soldier irked Prince Albert but this was nothing compared to the news that while in the camp, his son had slept with an actress called Nellie Clifden whom Charles Carrington

described as: 'a London lady much run after by the Household Brigade'.[41] Carrington himself was later to have a liaison with Nellie, which, given the furore that his own experience had caused, produced a nervously moralizing tone in Bertie, who wrote to his friend on two separate occasions saying: 'I also trust that you have cut the acquaintance of our friend N' and a few weeks later, 'I am sorry to see by your letter that you still keep up an acquaintance with NC as I had hoped that by this time that that was all over.'[42]

The fact that Nellie Clifden was an attractive commodity shared by the young Guards officers was of little relevance to Prince Albert; his only concern was that his son had 'fallen' and that people were openly talking about it. For some time Albert had been constantly prone to illness, brought on either by worry or depression. Now his worst fears were detailed in a letter to Bertie who had returned to Cambridge. As well as the personal failure and disgrace, Bertie's behaviour threatened the very structure of the monarchy which his father had worked to stabilize in foundations of untainted morality. The situation would have been marginally more bearable if it was a closed book but no, the evil girl might be pregnant and then:

> She will be able to give before a greedy Multitude disgusting details of your profligacy for the sake of convincing the Jury, yourself cross-examined by a railing indecent attorney and hooted and yelled at by a Lawless Mob! Oh horrible prospect, which this person has in her power, any day to realize! and to break your poor parents' heart.[43]

The letter was written on 16 November. Bertie's reply was suitably and genuinely contrite. Thus encouraged, but still profoundly depressed, Prince Albert visited his son at Madingley Hall on 25 November. He was not well and should not have travelled. Within a few days it was clear that he was suffering from typhoid. He died at Windsor on 14 December 1861. Bertie had only just arrived at the castle early that morning because Victoria had not informed him of his father's rapid decline over the last few days; only a telegraph sent in secret by his sister Princess Alice summoned him in time. He was grief-stricken: the educational regime had not crushed his filial devotion, while the succession of perceived failures or shortcomings, culminating in his father's reaction to his affair with Nellie Clifden heaped on a burden of guilt. On top of this, Queen Victoria laid much blame for Albert's death at his door and the irritation which he aroused in her increased out of all reasonable proportions.

Bertie's reaction to his father's death demonstrated that if his upbringing had suffocated his intellectual curiosity it had also stunted his emotional development. While his feelings were utterly genuine and heartfelt, they were shallow. This can be detected in any of the letters he was to write in answer to the thousands of messages of condolence. He replied to Charles Carrington: 'My dear Carrington, many thanks for your kind letter written at this sad moment and I hasten to answer it. I have received a sad blow in the loss of my father, who was always kindness itself, though I fear I have often given him pain in my conduct.'[44] Such emotional reserve was in marked contrast to his parents, both emotionally highly volatile people. Throughout the rest of his life it was concealed by the façade of impeccable correctness such as he presented to Carrington.

Prince's Albert death caused a sudden but fundamental change in his son's life. The hand which had ruled his every move from birth was no more. Significantly this liberation occurred at a time when, in his twenty-first year, Bertie was approaching the majority Queen Victoria so dreaded. If Prince Albert had lived there is no doubt that, adult or not, bachelor, married man or father, a large degree of parental control would have continued to be exerted over Bertie's life; indeed his main activities in the period immediately following his father's death were those which Albert himself had already planned for his son. His father's influence might have resulted in the Prince being given more rewarding employment than later proved to be the case – even perhaps some involvement in the activities of the monarchy – but at the time of his death Albert did not consider Bertie to be capable of shouldering any great responsibility.

Alone, Queen Victoria proved unable to control the activities of her adult son. Initially, she could not even look at him without horror. Memories of the background to Albert's premature death crowded in as she repeatedly showed in outbursts to Vicky: 'I can never see B. – without a shudder! Oh that bitterness – Oh! that cross!'[45] But as time went on, her complaints about his friends, his social activities and his many other failings were either ignored or dismissed by Bertie in a manner that he would never have contemplated showing to his father. And while the memory of Albert's qualities remained the touchstone of Victoria's life through forty years of widowhood, his death in some ways simplified her relationship with Bertie. She felt free to criticize him on the smallest of issues, but others had no right to do so, and when he was most under threat she instinctively gave him her public support.

Many observers, including leading politicians were certain that Albert had been the power and direction behind the crown throughout most of his marriage. Victoria appeared to confirm this when she immediately made it clear that her future conduct as Queen would be governed by what she considered would have been Albert's wishes. Nonetheless, and while there was genuine admiration for her husband's wide-ranging achievements, the fact was that his death removed a distraction from Victoria's individual status as the sovereign. She was the Queen and her son was the heir and there was no longer a third figure influencing this equilibrium. The Prince of Wales's position in relation to the crown may not have become any easier and for the rest of his mother's life he would, at times, feel frustrated at every turn. But his position was simpler than it could ever have been had his father lived into old age. For better or worse, he was free to become his own man and not a prince and future monarch in his father's shadow.

CHAPTER THREE

MARRIAGE AND THE PUBLIC GAZE

Queen Victoria and Prince Albert had held the view that the obvious solution to Bertie's future was an early marriage. This goal, however, initially proved elusive. For a start, given that the only acceptable wife for the Prince of Wales would be a royal princess and a Protestant there were very few candidates; in April 1860 Vicky, who took on the role of scout and later liaison officer in the search, wrote to her mother: 'What are we to do? Unfortunately princesses do not spring up like mushrooms out of the ground or grow on trees . . . I sit continually with the Gotha Almanack in my hands turning the leaves over in hopes to discover someone who has not come to light.'[1] Secondly when the question was first raised with Bertie he took a robustly individual line and surprisingly made it clear that he would not be forced into accepting a candidate of constitutional convenience alone. He would marry someone he found attractive and for love and he reinforced his views with a comment which could have come from Prince Albert's own lips, 'in these days if a person rashly proposes and then repents, the relations, if not the lady herself, do not let him off so easily.'[2]

And so the most beautiful but, from Victoria and Albert's point of view, the least acceptable candidate, Princess Alexandra of Denmark (or Alix as she was always known in the family) rose to the top of the list. Her disadvantages were twofold and enmeshed in the web of European political and dynastic rivalry: Denmark's dispute with neighbouring Prussia over the status of the twin duchies Schleswig-Holstein, and her relatives. The first was in uneasy abeyance after hostilities between 1848 and 1850 and was violently settled in 1864 when Prussia invaded Denmark and annexed the two duchies. Alexandra's father, Prince Christian, was an upstanding and kind but poorly educated and impoverished army officer (who remarked when his daughter was awarded an allowance of £10,000 per annum by parliament after her marriage that it was more than ten times his own income). He was also heir to the King of Denmark, Frederick VII, whom Philip Magnus described succinctly as 'a drunken and divorced debauchee'.[3] Her mother, Louise, was from the house of Hesse-Cassel, which of all German dynasties came in for Victoria and Albert's particular disapproval. In 1859 Victoria wrote to her daughter Vicky about Alexandra's mother and maternal family, 'not a word can, I believe, be breathed against the mother, but against her mother and sisters, plenty!!'[4] The focus of animosity was the Hesse-Cassel family home of Rumpenheim castle near Frankfurt, for reasons explained by Philip Magnus. 'Rumpenheim became a centre of anti-Prussian sentiment and intrigue. It was reputed to be a scene of gossip, lounging, gambling and unseemly practical jokes which offended the earnest spirit of the age.'[5] To Queen Victoria the Danish royal family was close to, and in all probability tainted by, bad blood; they were unsophisticated, trivial and poor and their country was the sworn enemy of Prussia, home of Victoria and Albert's eldest daughter and the German state towards which they naturally gravitated.

From these inauspicious beginnings was Bertie's future marriage born. Reassuringly, the prime advantage was Alexandra's beauty. Three years younger than Bertie she was, and remained, wonderful looking. Bertie's father's first comment on seeing the photograph of her sent by Vicky at the end of 1860 was, 'From the photograph I would marry her at once.'[6] Queen Victoria agreed, but was more circumspect adding, 'What a pity she is who she is.'[7] In May 1861 Vicky was able to send a personal description, having met Alexandra for the first time.

She is a good deal taller than I am, has a lovely figure but very thin, a complexion as beautiful as possible. Very fine white regular teeth and very fine large eyes – with extremely prettily marked eyebrows. A fine well-shaped nose, very narrow but a little long – her whole face is very narrow, her forehead too but well shaped and not at all flat. Her voice, her walk, carriage and manner are perfect, she is one of the most ladylike and aristocratic looking people I ever saw.[8]

Full of natural if unsophisticated charm, Alexandra was also possessed of even less intellectual or cultural curiosity than her future husband. Her life revolved around her family whom she adored. Competition emerged from Russia, for whom Alexandra was deemed a possible bride for the tzarevich, Nicholas. (Eventually, he had to settle for Alexandra's younger sister Dagmar and they became engaged. When he died suddenly before their marriage, she then married his younger brother who became Tsar Alexander III). Thus pressed into action, Victoria and Albert's objections rapidly fell away. Encouraged by the photographs and Vicky's glowing report, Prince Albert found it easy to defy his mentor, Stockmar, and pro-Prussian brother, the Duke of Coburg – who was told to mind his own business when he raised objections. In September 1861 Bertie left his army training in Ireland and travelled to Germany where, on the pretence of accompanying his brother-in-law the crown prince to Prussian army manoeuvres, he met his future wife for the first time in the cathedral of Speyer, watched by his sister Vicky.

Bertie was somewhat resentful that he was being pushed along, but told his sister that 'he had never seen a young lady who pleased him so much.'[9] With confidence in his future course of action clouded by his emotional immaturity and by warm thoughts of Nellie Clifden, he was clearly hesitant. Queen Victoria, as so often when she felt she was being thwarted, became impatient. Having noted in her diary that 'he seemed nervous about deciding anything yet'[10] she then wrote to Vicky: 'A sudden fear of marriage, and, above all of having children which for so young a man is so strange a fear, seems to have got hold of him'.[11] She continued petulantly 'as for being in love, I don't think he can be, or that he is capable of enthusiasm about anything in the world.'[12] Vicky made a perceptive comment immediately after the meeting, when she reported to her mother: 'I see that Alix has made an impression on Bertie, though in his own funny and undemonstrative way'.[13] Encouraged by Victoria she then, in her reply to her mother's letter, accused him of being incapable of falling in love: 'What you say about Bertie is true. I was quite sure it would be. His head will not allow of feelings so warm and deep, or of an imagination which would kindle those feelings which would last for a long time! . . . I love him with all my heart and soul but I do not envy his future wife.'[14] Finally, Prince Albert sent his son a characteristically long and emphatic memorandum on the subject, stressing how much effort had been made on his behalf, and that while he would agree to a further meeting in England to help Bertie make up his mind, thereafter it had to be a swift and definite decision.

The memorandum was presented to Bertie at the beginning of October; two months later Prince Albert died and the revelations about Nellie Clifden went some way towards explaining Bertie's reluctance to commit himself. While Queen Victoria was determined that the marriage should go ahead as her husband had wished, in the immediate aftermath of his death her most pressing desire was for her son to go abroad, out of her sight, for a period of some months. Albert had already planned a tour of the Near East for the autumn. This was now brought forward and Bertie left England in early February.

Prince Albert's death sharpened the edge of Victoria's relationship with her son and the public's perceptions of it in a manner that was immediately obvious in the early weeks of 1862. Even his sister Vicky dared take his side at times in her letters to her mother, but to no avail. When the Prime Minister, Palmerston, saw her for the first time after Albert's death at the end of January, specifically to talk about the Prince of Wales, he reported public concern that she was 'not on good terms' with her eldest son,[15] while Lord Clarendon voiced the fears of most politicians when he wrote to his regular correspondent the German-born Duchess of Manchester: 'It seems to be an antipathy that is incurable but quite unjustified – it is entirely her fault as the poor boy asks nothing better than to devote himself to comforting his Mother & with that object w[oul]d be delighted to give up his foreign expedition but she won't hear of it & seems only to wish to get rid of him'.[16]

Abject though he may have been during the weeks before his departure abroad, Bertie was not inactive and important plans for his future were developing. On 23 January he wrote to Charles Carrington, who was still at Cambridge, showing his anxious and touching gratitude for their continued contact: 'I was very glad to receive a letter from you yesterday, as I was afraid that you had forgotten your promise of writing occasionally to me, to let me know how you are getting on . . . I went over Marlborough House this morning (my future residence) and found all the improvements progressing very favourably.' Because of continued mentions of Nellie Clifden the letter closed: 'PS. You won't, I hope, forget your promise not to show anybody any of my letter. AE.'[17]

On the initiative of Prince Albert, Marlborough House had been allocated by an act of parliament to become Bertie's London residence when he reached his eighteenth birthday. The act was passed in 1850 in the face of opposition by some MPs who maintained there was plenty of room in Kensington Palace and Hampton Court. As a result of the opposition there was a delay of nearly two years between the birthday and parliament voting the £60,000 necessary for the extensive renovations he mentions to Carrington.

This apparent anomaly in Prince Albert's attitude to his son, that while in most matters he was strictly under parental control, once of age he should have suitable and independent residences, was even more apparent in his determination that Bertie should have his own country estate. Only days before his departure to the Near East, Bertie paid the first visit to Sandringham, soon to become his favourite home. When Prince Albert initiated the search for a suitable property this windswept estate near the Norfolk coast would not have seemed ideal. The house was an ugly hybrid of an undistinguished Georgian manor and later additions by the high-Victorian architect Samuel Sanders Teulon. Albert would have appreciated the potential for shooting but deplored the poor farming land. Proximity to Newmarket that was later so convenient for Bertie would not have attracted him. The main impetus for the purchase came through the shrewd overtures of Palmerston, for Sandringham belonged to his stepson The Hon. Charles Spencer Cowper, who had gone abroad with wife and former mistress of many years, Lady Harriet d'Orsay.

Given that it had been his father's wish for him to buy the estate, at this early stage Bertie had little option but to co-operate even if he had had any objections. Following his initial visit negotiations got under way. In the summer of 1862 an inflated price of £219,000 was paid for an estate of 7,700 acres on the basis that it should be bringing in total rents of around £10,000 per annum; in fact they were £7,000. Although it was to be Bertie's home the parental ties were not cut; Sandringham was bought in Queen Victoria's name and Bertie was to be tenant for life. The property became his only on Victoria's death.

Having inspected his two future homes, Bertie left England for five months, accompanied by General Bruce, three equerries and a doctor; the party was later joined in Egypt by Dr Arthur Stanley, who had been one of Prince Albert's chaplains, was Professor of Ecclesiastical History at Oxford and had particular knowledge of the Near East. Initially he was an unwilling member of the party, not least because he was apprehensive that this attendance on the Prince of Wales would be seen as undue influence from one quarter of the Church of England. But he was persuaded to go because, as he wrote to Cannon Hugh Pearson: 'I feel that I could not refuse such a contribution to a household plunged in grief as this.'[18] Stanley later became Dean of Westminster, when he revealed a fascination with opening the tombs of the distinguished figures buried in the Abbey, and he married the Queen's favoured lady-in-waiting, Lady Augusta Bruce, much against the royal will.

After travelling through Germany, where he met his younger sister Alice's future husband, Prince Louis of Hesse, Bertie paid his first visit to Vienna and was entertained by the Emperor Franz Joseph – against the wishes of Queen Victoria, who had intended him to remain incognito. At Trieste he boarded the royal yacht *Osborne* and sailed down the Dalmatian coast before crossing the eastern Mediterranean to Alexandra and going on to Cairo, where he stayed as a guest of the viceroy. From the pyramids, the party boarded two comfortable steamboats and set off down the Nile, visiting Thebes and Karnak before returning to Cairo a fortnight later. The second major destination of the trip was the Holy Land, where just over a month was spent before the demanding itinerary continued through Syria to Patmos, Ephesus, Smyrna, Constantinople, Athens and Malta, across the Mediterranean to Marseilles and on for a brief visit to Paris, where he shopped for his future bride and to the French Emperor and his wife at Fontainbleau. The party arrived home in England in the middle of June.

The expedition was the last that Bertie made under his father's plans. If he found the culture wearisome, there were compensations in the shooting – although he was disappointed that he failed to bag a crocodile – and the general excitement of travelling. He rode through the streets of Cairo on a donkey and climbed to the top of the Great Pyramid at dawn. For his ascent he spurned the customary help of a Bedouin boy, who followed with Dr Stanley. The young assistant obviously expected the Prince to be a man of great stature, exclaiming when Bertie was pointed out, 'What, that little chap!'[19] In the Holy Land he particularly enjoyed gaining access to the Mosque of Hebron which no European had entered since 1187, witnessing the Samaritan Passover on Mount Gerizim in his first sight of the Sea of Galilee (Lake Tiberias), where they celebrated Easter.

As much as anything, however, it was the novelty and at times unpredictability of the journey which most appealed to Bertie. In the Holy Land they travelled on horseback and camped each night in tents. The details were recorded by Dr Stanley.

You must imagine us winding down some hillside. In front is usually the Prince, in his white robe, with his gun by his side. Close by him, also in a white burnous, is the interpreter (Noel Moore) who must always be with him as we approach any town, to be prepared for the arrival of some petty governor coming out to meet us, and falling on his knees to kiss the Prince's stirrup. Not far off come Keppel and Meade, [two of the equerries] Keppel in his grey shooting-jacket and widewake, Meade in his flying white burnous, and a Kefieh (red and yellow silk handkerchief) round his head, looking exactly like a Bedouin . . . Teesdale, [the third equerry] in brown, is perpetually poking about on the outskirts for partridges, or vultures, or gazelles . . . Around, or behind, or before, but usually as we approach the encampment scampering over everybody in violent haste to be close to H.R.H., the long array of fifty mounted spearmen, their red pennons flashing through the rocks and thickets as they descend . . . They have been with us all the way from Jaffa.[20]

Stanley was an initially reluctant member of party, and a man of formidable intellect who travelled in search of culture. It was a reflection of the Prince's winning character that his unfailing courtesy and

58

consideration dominate Stanley's personal recollections about Bertie. In Cairo Stanley was devastated to hear of his mother's death; worries about her had been a prime reason for his original unwillingness. But: 'The Prince himself was to me as he had never been before'.[21] Later, as they rode together towards Lake Tiberius, they planned the Easter communion that they would celebrate there. He also noted with astonishment Bertie's remarkable memory. In Cairo the Prince recognized, on a chance meeting, someone with whom he had once played tennis at Oxford and insisted on stopping to talk to him. 'Certainly a most useful and king-like quality'[22] Stanley wrote. When they were travelling down the Nile he recorded: 'It is impossible not to like him and to be constantly with him brings out his astonishing memory of names and persons.'[23]

The expedition suffered another blow when General Bruce contracted a fever in the Holy Land. He remained dangerously ill throughout the rest of the journey and died a fortnight after the return home. Since Bertie was approaching his twenty-first birthday Bruce was not replaced with another governor, but a 'Comptroller and Treasurer', General William Knollys, a kindly 65-year-old soldier, whose son Francis, would later be the prince's private secretary.

Bertie's prolonged absence did much to heal his mother's animosity towards him concerning the death of his father. It also confirmed his willingness to proceed with his marriage to Princess Alexandra. At the beginning of September Queen Victoria met Alexandra for the first time at Leopold's palace of Laeken in Belgium and was suitably enchanted. A few days after his mother's departure Bertie arrived. On 9 September he proposed to Alexandra and was accepted. The public announcement that followed was received with joy in Britain and Denmark and scarcely concealed anger in Prussia. Because of this and Victoria's suspicions about most of Alexandra's relations, Bertie was forbidden to visit Denmark before the wedding, which was set for 10 March 1863.

Queen Victoria's determination to keep her son and his future bride apart for as much time as possible was successful. During the six months they were betrothed they spent three days together. In the autumn Bertie was sent to join his sister Vicky and her husband Frederick for a Mediterranean cruise in the royal yacht, *Osborne*. The Prussian Crown Prince and his wife were relieved to escape the wave of anti-British sentiment, stirred up in their country by Otto van Bismarck's recent policies, which focused personally on the British crown princess. Bertie was less happy, not least because it meant spending his twenty-first birthday away from home. Considering that he had recently become engaged, the tone of a letter to his sister Princess Louise, thanking her for her congratulations on his birthday, is revealing on how his father's death continued to hang over him. 'I was very sorry to have been prevented from spending it with you all at home as usual – But as this year is one of mourning and sadness, it is perhaps better than I should have been away.'[24]

Alexandra was summoned to England for three weeks in November. Well aware that she was on approval, she did not retain happy memories of the visit. Her father who escorted her to England, spent the night at a hotel as he was not asked to stay at Osborne. He then travelled back to Denmark before setting out once more at the end of the month to collect his daughter. A melancholy atmosphere hung over the royal homes and much time was spent listening to lectures from Queen Victoria about her future conduct as Bertie's wife with special emphasis on the dangers of trying to encourage pro-Danish sentiments.

The wedding was to take place in St George's Chapel, Windsor. Although no royal marriage had taken place in the chapel since Henry I's in 1122, Queen Victoria stated it was her late husband's wish, but her reason for expressly ordering that it was not to be London, was to avoid the inevitable public spectacle in the city, something she was not prepared to countenance. Public disappointment was partly mitigated when the betrothed couple processed through the city's streets in an open carriage after he had greeted her on arrival from Denmark at Gravesend. Charles Carrington recorded he was one of the four friends whom Bertie was allowed to invite to the wedding ceremony. Sidney Lee's biography lists him as one of six, the others being the Duke of St Albans, Lord Hamilton (afterwards the Marquess of Abercorn), Lord Henniker, Lord Hinchingbrooke (afterwards the Earl of Sandwich), and Charles Wood (afterwards Viscount Halifax).

Only Alexandra's immediate family was invited. For Queen Victoria the visit she paid with Bertie and Alexandra to Prince Albert's tomb in the newly completed mausoleum at Frogmore was of far greater significance than the wedding the next day, when she declined to abandon her mourning. The Prince of Wales wore his Garter robes and Alexandra, who was late, as she would be for almost every engagement of her married life, was unanimously admired although the Earl of Granville, a senior statesman and lord president of the council at the time, considered her dress 'too sunk in the greenery'. He also considered that the eight bridesmaids – all young English ladies – were with the exception of Lady Diana Beauclerk 'hideous when in full view' and only 'looked well in their uniform dresses when their backs were turned.'[25]

In 1869 Alexandra wrote to a young friend about to be married, 'And may you some day be as happy a wife as I am now with my darling husband and children, this is really the best wish I can give you for your future life.'[26] It was in the establishment of family life at Sandringham and Marlborough House that the links in their marriage were forged; links later to be strained but never broken. Neither Bertie nor Alix were prone to deep emotion and their partnership was one founded on affection rather than passion. They enjoyed each other's company and soon developed mutual pride, he for her beauty, she for his bonhomie and gusto and for the position he had given her by marriage. Their marriage also developed a code, difficult to understand today, but not unusual amongst their contemporaries. Alexandra was under no illusions that her husband would remain faithful or not be attracted by other women and nineteenth-century society was full of the good-looking, bold and witty ladies whose company he would enjoy for the rest of his life. But in the main she accepted his behaviour as normal and his indiscretions as inevitable. Only on the few occasions when she considered he had violated the code by either attracting an unacceptable degree of publicity and gossip, or by neglecting her to a wounding degree, did she register her despair and and displeasure. On such occasions she usually travelled abroad to visit members of her family, and her reaction brought swift – if sometimes superficial – apology from her husband.

Domestic independence came soon after their marriage. Within a few weeks of their return from honeymoon at Osborne they spent Easter at Sandringham, happy but in a state of relative discomfort later completely banished by his improvements to the house. The pattern of life at Sandringham, where close friends were asked back regularly and mixed with a cross-section of less familiar acquaintances to whom Bertie wished to offer his hospitality, often in return for some kindness or duty performed, was established at the outset. For this first visit Bertie wrote to Arthur Stanley asking him to Sandringham saying, 'It would be especially agreeable to me as last Easter Sunday we took Holy Sacrament together at the Lake of Tiberius.'[27] Through the next four decades the visitors book would be filled with the names of those similarly invited through Bertie's thoughtfulness. While many of the invitations were prompted by generosity, over the years the cross-section of people whom he was able to invite to stay and benefit from their conversation, brought considerable rewards for Bertie. Stanley wrote afterwards that the visit gave him intense pleasure and described Alexandra as this 'Angel in the Palace'.[28]

Marlborough House, whose refurbishment Bertie had carefully overseen (down to choosing the furniture), was ready in June and became the focus of their life during the London Season. Through the 1860s Queen Victoria withdrew into an existence based at Windsor, Osborne and Balmoral. She was surrounded by the small circle of her court and her younger children, her time dominated by her constitutional duties. Since Prince Albert's death she had no appetite for social court functions such as levées; they were the one aspect of monarchical life that she was prepared to delegate to her son and daughter-in-law.

For them, these court events became the formal pinnacle of an elaborate and exhausting social life. Such activity was partly a response to popular demand for a royal figurehead around whom society could focus. But from Bertie's situation it was further encouraged because he had nothing else to do. It was a role he and Alexandra initially carried out with enthusiasm. For both of them it was a dramatic contrast to their previous existences and the novelty of being fêted by society and by the larger public who so enjoyed the energetic prince and his beautiful, vivacious princess lasted for many years. This busy social life partly accounted for the calendar regularity that their life took on year by year.

In addition to the strenuous demands made upon her by society, for Alexandra the first years of their marriage were also taken up with almost constant child-bearing. In a period of just under six years five children were born, two boys followed by three girls. A third son was born in April 1871, but died hours later. This last baby had been premature, as were the first two. Albert Victor, the eldest, was born two months early in January 1864. Queen Victoria insisted on the two names, much to the father's irritation who protested 'you had settled what our little boy was to be called before I had spoken to you about it.'[29] When the second, called George, appeared six weeks early in June 1865, Bertie was better prepared and wrote to his mother: 'We are sorry to hear that you don't like the names that we propose to give to our little boy, but they are names that we like and have decided on for some time.'[30] The eldest daughter, Louise was born in February 1867 and Victoria in July 1868; the following year the family was described by Lady Frederick Cavendish while they were on a visit to Windsor.

> We saw all the Wales children in the corridor; the eldest is generally called 'Prince Eddy' which gives one hopes of having a King Edward again some day. He is like the Princess and very pretty; all have the most dazzling fair complexions. Prince George however, is hardly pretty, but looks a wag; Princess Louise a tiny edition of Princess Alice [her aunt]; and the baby a placid white creature, with prominent bright blue eyes, exactly like the Queen. All are terribly tiny and miniature in scale.[31]

The third daughter, Maud, was born a few months later in November 1869.

Alexandra was an indulgent mother and as her family grew so did her contentment. Her homes and children satisfied most of her needs and this satisfaction was completed by regular annual visits to her Danish family. Bertie was similarly indulgent as a father and many onlookers commented critically on the unruly nature of the royal household. But while he enjoyed family life it never captured his attention for long; rather it was part of a ceaseless, energetic round of activity. His wife and children were only one aspect of the new freedom brought by the death of his father and his marriage.

While life at Sandringham inevitably revolved around his family, in London the possibilities for entertainment were numerous. Most favoured were a dinner party followed by a visit to the theatre and a supper party afterwards. These evenings were spent with the group of friends who formed the membership of the Marlborough Club –

established by Bertie conveniently opposite the gates of Marlborough House in 1869 when he resigned from the previously favoured White's Club in anger at their refusal to allow smoking of either cigarettes or cigars in their morning room. Bertie loved the theatre and, like most of his contemporaries, was equally admiring of the individual actresses. When the Parisian actress Hortense Schneider first appeared at the St James's Theatre there were fourteen royal highnesses in the audience and when Bertie's younger brother Prince Alfred became too attentive his mother quickly saw to it that he should be sent on an extended naval cruise. Charles Carrington, a leading light among Bertie's set, enjoyed a decade-long liaison with an actress called Nelly Bromley. The progress of their affair: weekends in Paris; the establishment of Nelly in a villa at Winkfield near Windsor; and the birth of two children in 1870 and 1871, were recorded in his diary, as was Nelly's discreet departure abroad a few months before Carrington became engaged to Cecilia (Lily) Harbord in 1878.

The Prince of Wales also happily indulged in supper parties with actresses and other ladies disapproved of by the more prim members of society, and enjoyed being flirtatiously attentive to pretty clever women. But, unlike Carrington, his every movement was dogged by ceaseless public interest and comment. The small amount that he had to do to attract adverse attention and end up in embarrassing circumstances was brought home for the first time in 1870 when he was subpoenaed to appear as a witness in court in the divorce case between Sir Charles Mordaunt and his wife, Harriet. The case revolved round Sir Charles's determination to divorce his wife because of her self-confessed adultery with a number of the Prince's friends, and the opposing evidence that his wife was insane. Bertie's appearance as a witness resulted from some innocuous letters he had once written to Lady Mordaunt and Sir Charles's seeming determination to 'Make everyone he can share the disgrace with him'.[32] In the end he lost and had to wait five years for his divorce; his wife lived on in an asylum until 1906.

The significance of the Mordaunt case in Bertie's life has often been greatly exaggerated. It was, however, illuminating in a number of ways, not least in the manner in which Queen Victoria unequivocally supported her son, her loyalty only qualified by her accurate analysis of the public aspect of the case, which prompted one of her often-voiced beliefs:

ABOVE Queen Victoria,
Prince Albert and all their
children at Osborne
House, shortly after the
birth of the youngest,
Princess Beatrice, in
1857. Bertie stands next to
his father.

RIGHT Bertie, aged
thirteen, with his younger
brother Prince Alfred
(Affie) in 1854.

The Prince of Wales as an Oxford undergraduate.

By Royal Permission.

His Royal Highness the Prince of Wales. Photographed from Life at Buckingham Palace, July 4th the day before the departure of H.R.H. for America

The official photograph of the Prince of Wales released on the eve of his departure for Canada and the United States in July 1860.

ABOVE Bertie (2nd from left) with fellow undergraduates at Trinity College, Cambridge in May 1861.

LEFT Bertie wearing the uniform of an officer of the Grenadier Guards, at the time of the Nellie Clifden incident.

OPPOSITE ABOVE The Prince of Wales and his party in front of the pyramids during his tour of the near east in March 1862. The Prince is seated on the third standing camel from the left.

OPPOSITE BELOW The mosque of Omar in Jerusalem, visited on Bertie's near east tour.

ABOVE The wedding cake.

LEFT The Prince and Princess of Wales at their wedding, March 1863.

OPPOSITE ABOVE The Prince of Wales arrives in Bombay in November 1875 to begin his tour of India.

OPPOSITE BELOW Bertie proudly displays the first tiger he shot during his tour. Sitting to the left of the Prince of Wales is William Russell, *The Times* special correspondent during the tour. Charles Carrington sits at the front on the right and Lord Aylesford, whose marriage problems were to cloud the end of the tour, at the front on the left.

ABOVE Alexandra and Bertie with Queen Victoria beside a bust of the Prince Consort.

RIGHT Alexandra in 1872, three years after the birth of her youngest child, Princess Maud.

ABOVE The Prince of Wales's complete suite, with the Viceroy Lord Northbrook, at Government House, Calcutta.

BELOW A view of Columbo, Ceylon, at the time of Bertie's visit in 1875.

The young Gaekwar of Baroda, one of the many Indian dignitaries visited by Bertie during his Indian tour.

ABOVE Lord Charles Beresford, the dashing young naval officer.

BELOW Charles Carrington at the time of the Prince of Wales's visit to India in 1875.

Francis Knollys not long after his appointment as private secretary to the Prince of Wales, a position he held for forty years.

ABOVE The west front of Sandringham House in 1864, before Bertie's programme of improvement and enlargement had begun.

BELOW The west front of the house in 1889, after being rebuilt for the Prince of Wales.

ABOVE One of the Prince's 'toys' at Sandringham, the bowling-alley, added during alterations in the 1880s.

BELOW For much of his life as Prince of Wales Bertie enjoyed hunting as well as shooting. Here (seated on the second horse from the left) he attends a meet at Easton Neston.

Bertie and Alexandra's children in 1874. Prince George stands on the left and Prince Albert Victor on the right, with – from left to right – the Princesses Louise (the eldest girl), Maud, and Victoria, in front.

Still, the fact of the Prince of Wales's intimate acquaintance with a young married woman being publicly proclaimed, will show an amount of imprudence which cannot but damage him in the eyes of the middle and lower classes, which is most deeply to be lamented in these days when the higher classes, in their frivolous, selfish and pleasure-seeking lives, do more to increase the spirit of democracy than anything else.[33]

Her worries were justified; the case attracted enormous publicity and carping in the press. *Reynolds's Newspaper* gave a representative opinion:

Even the staunchest supporters of the monarchy shake their heads and express anxiety as to whether the Queen's successor will have the tact and talent to keep royalty upon its legs and out of the gutter. When, therefore, the people of England read one year in their journals of the future King appearing prominently in the divorce court and in another of his being the centre of attraction at a German gaming-table, or public hell, it is not at all surprising that rumours concerning the Queen's health have occasioned much anxiety and apprehension.[34]

Criticism was easily encouraged, to the extent that the Prince and Princess were booed at the theatre shortly afterwards.

While the Mordaunt affair attracted great publicity it diverted attention from the possibility of a more intimate liaison. In August 1866 Bertie wrote from Abergeldie to his sister Louise who was staying with Queen Victoria at Balmoral, 'We give on Thursday what is called here a Quality Ball, at 10 o'clock – and we shall be only too happy if you or anybody else at Balmoral like to come. You know best if Mama will allow you to come of not – at any rate I hope you will come. We have the Fifes, Farquharsons, Forbes, etc. – as we thought it better to get the 'smart' dance over first – before the ghillies ball later.'[35] The Forbes whom he mentioned were Sir Charles and Lady Forbes of Newe; she was Harriet Mordaunt's sister, one of eight sisters among the sixteen children of the energetic Sir Thomas Moncreiffe, 7th Bart. Helen Forbes had married her husband in 1864 and on March 1868 their second child was born, a daughter, christened Evelyn Elizabeth but always known as Evie, who enjoyed a relationship of unusual intimacy with Bertie and his family throughout her life, and was later to entertain them as Mrs William James at West Dean Park in Sussex. Bertie's letters to her were invariably headed 'My dear Evie'[36] – an unprecedented departure compared to his other correspondence with women – and his wife viewed her with similar affection writing to her as 'My dear little Evie'.[37]

Bertie's friendship with Evie Forbes' mother escaped public notice. But the attention and criticism aroused by the Mordaunt affair had given him a fright. The ability of public opinion to blow hot and cold was brought home to him by the fact that sympathy was not fully restored until he suffered a near-fatal attack of typhoid – uncannily exactly a decade after the disease had brought about the death of his father. The typhoid was contracted in October 1871 while staying with Lord and Lady Londesborough in Yorkshire. After leaving their home near Scarborough, Bertie decided to invite himself at short notice – as he was prone to do – to stay with Charles Carrington in Buckinghamshire.

> Fancy the Heir to the throne being in this ramshackle old house with nothing to do or practically to shoot when he has the whole of sporting England at his feet. A rowdy bachelor party – and not a woman he knows this side of London. I have only my father's rereboams [sic] of Lafite '48 to rely on. Shot Gayhurst Wood on the 15th but the Prince of Wales felt so ill that Doctor Oscar Clayton was sent for. [On] Friday 17th the Prince of Wales, who looks terribly ill, left for Sandringham with Doctor Clayton and the party broke up.[38]

Whether or not the racketing around at Gayhurst exacerbated his condition, by the end of the month Bertie was critically ill. It had been formally announced on 20 November that he was suffering from typhoid and on 29 November Queen Victoria hurried from Windsor to Sandringham. After a brief improvement which gave her the confidence to return home a sudden decline on 8 December brought her hurrying back, full of dreadful premonitions as the anniversary of Albert's death on 14 approached. Surrounded by so many of her husband's family that the Princesses Louise and Beatrice had to share a bed, Alexandra took up a bedside vigil broken only by brief bouts of

rest in an adjoining dressing-room and visits to Sandringham church just beyond the garden. Public apprehension and concern mounted as Bertie subsided into unconscious raving and it appeared to be only a matter of time before his death. But against all expectations the fever began to recede on the very evening of the 14, and from the next day the danger had passed.

For Alexander the recovery marked a watershed in her marriage which she described to her lady-in-waiting, Lady Macclesfield when she wrote in January in thanks for all her help.

> Thank God that it is of the past, and the Lord's name must ever be praised, Who was merciful to me and gave me back my all but lost darling. This quiet time we two have spent here together now has been the happiest days of my life, my full reward after all my sorrow and despair. It has been our second honeymoon and we are both so happy to be left alone by ourselves.[39]

From the very outset she realized that the occasions when Bertie would be content with such an existence would be rare and after the threat to his life she was happy to make the most of the situation.

The public had to wait slightly longer for the opportunity to express their loyalty, until 27 February 1872. A service of thanksgiving for the Prince's recovery was held in St Paul's Cathedral and he and the Princess drove with Queen Victoria through London at the head of a procession of carriages. Thousands – most of whom could not remember when they had last seen the Queen in public – poured into the city to line the decorated streets and cheer in a display of monarchical fervour that banished the sentiments aroused by the Mordaunt case and Victoria's reclusiveness. Inside the packed cathedral the Archbishop of Canterbury gave the address and prayed with suitable gravity:

> Father of Mercy and God of all comfort, we thank thee that thou hast heard the prayers of this nation in the day of our trial: We praise and magnify thy glorious name for that thou has raised thy servant Albert Edward Prince of Wales from the bed of sickness: Thou castest down and thou liftest up, and health and strength are thy gifts: we pray thee to perfect the recovery of thy servant and to crown him day by day with more abundant blessings both body and soul.'[40]

CHAPTER FOUR

IRELAND AND INDIA

'To speak in rude and general terms, the Queen is invisible and the Prince of Wales is not respected.'[1] This was the opinion of the Prime Minister Gladstone shortly before the Prince of Wales's illness. It was a situation Gladstone determined to change and the surge of public sympathy prompted by Bertie's recovery seemed the ideal stimulus. While he might privately admit that it would be impossible to convince the Queen of her need to appear in public he was confident he could capitalize on the current mood to argue that if the Prince of Wales were to be found gainful employment the public perception of him – and the status of monarchy in general – would improve.

As well as the difficulty in pinpointing any suitable activity for Bertie, the major obstacles to any appointment had been Queen Victoria who refused to allow him any involvement in her constitutional work owing to her conviction that he was indiscreet and unreliable over matters of importance. Bertie's support for his wife during the Schleswig-Holstein crisis in 1864, shortly after their marriage, demonstrated loyalty that the British public shared almost unanimously. Opinion was strongly on the side of the Danes in their opposition to German claims to sovereignty over the duchies of Schleswig and Holstein. In January 1864 German and Austrian troops invaded

Denmark and gained possession of the duchies after a campaign of some five months. Queen Victoria, however, like her daughter Vicky, strongly supported the German claims to the duchies. In his mother's opinion Bertie placed personal feelings before national interest and did so in a way that threatened dangerous indiscretion. In the same year Queen Victoria's fears were confirmed when, against her express wishes, he called on the Italian revolutionary Guiseppe Garibaldi who was visiting London and being lionized by his friend the Duke of Sutherland.

The background was therefore not encouraging when Gladstone began pressing his case. The Prince himself, while occasionally complaining about his impotence in affairs of state, was not unduly upset; his outbreaks of frustration were prompted more by irritation at not being as well informed as he would have liked than a genuine desire to be actively involved. He particularly resented hearing about important events from other people. He liked to be able to comment candidly about the events of the day, as he did to Charles Carrington in September 1870, about the Franco-Prussian War:

> What an awful state of affairs in France now. The Emperor a Prisoner, and virtually abdicated, and McMahon's army surrendered. I fear there will yet be a fearful carnage in Paris, if peace is not made and a revolution the final and invisible result. It is a sad sad business, and so unnecessary. France will not recover from this shock and humiliation for years to come. I pity the poor Empress and Prince Imperial very much, and I wonder how the former will ever get out of Paris.[2]

As such comments reveal, Bertie's views combined personal feelings and sympathies with an often incisive grasp of events. But, while ministers accepted the desirability of some kind of employment, any further involvement in political affairs was something they viewed with considerable suspicion. In the series of exchanges that followed Gladstone's initiative in 1871, Granville, the Foreign Secretary, recounted how when he had appointed Bertie to a House of Lords committee: 'He attended the first day. He then came to me to ask whether the Committee could not be adjourned for ten days. He had engagements and so on' and that when he agreed to send Bertie notes of information during the Franco-Prussian War the first one was handed round at a dinner-party at Marlborough House.[3] The Lord Privy Seal, Lord Halifax, voiced similar views on the possibility of Bertie being employed in the main ministerial offices: 'But do you suppose that the Prince w[oul]d. not pretty generally find some good reason for not going to the office in the morning, when in London?'[4]

Bertie had mixed feelings about how much work he actually wished to do, especially when it demanded regular commitment that would disrupt his well-organized social and sporting activities. But he was already voicing strong opinions on what he considered the most productive way forward for the monarchy as he made clear in a letter to Queen Victoria: '. . . we live in radical times and the more the People see the Sovereign the better it is for the People and the Country.'[5] Bertie believed that by being publicly visible the monarchy would most effectively combat the republican sentiments that led to occasional public demonstrations during the years before his illness. He felt that a popular monarchy would become increasingly asked for by British subjects. It was a view shared by Gladstone who saw the monarchy as an institution that could and should provide a unifying force within the kingdom. This, with the unsuitability of other options, added greatly to the case for Ireland providing Bertie's source of employment.

After discussion with Queen Victoria the options had been outlined with characteristic succinctness by her private secretary Henry Ponsonby. They were: 1. Philanthropy; 2. Arts and Science; 3. Army; 4. Foreign Affairs; 5. Ireland. Ponsonby himself was scarcely confident of success, not least because: 'To get the P. of W. to enter into a subject or decide on it is most difficult. They have to catch snap answers from him as he goes out shooting, etc. Then he runs off on his lark to Trouville where of course business is impossible . . .'[6] The reply to Ponsonby's suggested list from Bertie's own private secretary, Francis Knollys, shows that he was already realistic about what was feasible, despite only having been appointed in 1870. Knollys argued that the employment should be something for which the Prince had a 'natural inclination'.[7] It was a polite way of admitting that the Prince's own temperament and the peripatetic, if enjoyable, life that he had established over the previous years would rule out anything that he did not find appealing.

Gladstone was not alone among Victorian politicians in believing that a permanent or at least regular royal presence in Ireland would help solve the country's constant state of unrest, both political and social. Their ideal was for the political office of Lord Lieutenant, which commanded a seat in the cabinet, to be abolished. Instead, the Prince of Wales would become a non-political viceroy or governor of Ireland, and the combination of a royal presence and his personality would greatly encourage Irish loyalty. Gladstone's predecessor, Disraeli, had suggested such a scheme in 1868, with the carrot to Bertie that his residence should be in prime Irish hunting country. Bertie's opinions were, however, incidental as the idea was dismissed as 'quite out of the question'[8] by Queen Victoria.

Gladstone repeated the plan for a permanent royal residence where the Prince and Princess of Wales would spend a set period each year. Other members of the royal family could use it at other times. Queen Victoria had made it clear that she would not contemplate the replacement of the Lord Lieutenant by her son, so when Gladstone pressed on and suggested that Bertie should be made a titular viceroy, the problem of precedence arose as to his relation with the Lord Lieutenant, Queen Victoria's personal representative. In March 1872 Gladstone was told by Ponsonby that the Prince was 'even more opposed than the Queen to going in any official capacity to Ireland; and nothing but the most urgently expressed wish from the Queen would induce him to go.'[9] The possibility of Victoria expressing any such wish appeared remote, as she made clear in increasingly forthright terms. The only possible attraction was that it might get her son away from London during the Season. It was a measure of Bertie's natural instinct to be accommodating that, at the end of April 1872, shortly before he left with Alexandra for a tour of Europe, he told Knollys that he would: 'Discuss the Irish plan on its merits, and that, upon the whole, he looked on it in a more favourable light than was formerly the case.'[10]

Disraeli was not one to make ripples in his relations with the Queen, and after her chilly response to his suggestion he never mentioned the idea again. Gladstone, on the contrary, rarely allowed opposition from Queen Victoria to dissuade him from a course of action. Despite the discouraging response he pressed on. In July 1872 he outlined his plan in a long letter to Queen Victoria. Central to the plan was the suggestion that the Prince would assume an official position, but one in which any political controversy would be defused by the appointment of a new Irish minister with whom he would work. One of the main attractions would be: 'The nature of his duties would afford an admirable opportunity for giving the Prince the advantage of a political training which, from no fault of his own, he can hardly be said to have enjoyed.'[11] Gladstone's proposals were part of an overall plan for Bertie which, if put into effect, would have radically changed how he spent his life: '. . . four to five months in Ireland, two or three in London [officially deputising for Queen Victoria], the autumn manoeuvres, Norfolk and Scotland, with occasional fractions of time for other purposes, would sufficiently account for the twelve-month.'[12]

Despite Victoria's opposition, memoranda and correspondence flowed between Gladstone and senior politicians, in particular the Marquess of Hartington who was Chief Secretary for Ireland. Most of those involved agreed with the Earl of Bessborough, an Irish peer and Lord Steward of the royal household, that a royal residence was a good idea – for the reasons that he outlined in part of a long memorandum to Hartington:

People in Ireland complain of the habitual absence of Royalty, which gives the idea of its being an inferior country. This feeling is not confined to any class but is general from the highest to the lowest . . . What is wanted is to get the Irish to consider themselves an integral, not a distant part of the United Kingdom, which would be much encouraged by a habitual residence of some of the Royal Family.[13]

Gladstone found almost no support on the question of the Prince of Wales assuming the official position of Viceroy and by the autumn of 1872 his effort to give Bertie employment in Ireland was doomed to failure. He admitted as much to Hartington in a letter in September: 'The Queen has put an extinguisher upon my proposals with regard to the Prince of Wales, the Viceroyalty of Ireland, and the provision for a fuller discharge of the visible duties of Royalty.'[14] Further confirmation came from William Forster, at the time vice president of the council, who wrote to Gladstone in October after conversations with Queen Victoria at Balmoral where he was staying as official minister in residence: 'it is not now a question between our plan and the simple residence – if it were, my opinion would be worth very little, but it is a question of a Royal Residence in Ireland.' He went on to say that in his view an arrangement whereby the Prince of Wales spent a set period of time in Ireland would provide him with an ideal opportunity to demonstrate his best qualities: 'It would be no flattery to the Prince to tell him that he as well as the Princess have special gifts for winning personal attachment as in addition to good manners to which men can be trained, he has that which no training can give – real kindness of heart.'[15]

With the most ambitious thrust of Gladstone's proposals effectively scuppered by Queen Victoria's opposition, Bertie's lack of enthusiasm, and political obstacles, the secondary idea of a royal residence was equally destined to fail, although faltering discussion continued for some time. In reality Gladstone had failed to take into account what would be acceptable to either the Queen or the Prince of Wales when devising a scheme which he himself was certain had great political and constitutional merit and provided an answer to the problems of the Prince's lack of employment. The Queen had shrewdly strengthened her own opposition by supporting her son's right to retain independent control of his occupations. She could tell him how he should spend his time, but it was no business of Gladstone's to do so.

While the Queen caused Gladstone frustrated resentment at her unyielding stand over the affair, Bertie managed to come out of it on the best of terms with the Prime Minister. He invited Gladstone to spend the weekend of the Princess of Wales's birthday (1 December) at Sandringham. Francis Knollys, who supported the Irish scheme, reported to Henry Ponsonby with some irritation at a wasted opportunity: 'G. was evidently very much pleased at having been asked, particularly for the Princess's Birthday, and was I suppose reluctant, while stopping at the House, to do or say anything in any way he thought distasteful to H.R.H.' He went on to outline accurately the manner in which Bertie would in the future cement relations with politicians: 'The first political party here was I think altogether a great success and I hope it will induce H.R.H. to continue to ask the leading men on both sides to Sandringham.'[16]

Knollys' message to Ponsonby was representative of the close relations that the two private secretaries established which on many occasions smoothed over differences between Queen Victoria and Bertie.

And within a few years of his appointment Knollys had become integral not only in Bertie's relations with his mother, but also with the rest of the royal family, politicians, and all the other varied people with whom the Prince had dealings.

Knollys was descended from Sir William Knollys, Treasurer of the Household to Elizabeth I who made him Earl of Banbury. But Queen Victoria strongly disapproved of his appointment in 1870 as private secretary to her son. She considered him a bad influence, who would encourage Bertie's frivolous social life in London and impose his liberal political views. In the event Knollys served Bertie as prince and king for nearly half a century and became the linchpin of his royal employer's public and private lives. In his hands the position of private secretary was to change dramatically from the role carried out by Henry Ponsonby. He operated from within the confines of Queen Victoria's household on a highly formalized basis. Knollys developed a close personal friendship with Bertie whose children called him 'Fooks'. While never afraid to disagree with his employer when necessary, Knollys ceaselessly promoted his interests, and developed an unfailing sensitivity to Bertie's mood and wishes. This friendship and Knollys' humorous character removed the position of private secretary from the dusty confines of the court. During the years of Edward VII's reign, his position became integral to the King's establishment of a monarchy at home in modern democracy. Shortly after Edward VII's death, Lord Esher wrote in his journal, 'Francis was the only human being who could deflect his purpose. For 48 years Francis had served him, as well as any man ever served another, with complete disinterest and complete devotion, and the King knew it well.'[17]

Gladstone's Irish scheme was the most promising effort to find regular, long-term employment for Bertie. While advice and opinions continued to be offered from all sides, there was little change in the annual routine. Towards the end of 1874, however, he started planning an official visit to India. It would turn out to be one of the greatest successes of his period as Prince of Wales, as well as a tactical triumph against stern opposition from Queen Victoria and politicians. In January 1875 the Secretary of State for India, the Marquess of Salisbury drily reported to the Viceroy, Lord Northbrook: 'I spoke to the Queen a few days back upon the subject of the Prince of Wales' proposed visit to India. She did not at all encourage it and I suspect it will never take place'.[18] Nonetheless, Lord Salisbury, usually one to put a dampener on most of the Prince's activities, demonstrated his support for the scheme in a subsequent letter to Northbrook, in February 1875, when he argued that it would 'Increase his influence both in England and India'.[19]

Bertie got his way against considerable odds. His first success was to gain his mother's tacit agreement to the expedition. Since the beginning of 1875 he had been corresponding with the Prime Minister, Disraeli, about the trip. It is likely that Disraeli encouraged 'our young Hal' as he patronisingly referred to Bertie, confident that the idea would be vetoed by the Queen. After a visit by Bertie to Windsor, when it was clear that his mother had unexpectedly given her consent, Disraeli accused the Prince of persuading his mother by suggesting that the trip had been sanctioned by her ministers, when it had not.

As well as the boost it would give to the Prince's own position, the most important benefit of the tour would be the representation of the sovereign in India. In 1858 the Indian Mutiny had brought the question and nature of British rule to violent conflict. The atrocities carried out by both Indians and British soldiers were remembered with considerable bitterness. The events of the mutiny had stressed the urgent need for reforms in the way India was governed, and as a result the control of the East India Company, increasingly all-powerful since the end of the eighteenth century, was removed. The company was abolished and power was directly assumed by the British crown. And yet for the native Indian princes and their people, and the British soldiers and civil servants who administered the country, the crown was a distant figure with which India had no real contact. This would change with a visit by the Prince of Wales whose personality would undoubtedly strengthen the possibility of harmonious relations with all parties.

Discussion and planning continued throughout 1875. For Queen Victoria there were four points of particular importance; the Prince of Wales's status in relation to the Viceroy; the impossibility of Alexandra accompanying her husband; the possible dangers to Bertie's health; and the choice of people to accompany him. The question of precedence over the Viceroy was similar to the problem that had arisen in Gladstone's negotiations for an Irish position; the

Queen was adamant that Bertie would travel through India as the Viceroy's private guest, not as her official representative which would compromise the Viceroy's authority.

Her concerns about the Viceroy's status were strenuously endorsed by Northbrook himself. A Liberal politician, he had been appointed Viceroy in 1872 by Gladstone. But after Gladstone's defeat in the general election of 1874, Northbrook had had to deal with the Tory Lord Salisbury, with whom he did not enjoy the easiest of relations. In September 1875, weeks before Bertie's arrival in India, Northbrook announced that he would resign in the New Year.

Queen Victoria need not have worried about the question of Alexandra accompanying her husband, as Bertie had never envisaged that his wife would join the party, which she found hard to bear. Her correspondence shows how much Alexandra disliked the times when Bertie was away, even if it was only for a few days, as when she had written to Princess Louise from Sandringham in 1868; 'My *darling* husband left today for Kimbolton. I hate it when he is away, the home seems empty and desolate and lonely.'[20] Now, with the Indian trip planned to last many months, Bertie would be away for longer than ever before during their marriage. The separation was to affect her deeply even forty years later, in 1913, when she wrote to the wife of the then Viceroy, Lady Hardinge of Penshurst:

How I wish I could have paid you a visit in beautiful India – the one wish of my life to see that wonderful, beautiful country! But, alas, it was never to be, and when I might have gone – that time with my dear husband – he would not let me and to this day I do not know why, excepting that he said at the time it was difficult for ladies to move about there – as if that would have mattered to me![21]

The opinion of the Foreign Secretary, Lord Derby, was expressed in a note on the subject to Disraeli: 'and lastly "Hal" is sure to get into scrapes with women whether she goes or not, and they will be considered more excusable in her absence.'[22]

'The Queen is very much alarmed at the possible consequences to the Prince of Wales's health of his journey to India . . . His health is not very strong and he must be kept out of all risk of fever',[23] Salisbury wrote to Northbrook in March. In June Victoria requested

Northbrook to provide: 'an impartial opinion on the effect of the con-templated visit of the Prince of Wales to India upon His Royal Highness's health.'[24] Her Viceroy did so in reassuring terms, outlining the programme and concluding: 'Lord Northbrook has no hesitation in saying that such a programme as this would expose an ordinary traveller to no greater risk of illness than life in England or a tour of Italy.'[25]

Victoria's attention to who would accompany her son was equally intensive. She told Salisbury that the number and individuals involved was no official matter and therefore one over which she had legitimate control. She had no intention of sanctioning a number of the friends that Bertie had chosen to travel with him. Bertie fervently disagreed. Exasperated by a number of unwarranted interventions into the plans, he lost his temper with Disraeli when the Prime Minister attempted to support the Queen's right to choose the party. Faced with the unexpected outburst Disraeli advised the Queen to give way over the two friends who aroused particular disapproval, Lord Charles Beresford and Charles Carrington (in 1892, she was to appoint the latter her Lord Chamberlain and he and his wife, Lily, became two of Victoria's particular favourites during the last decade of her life).

Finally, the suite of eighteen was agreed. Overall control was assumed by Sir Bartle Frere, a senior India hand and member of the Council for India; the Queen's personal representative was General Lord Alfred Paget, the clerk-marshall of the royal household and until 1874 Victoria's chief equerry. The Prince's suite combined its regular members with a handful of friends: his two equerries, General Dighton Probyn (who had won the VC as a cavalry officer in the Indian Mutiny) and Colonel Arthur Ellis; Lord Suffield as Lord-in-Waiting; the private secretary, Francis Knollys; four ADCs, Colonel Owen Williams, Augustus FitzGeorge (son of the Duke of Cambridge), Prince Louis of Battenburg and Lord Charles Beresford. The Duke of Sutherland, the Earl of Aylesford and Charles Carrington travelled as personal guests. The group was completed by Albert Grey (Sir Bartle Frere's secretary); the special correspondent of *The Times*, William Howard Russell; the all-important physician, Dr Joseph Fayrer; an official artist Sydney Hall; a chaplain, the Revd Robinson Duckworth; a taxidermist, Mr Clarence Bartlett; and assorted servants including the Duke of Sutherland's personal piper.

The most controversial question was who would pay for the tour. Disraeli complained to Salisbury in March 1875: 'Where is the money to come from? He has not a shilling; she will not give him one'.[26] To make matters worse, the Queen made it clear she expected Parliament to vote sufficient funds for the trip to be carried out in a suitably imperial manner. The question became intensely political. Radicals were unanimous in their condemnation of public funds being used, while the Prince's Liberal friends, such as Lord Hartington, accused the Tory government of not offering enough money. In the end, Disraeli got a parliamentary vote which approved £52,000 for travelling expenses and £60,000 for personal expenses – including the problem of presents for the Indian princes whose own gifts in return were bound to be more lavish than those allowed for in the Prince's budget. The initial contribution that Salisbury secured from the Indian government eventually grew to over £100,000. The areas of possible conflict seemed endless, however, as one of Salisbury's missives to Northbrook during the lengthy discussions over the question of official presents demonstrated: 'Of course, if India pays for his presents, the presents he receives must be sold.'[27]

Disraeli's frustration boiled over when he discovered that Bartle Frere, of whom he had a dismally low opinion, had allowed Bertie to allot from the funds he, Disraeli had wrung out of parliament, £300 (£6,000 in today's money) to each member of the party to buy cotton underwear for the trip. Fuming about this to his adored correspondent, Selina, Countess of Bradford, Disraeli complained about the Prince of Wales: 'He cannot say "No" – or as I would put it Bo(o) [sic] – to a goose! This is the weak part of a character, not by any means deficient in intelligence or knowledge of men.'[28]

Bertie played the Sandringham trump card. Disraeli was invited for the last weekend before the party's departure on 10 October. He did not altogether enthuse about the stay, complaining in particular about his fellow-guests, but he had to confess that his host was 'the most amiable of mortals' and that, 'he truly loves'[29] Alexandra. Sadly, she was looking 'as though she were preparing to commit suttee'.[30]

In England many people considered the trip to be an unjustifiably expensive jaunt for Bertie. They agreed with the opinions of Henry

Ponsonby and Salisbury, 'The object of his mission is amusement', 'Yes, and to kill Tigers.'[31] In India, sentiments were different and expectations ran high. This is not surprising when one considers the opinion of Sir Alfred Lyall, who had a lifetime of experience in India. He commented that the Europeans who lived in more remote stations, always heavily outnumbered by native Indians, 'lead a dull life in their hutches, like rabbits.'[32] In the centres of British India, social life was paramount and, despite the pedantic regulations and hierarchy, constantly enlivened by scandals of inflated proportions; 'Alas we have had a terrible scandal here since three days, an officer seduced and tried to run away with Miss Hooper!!!'[33] Not surprisingly there was more than a frisson of excitement as the arrival of the leader of London society drew near.

Princess Louise reported the tearful family parting in a letter to Queen Victoria.

> The last day the 11th was the most painful for Bertie, and I know he was thankful when it was over. He was dreadfully overcome when he parted with the children; and he said goodbye to all his servants and Alix's people. They drove in an open carriage to the station, and there were crowds of people all along the streets, and in the station. Dear Alix kept up wonderfully, she was fighting with herself all the time.[34]

The Princess accompanied her husband to Calais. Thereafter the journey to India was first across Europe via Paris and Turin to Brindisi where the party arrived on 16 October. There they boarded HMS *Serapis* which continued the journey via Athens, where Bertie stopped to spend a day with the King and Queen of Greece, through the Suez Canal to Ismailia, where he disembarked to visit the Egyptian Khedive Ismail who entertained the Prince in lavish style, and on to Aden where they landed on 1 November. Here Bertie held a levée for Arab chiefs before setting out on the final leg to Bombay, where the *Serapis* docked on 8 November.

At first the mood of the party was subdued and Charles Carrington wrote to his mother about Bertie: 'He was tremendously low in Paris and even yet isn't up to form.'[35] Things improved by the time they were crossing the Red Sea and Albert Grey, Sir Bartle Frere's

secretary wrote in a letter: 'His temper is most amiable. He sits mop-
ping away as we steam along with the thermometer at 88 on the
bridge at midnight, not complaining like the others of the discomfort
of the heat – but congratulating himself as he throws away one wet
handkerchief after another – "what a capital thing is a good whole-
some sweat!" '[36]

Carrington had made an agreement with Disraeli to send him dis-
patches during the tour and from the *Serapis* he wrote: 'I am glad to
be able to say that the P of W is wonderfully well, in fact better than
he has been for the last 12 months – he takes great care of himself and
goes to bed earlier than he does in London. He seems very much
impressed with the importance of the journey'.[37]

Bertie did not only appreciate the significance of the trip.
From the very first day he was to confound all expectations with his
energy and ability to cope with the Indian climate. While threats
to his health remained Queen Victoria's constant worry and
prompted a stream of advice and warnings, threats to his life
were more widely viewed as a danger. Every possible precaution
was taken, as Carrington confirmed: 'Our orders are always to
be with him – always round him on all occasions. He is never on any
pretence to take any petition or address from a native's hand and
not to be out on any occasion after dusk except in a carriage in
Bombay.'[38] Later he wrote to Disraeli, 'I had yesterday a long
confidential conversation with HRH on the subject of precautions
in India without the least loss of that personal courage for which
he is so distinguished. He seems anxious no precautions should be
omitted that lend to his safety.' Carrington went on to tell Disraeli
that he had also reassured Bartle Frere on the subject, 'as he with
many others appeared to fear that HRH's love of independence and
natural dislike of personal restraint or supervision might lead him
into danger.'[39]

The *Serapis* arrived at Bombay the day before Bertie's thirty-fourth
birthday. He was welcomed to India by the Viceroy and other dignitaries and the constant round of official greetings began. It was to last
up to the day he departed in March the following year. The most
problematic were the planned audiences with Indian princes. A few
weeks after Bertie's arrival the Governor of Bombay, Sir Philip
Wodehouse, wrote to Salisbury:

I was certainly at one time under some apprehension that the harmony would be to some extent interrupted by expressions of discontent of the part of some of the Native Princes and Chiefs who had been summoned to Bombay to meet the Prince – Your Lordship must know well how extremely tenacious they are of their privileges and how ready to resent any question of their rights in matters of ceremony and etiquette.[40]

Wodehouse went on to describe how it was the Prince's behaviour alone that gave them satisfaction.

The Prince's ability to calm troubled waters was further tested ten days after his arrival when he made a previously unplanned visit to Baroda, due north of Bombay, which was in the throes of political and dynastic crisis. In January 1875 the then Gaekwar of Baroda had been implicated in an attempt to poison the British resident, Colonel Phayre. The Gaekwar had been replaced as ruler by a twelve-year-old boy, carefully watched over by his foster-mother – the widow of another former Gaekwar – and as Carrington wrote it was still 'a very disaffected place'. Amongst his reports home the Prince wrote to Lord Granville: 'The little Gaekwar of Baroda who is as old as our oldest boy, seems a really very intelligent youth, though only six months ago he was running about the streets adorned with the most limited wardrobe.'[41] The three-day visit was an unqualified success, Bertie got his first taste of Indian sport, hunting cheetah, pig-sticking and shooting quail, and Wodehouse was confident that it would 'have a most important effect on happier affairs and feeling at Baroda.'[42]

From Baroda the planned journey overland to Madras on the far-east coast had to be abandoned because of an outbreak of cholera. Instead the party travelled by sea to Goa and on to Ceylon before continuing up the east coast to Madras and then Calcutta which was reached on 23 December. At every stop a busy programme of official receptions and levées, handing out honours to dignitaries, reviewing troops and more humble visits to factories and new buildings was, wherever possible, enlivened with hunting or shooting. Ceylon provided the Prince of Wales's first elephant; scores more creatures were to follow. While his seemingly insatiable appetite for such sport either wearied or bored some his English companions, it served only to increase his prestige in the eyes of Indian rulers.

Calcutta, where he was once again greeted by the Viceroy, marked the official zenith of the tour. At all times the convoluted structure of Anglo-Indian society had to be upheld; not least on the day when a series of Indian royalties either appeared in person or sent a representative mission. As each party departed a salute of guns was fired, the number of salvoes depending on their relative importance. The day after his arrival Bertie held a durbar (the title of the official court gatherings of native Indian princes which was adopted by the British in India), in Government House. Then, as his biographer Philip Magnus wrote:

> A week of strenuous sightseeing, visits, races, and receptions followed, at the end of which, on New Year's Day 1876, the Prince held an investiture of the Order of the Star of India in camp on the Maidan. After joining the Viceroy and the Commander-in-Chief (Lord Napier of Magdala) in a stately procession of Knights Grand Commander, the Prince proceeded to invest new members individually with the different grades of the Order to which they had been appointed; and he rounded off the day by unveiling an equestrian statue of the Viceroy, Lord Maho, who had been assassinated in 1872; by watching a polo match on the Maidan and a display of fireworks on the racecourse; and by attending at 10.15pm, after a banquet at Government House, a performance of one of favourite farces, *My Awful Dad*.[43]

Such zest and stamina amazed most observers and one young officer wrote home, after seeing Bertie for the first time in Delhi: 'The Prince looks well, but very, very stout. I wonder this constant knocking about doesn't make him ill.'[44] Rather the opposite. In and out of uniforms and full evening dress in the most oppressive of climates, on horse or elephant, staying in permanent splendour at Government House or the temporary comfort of a tented camp in a remote province, meeting maharajahs or district commissioners, on all occasions the enthusiasm was irrepressible. In Delhi the chief entertainment was military manoeuvres on a massive scale, with Bertie taking part with his own regiment, the 10th Hussars. This came after he had visited northern India, including Lucknow, the city most scarred by the Indian Mutiny in 1857. During part of this trip north, the

Prince's host was Sir John Strachey, Lieutenant-Governor of Bengal, a member of an intellectual family whose wife revealed in a letter to her sister-in-law in England, the mixed feelings that Bertie so often aroused: contempt for his shortcomings and foibles blending with reluctant admiration.

> We only had HRH to stay for two days but John's opinion is that HRH is by no means the fool that he is made out to be. He is contemptible in other ways but no fool. John was agreeably surprised with his sensible remarks and appreciations of things which he saw & of his views in politics too. The Prince's tastes are low and childish enough – He has a perfect mania on the subject of dress. Dr Fayrer told me that he was quite sick of perpetually changing his clothes, as fresh orders come nearly every hour about what the suite were to wear & if a button is wrong it is at once noticed and remarked upon. His other tastes are for smoking & eating and drinking. He is at times thoroughly selfish & inconsiderate. On the other hand he has the gift of pleasant manners, a charming smile & can make himself most agreeable.

After saying how the Prince appeared happy with the arrangements they had made in Benares and describing Lord Alfred Paget as 'a horrible coarse-looking man', Lady Strachey continues on the subject that was the main topic of interest for ladies all over India, his morals.

> As for HRH's moral character, Major Bradford told us that he was as bad as possible & that the respectable part of the suite were always in an agony lest he should misbehave. He has set all Calcutta by the ears with his particular attentions to Nicky [a mutual friend]. He asked himself to luncheon with her at her lodgings . . . & he again went there with 4 of the most rowdy of his set. Then he again went there to say goodbye to her the last morning. Of course there are the most ill-natured remarks by ladies in high positions who have attractions and who blame Nicky. Do not repeat what I have told you of this affair to anyone.[45]

Given the nature of Calcutta society and the reputation that preceded Bertie to India it was inevitable that he would 'set all Calcutta by the ears' and do so by lunching with one of the most attractive young ladies in the city. But as the tour continued it was not his fancies for the ladies that aroused indignation among British Indians. They objected far more strongly to what they considered the undue attention and civility he afforded the natives, both rulers and more humbler people. His occasionally relaxed attitude towards the Europeans' rigidly hierarchical life was similarly unpopular. Long-established feelings that the natives were inferior and to be firmly kept in their place had been given a bitter, rancorous edge by the Mutiny the memory of which was still vivid. The attitude of superior indifference was noted with shock by Charles Carrington, who wrote to his mother, 'I cannot help thinking that with very few exceptions the English know nothing of the real character of a native.'[46]

The improvement of relations between different Indian states classes and religions, had been one of Bertie's primary aspirations for the tour. But he had not expected to find the attitudes of Englishmen to be major stumbling block to greater harmony and from the very outset his letters back to England were censorious. In November he wrote to Lord Granville: 'Because a man has a black face and a different religion to our own, this is no reason why he should be treated as a brute.'[47] To his mother he had earlier complained: 'Natives of all classes in this country will, I am sure, be more attached to us if they are treated with kindness and with firmness at the same time, but not with brutality or contempt.'[48] He was most indignant to Lord Salisbury on one occasion, when he brought his attention to: 'the disgraceful habit of officers in the Queen's service speaking of the inhabitants in India, many of them sprung from the great races, as "niggers"'.[49] It was unusual for such royal complaints – however justified or well-informed – to bring about any political action. But in direct response to the Prince's complaints the Resident in Hyderabad, a Mr Saunders, was recalled by the government in December 1876 for what Disraeli described to Queen Victoria as 'offensive behaviour to the princes and people'.[50]

The last few weeks of the tour were given over to hunting and shooting expeditions in the northern provinces, and into Nepal. On 5 February, mounted in a suitably decorated howdah on an elephant's back, the Prince shot his first tiger. More were to follow; six in one day in Nepal, where Carrington described an elephant hunt on

24 February as 'probably the finest day's sport ever seen.'[51] Before he left India Carrington also chronicled the extensive list bagged by Bertie and his suite. 28 tigers, 2 leopards, 3 wild cat, 1 civit cat, 4 mongoose, 1 jackal, 1 otter, 6 bears, 1 porcupine, 44 hares, 35 boar, 4 black buck, 4 sambre deer, 4 ferror deer, 2 pona, 1 swamp deer, 41 cheetah, 213 partridges, 11 quail, 19 jungle fowl, 12 pea fowl, 6 florican, 3 plover, 69 snipe. In addition 14 elephants were captured. Finally, as they left Bombay on 13 March, Carrington wrote to his mother: 'There is a good deal of smallpox in the town and they are anxious to get the Prince of Wales off. He is remarkably well and in very good spirits – and has certainly stood all his work very well'. Carrington concluded;

> Just this day 17 weeks ago the Serapis cast anchor in Bombay Harbour. The Prince has travelled 7,600 miles by land and 2,300 by sea, knows more Chiefs that all the Viceroys and Governors put together and has seen more of the country in the time than any living man. His health, courage, spirit, tact, and power of memory have been wonderful. He has proved himself a man in 100,000.[52]

These were all qualities that had been similarly noted after his tour of America in 1860. For the Prince of Wales, again, the novelty and excitement of travel, a constant pageant of new places without his ever being in any one of them for too long, gave him constant stimulation. He confirmed that giving brief but long-lasting pleasure was something at which he was supremely accomplished. Even critics such as Lady Strachey who saw him for long enough to conclude that he was shallow and dissolute, were forced to agree that there were attractive elements in his demeanour. Above all the ceremony, the tour saw him translate by dint of character a gesture by the crown into a personal statement of interest and enjoyment.

His efforts were especially enjoyed by the Indians, with whom his relations were a genuine and conspicuous success. Many felt that the Prince of Wales showed them more interest and courtesy than the district commissioners and other officers of British India.

This counted for an inestimable amount and gave them a brief, if transient, impression that the Raj did not purely exist at their expense for the benefit of the English. Individually, many were to retain fond memories for the rest of their lives, as two instances reported by later Viceroys demonstrated. In 1882 the Marquis of Ripon wrote to the Prince of Wales about 'the very lively and pleasant recollections which the native chiefs everywhere retain of your visit'.[53] In 1903 the Viceroy, Lord Curzon, recounted to the King how a Gurkha has produced with immense pride a silver knife which Bertie had given his father in the same place in 1876.

The anger which the Prince's attentiveness towards the natives aroused in some Anglo-Indians was confirmed by Lord Lytton, who took over as Viceroy in March 1876, in a letter to Lord George Hamilton written a year later:

> The fact is, the whole of Anglo-Indian society is mortally offended with the Prince of Wales for not having sufficiently appreciated its superiority to everything else in creation. His vision has left a deep rankling sore in the Anglo-Indian mind, which has got an idée fixe that I came out with secret instructions from his Royal Highness to snub and aggravate the whites, and pet and spoil the blacks.[54]

Lytton exaggerated when he talked of 'The whole of Anglo-Indian society', and the feathers that the Prince of Wales did ruffle were of little consequence in comparison to those he smoothed. One of the rare occasions when, as Prince of Wales, he was able to take on an ambitious project of real importance on his own, the tour gave a pointer to the future style of his monarchy. His success was founded on his common touch and his ability to convey unflagging interest and enthusiasm. There were also political benefits for Disraeli's government; not least that such a high-profile visit by the heir to the throne clarified Britain's firm commitment to India and countered any territorial ambitions the expansionist Russian empire was harbouring towards the border territories along the Northwest Frontier with Afghanistan.

Any feelings of achievement or that his habitual position had changed were swiftly banished. Shortly before his arrival home in England, Bertie read in the newspapers the announcement of the Royal Titles Bill. The bill was announced by Queen Victoria at the opening of parliament in February 1876, conferring on the Queen the title of Empress of India. After all Bertie's tour had involved – not least elevating the status of the monarchy in India by its visible representation – it was not surprising that the Prince was both angry and upset. Invariably sensitive to possible slights, he had not even been informed – let alone consulted – by either his mother or her Prime Minister.

Opinions in India on the Queen calling herself Empress counted for little in Britain. (Indeed, the remoteness of events in India accounted for the lack of response which the Prince's tour generated in many quarters.) Although from the outset the bill provoked considerable opposition in parliament and more widely, it was eventually passed. Disraeli comes out of the affair in a shabby light for not having the courtesy to inform the Prince of Wales who, after all, would be the next holder of his grandiose title. Queen Victoria, while obsessively indulgent about Bertie's health throughout his tour was now capable of ignoring him over a matter of real gravity. In so doing she demonstrated the fluctuating feelings towards him that she had retained since his childhood.

Bertie might have been forgiven for suspecting that fate was conspiring to overshadow any beneficial outcome from the tour. Prior to the political furore over the Royal Titles Bill, even before he left India, he was being drawn into a social scandal of others' making. In February, while the royal party was at a camp in Nepal, Lord Aylesford had been informed by his wife that she intended to elope with the Marquess of Blandford, eldest son of the Duke and Duchess of Marlborough. Blandford had similarly written of their intentions to Lady Aylesford's brother, Owen Williams, also travelling with the Prince. While it did not become as public as the Mordaunt case or result in legal action, the Prince's involvement ensured that it dominated society gossip and exercised the minds of Disraeli and other politicians throughout most of 1876. The potential scandal effectively overshadowed the positive achievements of the tour.

As in the Mordaunt case, the cause for concern was the Prince's previous familiarity – in the form of letters to Lady Aylesford – which was used as evidence of indiscretion and involvement in the couple's marital crises. He was also acquainted with all those involved. With the real possibility of public scandal resulting either from Blandford and Lady Aylesford continuing their elopement plans or Lord

Aylesford's intention to press for public divorce, the temperature was raised. Bertie refused to persuade Aylesford to drop his plan for divorce and roundly condemned Blandford as the guilty party. This aroused Blandford's younger brother, Lord Randolph Churchill, the Member of Parliament. When Lady Aylesford, desperate to avoid the social ostracism that would result from divorce, handed to Blandford the packet of letters written by Bertie, he in turn passed them on to Lord Randolf who determined to use them to coerce the Prince into taking action to prevent the divorce. With the Prince still on his return journey he made a threatening visit to Alexandra at Marlborough House and announced that he had evidence he was prepared to use against her husband in order to prevent a divorce. He told her that the letters were 'of the most compromising character' and that in the opinion of his lawyer, if made public, Bertie would 'never sit upon the Throne of England'. Elsewhere he bragged that he 'had the Crown of England in his pocket.'[55]

The furore that ensued did not become a public scandal. While Churchill was demonstrating such unforgiveable disrespect towards his Alexandra the royal party was marooned in the Mediterranean, which drove Bertie to such distraction that he challenged Churchill to a duel. On a more practical level Bertie's arrival home was delayed, on the advice of Queen Victoria, who was equally outraged by the 'villains' and fearful that her son would come home to a critical reception. In the event, his return on 11 May was as happy as he could have wished; after Alexandra had received in April what she told Victoria was 'a very dear letter from my Bertie',[56] she boarded his ship alone to greet him first, before any others of the welcoming party. That evening in London, in a characteristic display of bravado and of his firm belief that such problems should be faced in public, they attended the opera and received a tumultuous reception.

The unpleasant reality for the Prince of Wales was that, however, much problems like the Aylesford affair were of other's making they could, on the smallest premise, focus on him and provoke fierce criticism. Disraeli complained wearily that the Prince of Wales's private affairs were almost as troublesome as the Balkan crisis. The Aylesford affair was remarkable for the way in which it emphasized the close links between society and politics. The Prime Minister, the Foreign Secretary and the Lord Chancellor all personally took part in the negotiations between the parties. The Queen was closely involved: in addition to her concerns for her son's reputation the Duke and Duchess of Marlborough were her close friends. At the beginning of Disraeli's government the Duke had been offered the position of Viceroy of Ireland. He had refused on financial grounds; as Disraeli explained, 'to carry out the duties in a becoming manner requires £40,000 a year and the salary is only half that sum.'[57] Now Disraeli decided that: 'the dignified withdrawal of the family from metropolitan and English life at the moment and for a time' was imperative and the Duke was re-offered the position of Viceroy when it became vacant at the end of 1876. The Duke, not as rich as many of his peers, accepted without question although he had to sell works of art from Blenheim Palace to finance his term of office.

Although a convoluted form of apology and its acceptance were established between Lord Randolf and the Prince of Wales, the former's behaviour was not to be forgiven. He went off to the United States with his American wife but the Prince made it known that he did not expect to meet either of them. Nor did he for eight years. Lord Randolf's future political success assisted his social rehabilitation but the ostracism imposed by the Prince left its scars and accounted for much of his bitterness. In the end, Lady Aylesford did not elope with Blandford. There was no satisfaction for Bertie in any of this. The problem had taken the edge off his return from India and reminded him most unpleasantly how vulnerable he was to innuendo.

CHAPTER FIVE

SANDRINGHAM

If there was one place that offered respite from the intrusions and pressures of society and the Prince's public life it was Sandringham. From the day of purchase it was Bertie's exclusive domain and only his wife was allowed any say in the affairs of the estate. When Charles Carrington paid his first visit, immediately after Christmas in 1864, he described the house as 'very small and inconvenient.' Some thirty years later it was, in his opinion, 'the most comfortable house in England.'[1] During those three decades Sandringham developed from being a modest country house to being a great seat and the centre of a model estate. Above all, it became integral to the public perception of royal life, as it has remained ever since. Using the house to entertain a succession of people was one way in which Bertie created an active role as Prince of Wales. The atmosphere of splendid bonhomie that he engendered never failed to touch his myriad guests.

It was also the family home, where Alexandra increasingly spent her time and where Bertie was best able to relax and indulge his children. Almost immediately after his marriage he established an annual pattern whereby he based himself at Sandringham from early-November, shortly before his birthday, until the following February. In letters over the years he constantly referred to settling in for the winter at Sandringham. He also made other spontaneous visits at different times of the year, often for both Alexandra and himself to relax, as he described to Charles Carrington in April 1886: 'We shall go to Sandringham next week for three weeks to get some bracing air before encountering the London Season.'[2] But his children – and after a time Alexandra as well – spent much more of the year there. For all of them the most vivid childhood memories were of their life in the Norfolk countryside.

One trait that Bertie inherited from his father was a passion for organizing and undertaking constructive projects. One of the most productive outlets for this passion for both men was estate improvement. As Prince Albert had derived pleasure and pride from his diary at Windsor, his work at Balmoral and, in particular, his projects at Osborne, so his son did at Sandringham. The programme was begun after his first visit with Alexandra in 1864 and continued until his death, periods of intense activity alternating with quieter ones. The extension of the estate did not come until quite late. With only minor additions, it remained effectively the same size until the late-1890s when the purchase of the neighbouring Anmer property added around 2,000 acres and then in 1905 the two farms of Flitcham and Harpley Down added another 3,000. But its appearance began to change immediately and the period from 1864 until the end of the 1870s saw the most intense development: there were over twenty building projects in the decade from 1864. In the first year the Alexandra cottages were built in the village of West Newton, thereafter the improvements included more substantial houses – Park House and York Cottage – and the station at Wolferton where guests arrived by train from London.

The provision of sport had always been a priority. In the first years Bertie was content to concentrate on hunting which throughout the 1860s he continued to enjoy as much as shooting. He offered his guests the initially modest shooting on the estate, or rented sport on the estates of near-neighbours such as his friend Lord Suffield at Gunton Hall. During these early years there were also events in the summer and in 1866 Bertie opened the batting in a cricket match at Sandringham, playing for the touring club I Zingaria against the Gentlemen of Norfolk. Unfortunately he did not score and the match was over so early that he suggested an improvised game between the visitors and twenty-two members of his household. As the IZ records describe: 'Every grade of employee was marshalled into service, from F. Knollys down through Francatelli, who sounds like a cook, to the humble Coggs, whose name is specifically mentioned as being real, not assumed. The result was the most cheerful match with IZ easy winners over the twenty-two members of the household. HRH contributed 3 runs for IZ.'[3]

Despite the pace of change all over the estate Bertie was initially hesitant to carry out major alterations to the house itself. In the end he was forced into action when Alexandra developed the first symptoms of illness that had sad and permanent effect. Staying at Sandringham over Christmas 1866 and expecting her third child the following February, she began to suffer acute rheumatism brought on by chronic damp and was forced to leave for Marlborough House. She remained unwell through the ensuing weeks but the situation became critical only days before the baby was due when it was clear that she was suffering from rheumatic fever. The baby, Princess Louise, was born in 20 February but Alexandra was in pain for months afterwards and never made a full recovery. The rheumatic fever left her with a stiff knee and pronounced limp. In November 1867 she wrote to Bertie's sister, Louise: 'I have to go about on two sticks which makes me rather *shy* before people.'[4] More serious, it so badly aggravated the congenital form of deafness, otosclerosis, from which she suffered, that the affliction steadily worsened until she eventually became totally deaf. For someone who thrived on human contact and whose alternative sources of inspiration were limited, it was a cruel blow.

Alexandra's slow recovery spurred Bertie into action to set about improving Sandringham's comfort. In 1867 plans were drawn up for the old house to be demolished and replaced. His architect was A. J. Humbert, who had been one of the two designers of Prince Albert's mausoleum in Frogmore. His other work at Sandringham included a circular camellia house in the gardens, the first block of stables, a hexagonal game larder, an ice house, a venison house and the estate's school. Work began on the new house in 1868 and was completed in time for Bertie's birthday in 1870. Built in the 'Tudorbethan' style, with gables and balconies, and with ornate stone dressing to enliven the local brick and carrstone, it was far more substantial than its predecessor, of which only the old conservatory was preserved and transformed into a billiard room.

The saloon which visitors first entered had a minstrels' gallery. Beyond the saloon the long corridor through the centre of the house was hung with arms – mostly presented to Bertie on his tour of India. The main drawing room was decorated in the currently fashionable wedding-cake style of white with rich plasterwork and painted panels containing chubby cherubs. Three of these panels were later filled with glamorous but mediocre portraits of Alexandra and the younger daughters, Victoria and Maud. The Prince of Wales was no aesthete and throughout, the decoration and furnishing were notable for quantity rather than quality. The chairs were large and comfortable and he liked pictures of his family along with scenes that reminded him of his travels and sport. There were plenty of books, but they were read only by guests. The source of greatest pride for the Prince was his own gasworks which lit the house. After his near-fatal attack of typhoid he took no chances with the water and a new supply was drawn from a huge tower built at some distance from the house on Appleton Farm and incorporating a purification system. New gardens followed the building work; W. B. Thomas, who had previously worked at Buckingham Place, made sweeping changes. The original lake was filled in and replaced by two large flower parterres below the long terrace on the west front, while two new lakes were dug beyond the parterres with suitable rockworks and cascades.

Humbert the architect died in 1877 by which time his royal employer was already planning extensions to the new house and other projects. He wrote to Charles Carrington in the same year: 'All my improvements here are getting on very well but there is still much to be done'.[5] The extensions were begun so that they would be ready for his fortieth birthday in 1881. His new architect was a local man, Colonel Robert Edis who added the square wing on the southeast side containing a ballroom and a new conservatory considerably larger than the old one. Edis built another of Bertie's favourite additions, a bowling alley (an idea copied from Trentham in Staffordshire, one of the many homes of Bertie's friend the Duke of Sutherland). The final additions came after a fire in November 1891, which broke out when preparations were being made for the Prince's fiftieth birthday celebrations. A dozen or so bedrooms were burnt and the water applied by the estate's fire brigade caused even more damage downstairs. Bertie was not to be put off, and the party went ahead with a temporary roof of wood, tarpaulins and corrugated iron over the exposed areas. In his rebuilding, Edis balanced up the west façade by adding a long upper storey containing bachelor guest bedrooms over the old conservatory and bowling-alley.

The programme of works was impressive and necessary in order to provide the heir to the throne with a suitable home. But it was also expensive. During the first major flurry of activity, Bertie's Comptroller Sir William Knollys, who had primary responsibility for the royal finances, wrote in 1867: 'Were it not for the outlay at Sandringham, I should have no difficulty up to the present time in keeping the P's expenditure within his Income.'[6] This corrected exaggerated rumours about Bertie's perennial indebtedness; it also indicated the strength of the Prince's commitment to Sandringham. Knollys estimated at that time the cost of the work on the estate currently in progress was £80,000 and that for the four years to May 1867 the Prince's expenditure had exceeded his income by £20,000 per annum. In 1888 Bertie showed a degree of sensibility to the concerns of his advisers when he wrote to Charles Carrington – rather prematurely as things turned out: 'I have, I think, finished all my improvements here, much to the relief of Probyn [Sir Dighton Probyn who that year succeeded Knollys as Comptroller and Treasurer] and Beck [Edmund Beck, the agent at Sandringham] and I think I have every reason to be satisfied.'[7]

The shooting may have been modest when Bertie first bought the estate, but it did not remain so for long. In 1870 three consecutive days in November produced a total bag of 1,029 pheasants, 142 partridges, 5 woodcock, 400 hares, 83 rabbits and 22 various. Over the years new woodlands were planted to improve the cover for game, particularly pheasants and thousands were reared every season. The estate was naturally suitable for partridges which were as important a quarry as the pheasants. For Bertie every aspect of the shoot was paramount; from the uniforms of his keepers and beaters, to the arrival of the ladies for luncheon eaten off armorial plates and served by footmen in a decorated marquee erected on some judiciously chosen site.

The period was notable for a group of men – among whom Bertie was not numbered, but his son Prince George most certainly was – whose shooting was faultless and their interest in the sport obsessive. They included Lord de Grey, who became the Marquess of Ripon and Lord Walsingham. (The latter, when not slaughtering quantities of game in England, amused himself on expeditions to South America where he 'shot' humming-birds with an air-gun for the British Museum's collection.) Such was the cachet of an appearance at a shooting party by any in this elite, that they were able to chose where they went. Sandringham never competed to produce either the largest bags or the most challenging birds. But a day's shooting there was unrivalled for the sheer scale and pageantry, which the royal host enjoyed with gusto, and invitations were coveted by all.

Great as was his own satisfaction, as important for the Prince was that other people enjoyed themselves and were impressed by his efforts. From his childhood the desire to please was intrinsic. Then it was caused by his own disposition and the worry of having caused displeasure. So too was the sense of security that he derived from being able to make people happy. Throughout his life this was manifested in impetuous generosity – usually a personal momento – a tendency equally marked in his wife who was well known for spontaneously pressing money into the hands of servants she suspected of being in need.

All these impulses came out in his role of host at Sandringham. People left with varied memories; of the commotion caused by the royal children or the Prince's pack of dogs, of Alexandra's menagerie of creatures including parrots and monkeys, or his prize cattle and sheep. Some, like Disraeli, did not always enjoy their fellow-guests: 'a strong brigade of the dark sex: buffoons & butts & parasites & swashbucklers . . . & Sykes & Co., & nameless toadies in the shape of mysterious Polish Counts picked up at the Roulette Baths.'[8] But no one, it seemed, was immune to the charm of their host and hostess. The Gladstones stayed on a number of occasions when he was Prime Minister and after a visit for the Prince's birthday in 1880 she remembered: 'the wish to make guests happy and the absence of much form or ceremony' and in particular, being tucked up in bed by Alexandra.[9] A few years later, in January 1884, the Prime Minister's private secretary, Edward Hamilton, was able to enjoy the royal hospitality for himself.

'I have received to my surprise and not a little to my alarm, a summons to go to Sandringham next Saturday. I only hope the reality will not be as formidable as the prospect.' A few days later, after registering his thorough approval of Francis Knollys – an enthusiastic Liberal – and mentioning other guests who included the Russian and French ambassadors and their wives, he continued:

> We were received in the entrance hall by the Prince and Princess. It was a little shy work going in, but the presence of Gladys Lonsdale [the widow of the Earl of Lonsdale who would, in 1885, marry Lord de Grey] already staying here made it easier for me, and the Prince – a model of hosts – soon put one at one's ease.
>
> It is a charming country house – nothing more or less. I am quartered in the cottage, which is a comfortable overflow house close by.

The visit appeared subdued in the extreme; dinner followed by polite conversation and then billiards and bowls for the men. The following day there was church in the morning and at lunch:

> Our numbers were increased by the presence of the three young princesses – nice looking and so simple and unaffected – evidently brought up in the best of ways. After luncheon we all turned out "to do the rounds" – kennels with dogs innumerable, a small menagerie, kitchen garden, dairy, farm and stables in which the princess fed almost all the horses with her own hands. She is devoted to animals.

Finally, on the morning of departure,

> Before starting we all wrote our names in the visitors book having previously registered our weight in another book. My visit was certainly most enjoyable and interesting. Nothing could have been kinder or more gracious than the prince and princess. Every time one sees her one is more struck by her refined beauty and her extraordinary youthful appearance.[10]

The three princesses to whom Hamilton referred – Louise, Victoria and Maud – all looked uncannily alike and bore a strong resemblance to their mother, without ever rivalling her beauty. Their formal education was rudimentary. As a result and because of their sheltered, yet light-hearted upbringing they grew up without affectation but with only a natural sense of fun to overcome dullness. For these reasons, while Bertie loved them as daughters, his feelings did not go any further. A man so devoted to the company of sophisticated and beautiful women and with a tendency toward impatience was hardly likely to be otherwise.

Not least because Alexandra was so possessive a mother, the three daughters' upbringing centred on their family life together. One close friend that they all shared, however, was Evie Forbes, who was exactly the same age as Princess Victoria. In 1886, when she was aged seventeen, the youngest, Princess Maud wrote two letters to Evie, the first to thank her for a sending her photograph. Maud enclosed one of herself with her reply. 'My darling Evie, how dare you call me "dear Madam" you nasty little monkey . . . I am sending you a horrible little photograph of myself which I thought you might like. Ever your loving little friend, Maud'.[11] Later in the year Maud wrote again to complain about a visit she and her sisters were making with her mother to a German spa town.

> It is such an awful nuisance that we are here at this old, dour place. I hate being here and we all feel very ill instead of feeling well – it shows what a horrid place this is . . . We have been here nearly a week and have to take the waters every day which is horrid stuff and I always long to spit it out – we also take the baths which is supposed to make one strong but I don't feel it. I nearly drowned myself the other day as it was too deep and I fell over in my little chair and I called for help but nobody came, but I struggled up all the same.

She goes on to describe the Germans in tones of which her mother would have undoubtedly approved. 'You never saw such frights (just like Germans always are!) I hate every sort of German and I must say they are such vulgar people I think.'[12]

Given his daughters' lack of worldliness and sensuousness, which were so much the hallmarks of society beauties, the Prince knew that their royal status would be responsible for future marriage and position. Nonetheless, it was a significant departure for his eldest daughter, Louise, to marry outside the network of European royalty. An Englishman was a far more suitable prospect to Edward than a continental prince. It was typical of the Prince that while he would never have contemplated pushing his daughter towards a dynastic match, he was happy to encourage her choice of one of his friends, Alexander, Earl of Fife. Aged forty when he married Princess Louise in 1889, Fife was eighteen years her senior, but only eight years younger than his father-in-law. The Prince of Wales was immediately enthusiastic and wrote to Charles Carrington, 'Nothing has given us greater pleasure and satisfaction than our daughter's marriage. It is a complete "Love Match" and we did nothing to bring it about, but you know what an excellent fellow Fife is and I am convinced that they will be very happy. It is also a popular marriage throughout the country and instead of losing a daughter we have gained a son!'[13]

Others agreed with Bertie. The often acerbic Lord Rosebery wrote generously,

> Macduff's [Fife's junior title and the name by which he was known to his friends] marriage seems to me sensible enough. It is really a marriage of affection – she has always been devoted to him, and he on his side is very fond of her and determined to secure a sensible position and not decline into the anomalous servitude of a Lorne [referring to the Marquess of Lorne who was married to Bertie's sister Princess Louise]. They will be married almost before the dowry is voted.[14]

Rosebery's predictions proved accurate. The Fifes – he was elevated to a dukedom by Queen Victoria just before the marriage – established an independent life at his various homes in England and Scotland and he was rich enough in his own right to support the eldest daughter of the heir in suitable style. Louise was thankful to be released from the over-protective and demanding affection of her mother. Although she blossomed into a doting mother herself she never shook off the hesitancy that characterized her girlhood. This shyness notwithstanding, the success of the match was confirmed by Francis Knollys a year after the wedding. 'Princess Louise and Macduff are as happy as possible together, and I don't suppose any marriage could have turned out better.'[15]

While Princess Louise married a friend of her father, the youngest, Princess Maud, married a relation she had known since childhood. Prince Charles of Denmark was her first cousin and a junior officer in the Danish navy when he proposed to Maud in 1895. Although three years his senior she had long enjoyed his company at family parties and happily accepted. She did not, however, take so readily to leaving England and in particular, home at Sandringham. Bertie, happy to indulge his wife's determination that her daughter would return for visits on a regular basis, gave Maud Appleton House on the Sandringham estate as a wedding present. The wedding took place in July 1896. After what was supposed to be a few weeks honeymoon at the house, Maud and her husband were still there in December. He only just persuaded her to leave for Copenhagen in time for Christmas. Quite unexpectedly, in 1906, Charles was elected to the throne of Norway and became King Haakon VII. A few months after the coronation his new Queen wrote to her sister-in-law, Princess May of York, with the artless naiveté which often characterized all three sisters. 'Behold I am a Queen!!! Who would have thought it! and I am the very last person to be stuck on a throne. I am actually getting accustomed to be [sic] called Your Majesty! and yet often pinch myself to feel I am not dreaming!'[16]

Princess Victoria never married; the widespread conclusion was that while Alexandra would put up with losing two of her daughters, like her mother-in-law, she would never give up them all. Victoria was unfortunate as the last to be left single. Indeed, once her sisters had both left the nest it appeared to many observers that the companionship she provided for her mother was both beyond the call of duty and the only case of Alexandra's legendary generosity failing her. In December 1896, after staying with his sister-in-law Nora (Eleanor) Lady Musgrave who was Victoria's lady-in-waiting, Charles Carrington wrote in his diary, 'The situation in the Royal Family seems strained. The Princess is now getting to the "temps de la vie" and is difficult to manage. Princess Charles is gone off to Denmark and Princess Victoria is left alone with "dear Mama" '.[17]

At one time it was thought she might marry Prince Max of Baden (a nephew by marriage of Bertie's eldest sister Vicky) but when Victoria went on an autumn holiday to the Continent, and there seemed an opportunity for their betrothal, he did not turn up and thereafter the always tenuous possibility of a match fell through. There was far more speculation that she would marry Lord Rosebery, whose first wife, Hannah Rothschild, died in 1890, but Rosebery himself consistently denied the rumours and Bertie was certainly opposed to the match. Potential husband or not, however, Rosebery was clearly close to the Princess and fond of her. His loneliness after his wife's death, his natural aloofness and increasing political disillusionment together struck a chord with her own poignant circumstances, despite her not sharing his wide intellectual interests. On more than one occasion he voiced sad concern at her lot to Charles Carrington, his cousin and close political friend, twice within a few weeks in 1897. Carrington wrote afterwards in his diary: 'Of course he brought in Princess Victoria, who is so unwell that she had to stay behind at Sandringham when the Princess went to Copenhagen and she does not seem to be looked after or taken care of, any more than in the old days.' Two months later; 'He gives a bad account of Princess Victoria, who is evidently in a very bad way. No care whatever is taken of her, and she will one day slip through their fingers, then a mausoleum will be built in her memory. It is very sad to see so good a woman so utterly neglected.'[18]

If the three girls were overshadowed by their mother, the two boys similarly suffered in relation to their father. The elder, Prince Albert Victor who was always called Eddy was tall and pale to an effete degree. It is ironic that comments about the young Prince Eddy were similar to those about his father at the same age; he was described as well-mannered, childish and delicate looking. The difference was, however, that while his father overcame his early faltering and developed an expansive personality, Eddy's progress was slow, even as he approached adulthood. He appeared completely listless. His younger brother Prince George, sixteen months younger, was considerably more lively. In the hope that some of this vitality would rouse Eddy from his habitual lethargy, they were educated together. Early years with a private tutor, John Dalton, was followed by a debate about their formal education. Queen Victoria strongly advocated that Eddy should go to Wellington College (founded by the Prince Consort), an unprecedented step for a royal prince. But Dalton's advice won the day and he joined his brother as a naval cadet on board HMS *Britannia* at Dartmouth. Two years later, as it had already been decided that

Prince George would pursue a career in the navy, both princes began a period of three years based on board HMS *Bacchante*, during which they visited the far corners of the British Empire, including South Africa, Australia and the West Indies. Their parents were vexed by a rumour recalled at the time by Lord Esher in his journal: 'It appears that Lord Napier of Magdela, who has been staying at Sandringham, told the Princess of Wales that her two boys have had anchors tattooed on the ends of their noses and that they came and showed him with great pride. The Prince and Princess are in despair and furious.'[19] The Princess wrote to her favourite, George, 'how dare you have your impudent snout tattooed'.[20] But she need not have worried; it was a rumour.

The time aboard the *Bacchante* did little to further the academic education of the boys and after their return in 1882, the aim of sending Eddy to Trinity College, Cambridge, to follow in his father's footsteps, necessitated some intense cramming at Sandringham. One of his tutors considered the idea of Cambridge a waste of both the Prince's time and those who would have the task of teaching him as, 'he hardly knows the meaning of the words "to read".'[21] The tutor's fears were proved correct. Cambridge was not a success and, concerned by accounts of Eddy's wayward behaviour, Bertie removed him early and he joined the 10th Hussars, of which the Prince of Wales was Colonel-in-Chief.

By 1890, when Queen Victoria created Eddy Duke of Clarence and Avondale, it was generally acknowledged that he was a problem. Certainly she preferred to try to not think about the possibility of him inheriting the crown. While people sympathized with Charles Carrington's assessment after Prince Eddy had visited him at Wycombe Abbey in May 1891, few would have joined in his confident conclusion. 'It is pathetic to see how little confidence he has in himself. At Cambridge and in the army he was always "chaffed" and supposed to be a "duffer" – and the P of Wales is hard on him. But there is a great deal in him. He is a great gentleman and will develop later.'[22]

Eddy shared his father's obsession with dress in general and uniforms in particular but otherwise his main predilection appeared to be unsuitable romantic attachments. In August 1890, encouraged to a degree by his mother and more obviously by his sister the Duchess of Fife, he became unofficially engaged to Princess Helene d'Orleans while staying at Mar Lodge, the Fifes' Scottish home. The Princess was attractive and the couple were equally fond of each other. But she was Roman Catholic and the daughter of the Comte de Paris the pretender to the French throne, who had settled in England after banishment from France in 1886. Neither were ideal recommendations for Eddy's future bride.

The union did not founder on opposition from Eddy's parents, who were on friendly terms with the Comte de Paris and his family. But the Comte was implacably opposed to the idea – particularly because his daughter had offered to renounce her Catholicism. Eddy's shortcomings made hasty action a priority for his parents and an alternative bride was found in Princess May of Teck; a sensible, intelligent, but plain daughter of one of Europe's minor and more impoverished royal families. Her parents also bore the ultimate stigma for nineteenth-century continental royalty, a morganatic marriage.

May had known Eddy since childhood and while that did not make the prospect of becoming his wife any more attractive she realistically accepted that she had little option but to comply with parental wishes. Throughout the second half of 1891 the plan unfolded in an uncannily similar manner to the one which preceded the Prince of Wales's marriage thirty years earlier – although the thought that he was using an early marriage to control his son's behaviour in the same way that Victoria and Albert had done with him never crossed his mind. On 3 December Eddy's brother George recorded in his diary that the couple were engaged. Any happiness was short-lived. That Christmas saw an unusually virulent and widespread outbreak of influenza to which the unhealthy young Prince fell victim. At Sandringham where many others among the party were also suffering, his condition worsened rapidly during the early days of the new year. On 14 January, a week after his twenty-eighth birthday, he died after many days of fever and delirium.

The engagement of Princess May to Eddy's younger brother George in May 1893 and their subsequent marriage in July, the widespread relief that an eminently more suitable candidate had now assumed the position of heir-presumptive, and the fact that Eddy's behaviour had too often connected him with scandals, publicly obscured the grief felt by his parents. They had already lost one son, albeit newborn, but this was a far greater blow to the unfailingly happy atmosphere of the family's home. At Eddy's funeral Bertie 'broke down terribly during the ceremony'[23] and for both parents the shortcomings of their son did not make his death any easier to bear. Their affection for him is made understandable by Edward Hamilton's verdict after playing billiards with him at Sandringham that he was 'a pleasing young fellow and un-stuck up'.[24] But as Queen Victoria commented shrewdly in a letter to her daughter Vicky: 'Poor Bertie – his is not a nature made to bear sorrow, or a life without amusement and excitement – he gets bitter and irritable.'[25] Not only did time heal the sadness, but, now that Prince George was his heir, their relationship took on a new significance and intimacy.

CHAPTER SIX

POLITICS, WOMEN AND HORSES

Towards the end of 1890 the Prince of Wales entered his fiftieth year. He reflected on inevitable change when, towards the end of the season, he wrote to Prince George that at all the London balls he had danced, 'not a single valse . . . because I am getting too fat.'[1] An expanding waist-line accompanied by a slight thinning of the hair and appearance of grey in his beard were the visible signs of the onset of middle age. If not exactly vain, Bertie was punctilious about his personal appearance and no detail was too small to merit attention. He was faultless on the convoluted niceties of court dress, uniforms, and what was socially correct for all occasions. After he had become King Sir Henry MacMahon reported to give him a full account of the Amir of Afghanistan's visit to India in 1907, which Sir Henry organized. Fascinating though the account was the King could not restrain himself from replying: 'It's all very interesting Sir Henry, but you should never wear a coloured tie with a frock coat.'[2]

Where court dress was concerned it always paid to check what was the order of the day, as a brief exchange between Sir William Harcourt and the Queen's private secretary, Henry Ponsonby, illustrates. Harcourt was about to become minister in attendance and wrote, 'Dear Ponsonby, "Is it knees?", Yrs W.V.H.' 'Dear Harcourt "As no ladies will be present trousers will be worn", Yrs H.F.P.'[3]

Ponsonby was famously uninterested in his appearance and re-garded by Bertie as sartorially unreliable. Together at the Emperor Frederick's funeral in 1888, Ponsonby wrote afterwards.

> I appeared in uniform. Prince of Wales pleased but critical. I sat at the breakfast at Cologne between the Princess of Wales and Prince Christian. Oliver Montagu, inspired no doubt, objected to my for-age cap. I admit antiquated. Before we got to Hanover I removed superfluous cape and my medals blazed forth. At dinner I sat next to Probyn who said "You have something wrong – I don't know what it is; the Princess of Wales is laughing". I looked at myself and saw that I had two Jubilee medals on. I removed one quickly. She at the end of the table laughed aloud and Prince Albert Victor was happier. The Prince of Wales spoke to me about it.[4]

From the 1880s a constant problem for the Prince of Wales was con-trolling his weight which, at worst, reached around fourteen stone. In 1887 he wrote one of his regular letters to Charles Carrington, who was serving as Governor-General of New South Wales, and ended, 'Tomorrow the Princess and our daughters start for Copenhagen – and I am going to Homberg to try and reduce my weight, which is alas not on the decrease.'[5]

There is no doubt that Bertie's appetite was the main culprit. When faced with some of his favourite food he could rarely resist the tempta-tion to over-indulge. Occasionally brave hosts dared to remonstrate, as when he visited Egypt where Sir Evelyn Baring (who later became the Earl of Cromer) ruled as British Agent-General. A member of Baring's staff recalled that when the Prince was greeted by Baring at Port Said he immediately expressed the desire to savour prawn curry, for which his host's table was renowned. Baring accordingly telegraphed ahead to his wife in Cairo: 'Prawn curry for lunch, extra supply.' His appetite sharpened by the journey, when they arrived and found the curry duly ready: 'The Prince took a huge helping and liked it so much that he asked for a second helping. Having finished it he called to Lord Cromer, "I want some more of that excellent curry of yours", to which he got the cool answer, "You had better not. It is rich enough, and you have already had two helpings".'[6] The Prince later described Baring as 'a very able man but with no manners'.[7] Even when he attempted to diet on his doctors' recommendation, the result was normally only that food was cooked less richly, rather than reduced in quantity. In 1893 he wrote to Lady Cadogan a few days before going to dinner with her: 'As you kindly ask what I am allowed to eat under Sir Thomas Smith's regime? When I dine with you on Tuesday the menu would be the following: clear soup, grilled fish (whiting or sole); grilled beef or roast mutton or beef; roast chicken, gammon partridge or pheasant; fruit.'[8]

Lack of activity was not a reason for the weight problem. Through the 1880s and 1890s the Prince's annual schedule showed no sign of flagging – as was to be the case for the rest of his life. Later it would be dominated by the duties of kingship, but at the moment the constant desire for activity was partly borne of frustration at not being allowed a serious role by Queen Victoria or her ministers.

The Queen and most of her ministers still considered Bertie to be unreliable and indiscreet. Unfortunately, he occasionally proved them right. His attitude over major issues, both at home and abroad, and his choice of friends or informants, was sometimes held up to show either personal bias or lack of judgement. In the autumn of 1879, with memories of the near outbreak of war between Britain and Russia still strong, Bertie broke what had become an annual habit of going to Homburg for a three-week cure, and accompanied his wife to Denmark. Also visiting Alexandra's parents at Bernstorff were her sister Minny and her husband Sasha, the Russian Tsarevich (who would become Tsar Alexander III). Queen Victoria and, more particularly, her Prime Minister, Disraeli, thought the meeting unwise. Bertie revealed his weakness for personal preferences when attempting to pacify his mother before leaving England. 'I shall, of course, avoid politics as much as possible, but as he married our dear Alix's sister, who I am very fond of, I am most anxious that our relations should not be strained.'[9]

The reason why Bertie had broken with habit and accompanied his wife to Denmark, where he was invariably bored, was to atone for his relationship with Lillie Langtry. They had first met in May 1877 at dinner with the Arctic explorer Sir Allen Young. She was then twenty-three and recently married to Edward Langtry. The marriage offered her the means to escape from the parochial dullness of her native Jersey but little else; after being abandoned by his wife during her comet-like rise through London society, Langtry eventually died in 1896 in an asylum in Chester, having been taken in as a vagrant alcoholic.

Lillie Langtry personified the contemporary comments of J. B. Booth that there was, 'at the time of the Marlborough House Set, a cult of feminine beauty.'[10] Within a matter of months she rose from obscurity to become the most talked-of person in London society, purely on account of her looks. The major impetus to her rise came from her association with the Prince of Wales, and knowledge of his wife's tacit acceptance of the situation. He arranged for her to be presented at court and her status as his 'official' mistress was acknowledged – if not approved. The Princess entertained her at parties at Marlborough House. Public attention was enormous, amongst not only the idle curious but also grandees of society. Margot Tennant, the waspish commentator who later married the future Prime Minister, Herbert Asquith, remembered 'great and conventional ladies like old Lady Cadogan and others, standing on iron chairs in the park to see Mrs Langtry walk past'.[11]

Lillie Langtry's looks – her pale complexion and hour-glass figure – were matched by ambition. She befriended the Prime Minister, Gladstone, whose innocent indulgence infuriated his secretary, Edward Hamilton. In April 1882 Hamilton recorded in his diary,

I have been concerned again about the Langtry affairs. Mr G presented her with a copy of his pet book, *Sister Dora*. She is evidently trying to make capital out of the acquaintance which she has formed with him. Most disgreeable things with all kinds of exaggerations are being said. I took the occasion of putting in a word cautioning him against the wiles of the woman, whose reputation is in such bad odour that despite all the endeavours of HRH nobody will receive her in their houses.[12]

Despite his disapproval, Hamilton, along with the rest of London society, went to watch Mrs Langtry's performances on the stage. She made her debut in December 1881, in Goldsmith's *She Stoops to Conquer*, her role championed by the Prince of Wales who ensured that the first night was attended by what *The Times* reported to be 'the most distinguished audience ever seen in a theatre.'[13] In April the following year Hamilton was in the audience again and commented afterwards, 'she is certainly lovely on the stage in appearance and very capable as an actress.'[14] A few months later he repeated his opinion after watching her in *Unusual Match*.

Mrs Langtry's stage career was prompted by shortage of money and the waning of her star. Especially given her liaison with Bertie, gossip circulated freely, much of it intimate and malicious. Reginald Brett, later Lord Esher, recorded in his diary that she had acquired 'a certain complaint' from one lover called Peel. 'She thereupon slept with Abington and accused him of having made her the unwelcome present. He paid her £12,000 which she divided with Peel.'[15] Such liberty with her favours encouraged the rumours and went on even when the Prince of Wales was in attendance. On one occasion he arrived to visit her when she was entertaining Sir George Chetwynd, a weathly racing baronet well-known for his philandering. The Prince was discreetly told by a servant that she was indisposed. Towards the end of the 1890s she took up with the disreputable George Abington Baird mentioned by Esher, a boorish but weathly racehorse owner. He subjected her to regular physical violence, but when asked by a friend why she put up with such treatment, she replied, 'I detest him, but every time he does it he gives me a cheque for £5,000.'[16]

Characters like Abington were beyond the pale for society and even among the racing world, which perpetuated a raffish flavour throughout the nineteenth century, he was generally regarded with disapproval. But the atmosphere of race meetings and the potential excitement of owning racehorses attracted Bertie. Having first registered his racing colours in 1875, a decade later he was an enthusiastic but unsuccessful owner. His attendance at meetings, in particular the annual succession of the Newmarket Classics in May, the Derby then Royal Ascot in June, Goodwood in July, and the Doncaster St Leger in September, gave racing enormous social cachet which could eclipse the sporting element. From the 1870s Bertie gave an annual dinner for fellow members of the Jockey Club on the evening of the Derby. Whether staying in his own suite of rooms at the Jockey Club in Newmarket or with the Duke of Richmond for Goodwood, he always found the social element of race meetings enjoyable.

Although the Prince of Wales bet regularly it was never in excessive amounts and neither the costs of gambling nor his horses in training had any real bearing on the shortage of money which continued

throughout the 1880s and 1890s. In the past the annual excess of his expenditure over income (usually around £20,000) had been covered by the capital sum available in the Duchy of Cornwall funds. The Prince of Wales's second title of Duke of Cornwall entitled him to the revenue from the duchy's estates, composed of extensive farming properties, mainly in the south-west of England, and other lucrative urban areas such as those of Kennington and Lambeth in London. During Bertie's youth the management of the duchy had been overhauled by his father. As a result the annual income increased from £16,000 per annum at the time of Bertie's birth to nearly £60,000 when he took over personal supervision on his twenty-first birthday. During the same period the estate had built up a capital fund of £600,000.

As the duchy capital diminished so expenses increased. Bertie's children were growing up and required funding. There was also the contentious question of the cost of duties he carried out as a result of Queen Victoria's seclusion. This was aggravated by her fixed view on the subject, that any extra money should be voted by parliament, which was matched by Gladstone, who was equally insistent that the money should come from the Queen.

Throughout the 1880s Gladstone's secretary, Edward Hamilton, makes anxious references to the situation in his diary. In January 1884 he wrote:

> I have long held that the affairs are urgent. It is impossible that H.R.H. can be otherwise than heavily insolvent and it always appears to me that the primary considerations are 1. that the sooner the condition of these affairs is disclosed the better and 2. that Mr G is the best, if not only person who can right them . . . My own relief is that the country would be far more willing to vote a substantial sum for the Prince to discharge his liabilities, and to increase his income than to make these periodical grants to junior members of the Royal Family. The Prince is popular, the British public know him, his zeal in discharging his duties and making himself useful is recognized.[17]

His diary entry a few weeks later shows that his master did not share his views.

> On the way to the Chapel Royal this morning Mr G was led to refer

to to the Prince of Wales's affairs again . . . He thinks it would be a most serious matter to have to approach Parl. on the subject. Parl. would be sure to insist on the appointment of a commission of inquiry. No case would be made as to the Prince's being put to any material expense by the retirement from public life of HM. They would probably find a total absence of economical management of his affairs and would be sure to insist in future on the strict appropriation of the grants made to him.[18]

Five years later Gladstone did put the matter to parliament and – in the face of radical outrage – succeeded in obtaining a grant of £60,000 capital and an extra £36,000 annual income for his children. But it did not solve the problem and Gladstone argued that Victoria should add £50,000 per annum, 'in consideration of the extent to which she allows him to discharge her social duties for her.'[19]

On the racecourse, the Prince of Wales finally had his first winner in 1886 with a horse called Counterpane. The following year another success, in the Grand Military Hunt Cup run at a new course at Sandown Park brought undeserved embarrassment. The victory was objected to by the owner of the second horse on the grounds that the race was only open to owners who had seen active military service. The objection was upheld and the Prince's horse disqualified.

The embarrassment was all the harder to bear because the incident came when Bertie had been pressing to be allowed to take active part in the British campaigns in Egypt and the Sudan. In July 1882 Gladstone had reluctantly ordered the bombardment of Alexandria. Egyptian unrest had been boiling up since 1875, when his Tory predecessor, Disraeli, had cunningly acquired the bankrupt Egyptian Khedive's interest in the Suez Canal, giving Britain a controlling interest. The bombardment only exacerbated the trouble as in August an army was sent to Egypt under the command of Sir Garnet Wolseley. Bertie's brother, Arthur Duke of Connaught – a serving brigadier at the time – led the Guards contingent. The Prince of Wales's lack of military experience, however outweighed by his enthusiasm, meant that there was not a place for him, even if Queen Victoria and Gladstone's ministers had not considered it politically impossible. The rebuff was repeated in 1884 when English garrisons in the Sudan, established by Wolseley's expedition to maintain order, were threatened by fanatical nationals and Wolseley once again set out from England, this time on the ill-fated attempt to relieve General Gordon in Khartoum.

Military service was a dream denied the Prince of Wales throughout his life and he was mortified by his rejection. Tactless comments by some senior officers about his military uselessness, and vulgar cartoons in the European press, lampooning him as a pleasure-loving coward increased his discomfort. Frustration at never being allowed any military role beyond the purely ceremonial partly accounted for his obsession with uniforms, decorations and regimental rank.

The Prince of Wales was equally unsuccessful in his efforts to persuade Queen Victoria to give him some useful involvement in matters of state. Jobs with any real degree of responsibility were few and far between, one being the official tour of Ireland in 1885 that the Prince carried out with Alexandra and their eldest son Prince Eddy. In 1882 the murder in Phoenix Park, Dublin of the newly-appointed chief Secretary for Ireland, Lord Frederick Cavendish and the permanent Under Secretary Thomas Burke, by nationalist extremists, was a shocking illustration of the strength of feeling among nationalists who were politically drawn up behind the fiery MP Charles Parnell.

Much opposition to English rule was focused on the Lord Lieutenant, Earl Spencer, holding the post for the second time and an old friend of the Prince of Wales. When Irish American supporters of the nationalists were waging a campaign of dynamite explosions in London, Spencer was hopeful that a visit to Ireland by the Prince of Wales would have the beneficial effect of drawing together loyal support and thereby countering the nationalist efforts. Spencer's confidence was not shared by either Queen Victoria or her Prime Minister, Gladstone and Bertie had no enthusiasm for a visit unless it was clearly supported, and paid for, by the government. In January 1885 Francis Knollys outlined the Prince's frustration in a note to Henry Ponsonby: 'I have written to Lord Spencer with the Prince's approval, that the government (with one or two exceptions) are invariably indifferent to what H.R.H. does, or does not, do; and that this is annoying to him sometimes.'[20]

The government eventually agreed to support and finance the tour and on 7 April Bertie and his party arrived at Kingstown, two weeks after Dublin City Council had voted to take no official part in his reception. In the event the city's welcome was warmer than had been hoped but in the south of the country protests were frequent. During one train journey black flags painted with the skull and crossbones were waved at the passing royal carriages and in Cork the nationalist demonstrations and shouting were so offensive that the Prince's equerry, Arthur Ellis, wrote to Queen Victoria: 'No one who went through this day will ever forget it, it was like a bad dream'. Ellis went on, however: 'The Prince of Wales showed the greatest calmness and courage.'[21] After Cork the reception was calmer in Killarney and Limerick, while in the north, visits to Belfast and Londonderry were cheered by enormous and enthusiastic crowds.

The three-week tour of Ireland confirmed the Prince's ability to make the most of such public appearances and to cope equally well with hostile receptions as well as friendly ones. Gladstone's admiration for Bertie's achievements once again prompted the Prime Minister to suggest to Queen Victoria that it was time for the Prince of Wales to be given access to Cabinet and Foreign Office papers. The royal reply was predictably consistent with her past opinions. The Queen was proud of her son, but saw no reason to sanction his access to papers. As before, Bertie was left gleaning information as best he could from senior politicians who were his friends or acquaintances. It was largely through the efforts of two of these, Charles Carrington and Sir Charles Dilke, that in 1884 he was given the rare opportunity for worthwhile service, becoming president of a royal commission on the housing of the working classes, a subject which aroused considerable public outcry throughout the early 1880s.

Carrington, a Liberal peer who was responsible for local government business in the House of Lords, suggested to the Prince of Wales that it would be useful for him to see at first hand the appalling conditions in which much of London's working class was housed. Writing afterwards to his wife Carrington described how, 'I bought him some rough clothing into which he changed at my house at Whitehall and we started off to visit some of the worst courts in Clerkenwell and Holborn. The first room we went into had no fire, or furniture and was inhabited by a gaunt, half starved woman with three little children practically naked lying on a heap of rags in the corner . . .' When the landlord told the visitors that the woman could not pay and would not leave, 'the prince was so horrified that he wanted to give her a £5 note. Had he done this, I don't think we could have got out alive as the news would have spread like wildfire . . .' Carrington concluded: 'The visit was a great success. HRH was not recognized and in no way interfered with or molested. He went into some horrible places and showed great interest and pluck. I hope it will do him and the cause of the suffering poor great good.'[22]

His involvement with the commission gave Bertie his first – and only – opportunity to make a major speech during a debate in the House of Lords. In often emotional language he described his visit: 'I can assure your Lordships that the condition of the poor, or rather of their dwellings, was perfectly disgraceful'.[23]

In the early stages of the commission's work the Prince regularly attended meetings but he soon absented himself. When his younger brother Leopold, Duke of Albany died in Cannes in March Bertie travelled out to accompany the body home. In April family duty called again; this time the wedding in Darmstadt of his niece Princess Victoria of Hesse to his cousin and friend Prince Louis of Battenberg. In the autumn he put off his annual visit to Homburg in order to attend. When the commission reported at the end of the year he had only been present at nineteen out of a total of fifty-one meetings, which many senior politicians held up as evidence that any such roles for him would be compromised by his social life and family duties.

At those meetings that he did attend, one of Bertie's most notable contributions was his easy ability to get on with all the committee's members. They ranged from Lord Salisbury to Cardinal Manning, the Roman Catholic Archbishop of Westminster, and the radical MP Henry Broadhurst. In November all the members were invited to Sandringham, in Broadhurst's words, 'in the first place, I presume, as an act of hospitality, but secondly that the Commissioners might inspect for themselves the cottages on the Sandringham estate.'[24] Bertie was understandably proud of the new cottages with which he had replaced the estate's previous hovels.

In clear evidence of the sensibility which was his greatest as both Prince and King, when Broadhurst was unable to join the group, Bertie wrote to him shortly afterwards. 'Hearing that I made it a rule not to dine out, and that I did not possess a dress-coat, the Prince of Wales renewed his invitation in a form which I could not refuse without being guilty of unpardonable rudeness.' He goes onto describe how,

On my arrival His Royal Highness personally conducted me to my rooms, made a careful inspection to see that all was right, stoked the fires, and then, after satisfying himself that all my wants were provided for, withdrew and left me for the night. In order to meet the difficulties in the matter of dress dinner was served in my own rooms each night.[25]

Broadhurst was given a detailed tour of the estate. After a long walk and after visiting a number of cottages they ended up at the village club that Bertie had built where, Broadhurst recalled: 'We had, I think, a glass of ale each and sat down in the clubroom where we found several farm labourers enjoying their half-pints and pipes.' The whole trip was a revelation to the gruff, working-class Member of Parliament. 'I left Sandringham with a feeling of one who had spent a week-end with an old chum of his own rank in society rather than one who had been entertained by the Heir-Apparent and his Princess.'[26]

The royal commission had been chaired by Sir Charles Dilke, fervently disliked by Queen Victoria for his radical views. In 1871, at the height of republican agitation against the monarchy, he had accused her in a speech of 'dereliction of duty'. Neither did the Queen appreciate his overbearing manner. After Dilke's first visit to Windsor as a cabinet minister the Queen's secretary Henry Ponsonby recorded with amusement, 'I think HM thought his conversation a little loud. We subdue our voices considerably here while eating the royal beef.'[27] Bertie, despite his mother's views, was content to overlook Dilke's previous outbursts and cultivate his friendship. Dilke was congenial company and appreciative of good food; more important, in 1880 he was made Under Secretary at the Foreign Office to Lord Graville. Unlike his superior, who was not prepared to defy Queen's Victoria's orders about her son's access to Cabinet papers, for the sake of his own friendship with the Prince, Dilke was happy to do so. He became a regular guest at Marlborough House and formed an incisive opinion of the Prince.

He has more sense and more usage of the modern world than the Queen, but less real brain power . . . It is worth talking seriously to the Prince. One seems to make no impression at the time but he does listen all the same, and afterwards, when he is talking to somebody else, brings out everything you have said.[28]

But in 1886 Dilke's career was ruined when he was cited as co-respondent in the divorce case of a fellow Liberal MP. The Prince remained characteristically loyal after most others had turned their back on Dilke. After his accession in 1901 he reinstated him at court. But his association with the discredited minister did not help his efforts to be taken seriously by the Queen and senior politicians.

It seemed that all such efforts were doomed to end unhappily. In 1884 Bertie had agreed to a reconciliation with Lord Randolf Churchill, whom he had ostracized for his part in the Aylesford affair nearly ten years earlier. Reconciliation was encouraged by Bertie's admiration for Churchill's wife and his political skills which propelled him to seniority in the Tory party during the early 1880s. Liberal opponents did not share the Prince of Wales's enthusiasm. In November 1881 Edward Hamilton recorded in his diary, 'It is sickening to think that a man of such unscrupulousness and with such want of seriousness could be coming to the front in politics.'[29] For his part Churchill was happy to keep the Prince up to date and his information was given considerable weight when he was made Chancellor of the Exchequer and Leader of the House in Lord Salisbury's government of 1886. Only months later, however, Churchill attempted to pressurize his Cabinet colleagues into reversing their earlier opposition to his cuts in the service estimates for the armed forces. While staying at Windsor Castle, he sent a letter of resignation to Salisbury. The Prime Minister was not one to get involved in theatricals and was already finding his Chancellor's abrasiveness wearisome. Much against Churchill's expectations, he accepted the resignation. Queen Victoria, for whom Churchill was – like Dilke – another *bête noire*, was furious when she learnt that the resignation had been sent from her castle on her writing paper. She vented a good degree of her rage on Bertie, to whom Churchill had belatedly written an explanatory letter, and who loyally, but inadvisely, attempted to intercede in support.

The associations with Dilke and Churchill, both of which ended with unsatisfactory effect on Bertie's reputation were largely brought about by his formal exclusion from the affairs of state. So too was his constant habit of recommending people for honours and pestering prime ministers of the day to elevate his friends and acquaintances. In November 1882 Edward Hamilton wrote in his diary: 'In deference to the Prince of Wales Oscar Clayton [the Prince's physician] has been submitted for a knighthood. It is to be hoped that no disagreeable stories come out about him.'[30] When Lord Salisbury took office in 1886 Bertie canvassed for three friends, all of whom were rewarded, arguably above their merits; Lord Cadogan became Lord Privy Seal, Lord Londonderry, Viceroy of Ireland and Lord Charles Beresford Fourth Lord of the Admiralty. (Bertie had originally suggested that the command of the Irish Police Force would be suitable.)

The appointment of Charles Beresford was not a success. With a past career as a swashbuckling naval officer – he had commanded a gunboat during the Egyptian campaign – and his stormy Irish temperament, he ruffled numerous feathers at the admiralty. In 1888 he resigned and the following year took up the Prince's suggestion to return to active service. This was not only prompted by his being better suited to a sailor's than a politician's life. For some time Beresford had been carrying on a passionate and widely known affair with Lady Brooke (universally known as Daisy) who was married to the heir to the Earl of Warwick. At a point when open scandal – and the likelihood of Lord Brooke seeking a divorce – seemed imminent, Beresford decided to return to sea. Among those contemporaries who looked on with interest was the future Lord Esher, who committed his impression of events to his journal in 1892.

The facts of the Brooke Scandal are these. Two years ago Lady Brooke was the mistress of Charlie Beresford. Lady Charles was about to be confined, upon which Lady Brooke wrote to Charlie and in strong – open – coarse and abusive language accused him of unfaithfulness to her. It is probable that she wished to break off relations with him in favour of George Chetwynd. Lady Charles opened and confiscated the letter. She took it to George Lewis [the leading society lawyer whom Beresford later accused of 'lickerish servility']. He spoke to the Prince of Wales about it whom he knew to be an intimate friend of Lady Brooke. The Prince remonstrated with Lady Charles but was met with nothing but abuse of Lady B. Ultimately the matter was hushed up. But the P of W and his set had the imprudent idea of cutting Lady Charles; gradually she dropped out of society. So infuriated at her treatment, she printed or typewrote a pamphlet containing many libellous statements about Lady B and embodying Lady Brooke's letter.

Here was a difficult and dangerous situation. Many people saw the pamphlet. Would it be published? Involve a libel suit? Charles Beresford who commanded a Queen's ship returned. He wrote an insolent reply to a letter from the P of Wales. Lady Charles wrote to the Queen. Now Salisbury interfered – and after a long negotiation settled the matter on the basis of an apology from Lord Charles to the P of W, from the P of W to Lady Charles, the temporary exile of Lady Charles and the exclusion from court of Lady Brooke. Lord Salisbury brought peace, whether with much honour or not may be questioned.[31]

Like most accounts, Esher's was accurate in the main, but omitted certain elements. Beresford was so incensed at the treatment of his wife that on 12 January 1890, he called unannounced at Marlborough House and, according to Lord Salisbury's recollections, roundly abused the Prince and came close to striking him. The threatening pamphlet was not put together by Lady Charles Beresford, but by her sister. And rather than interfering, Lord Salisbury was drawn in to negotiate much against his will and did so with considerable discretion, including dealing with Queen Victoria.

The Beresford affair lasted from 1889 until 1892 and at some date early in the preceedings Daisy Brooke became Bertie's mistress. Certainly it was before March 1890 when Charles Carrington's brother Bill, a long-serving courtier and at the time an equerry to Queen Victoria reported to his brother in New South Wales, that, 'In the last drawing room Lady Brooke looked the best but her reception by the Princess of Wales and daughters was dreadful. The expression of the P of W made up for it.'[32]

Throughout his life Bertie demonstrated a weakness for falling for women, but at no other time did it cause him to be so blind or bring him so much trouble as in the case of Daisy Brooke. Unquestionably beautiful, licentious and unscrupulous, she ensnared the willing Prince with consummate ease and it defies belief that she was later to write in her memoirs, 'we obeyed our parents, respected our elders, and kept our promises, even our marriage vows.'[33]

Daisy Brooke drew Bertie into the Beresford affair, albeit with little resistance on his part, and she was also instrumental in the most damaging blow that his reputation and popularity ever received, the Tranby Croft affair.

Traditionally Bertie had stayed for the St Leger meeting at Doncaster with his old friend Christopher Sykes, but by 1890 the hopelessly generous Sykes was virtually bankrupt – largely through the strain of royal entertainment – and was not able to accommodate the Prince in sufficient style. Daisy therefore organized for him to stay at Tranby Croft, the home of a shipping magnate named Arthur Wilson. She, however, was prevented from being there as a few days before the meeting her stepfather the Earl of Rosslyn died. Old acquaintances such as General Owen Williams, the Earl of Coventry and one of Bertie's favourite wealthy Jewish friends, Reuben Sassoon, hardly made up for her absence.

At the Prince's suggestion the after-dinner entertainment on the first evening of the party was a game of baccarat which was illegal in England. Bertie, however, enjoyed it to the extent of having his own set of counters bearing the Prince of Wales's feathers. They were used on this occasion. During play one of the guests, Sir William Gordon-Cumming, was suspected by Wilson's son of cheating. His suspicions were upheld by other members of the party whom Wilson alerted. After another game on the second evening when Gordon-Cumming was closely observed at the table, he was formally accused of cheating and forced to sign a paper in which, while he did not actually confess, he swore 'never to play cards again as long as I live.'[34]

Gordon-Cumming was a colonel in the Scots Guards and a long-time acquaintance of the Prince of Wales. He also had many enemies mainly because, as one observer remarked, 'He had cuckolded so many husbands and been witty at the expense of so many fools.'[35] He was forced to sign the paper by the party's two eldest members, General Owen Williams and Lord Coventry, to which they and the other players – including the Prince – added their names, in the vain hope that the scandal could be contained.

This would have been difficult in any event; the fact that Gordon-Cumming was not universally popular in society made it all the more unlikely. In a short time it was clear that the story was widely circulated. Towards the end of 1890 and in the early weeks of the following year Gordon-Cumming felt compelled to take action in an attempt to clear his name, given that the silence which had been assured him by other members of the house party had not been maintained. His decision, in February 1891, to issue an action for slander against his accusers caused panic, not least because it would call the Prince of Wales into the witness box in a civil court. Frantic attempts were mounted – with the Prince's support – to settle the case in other ways; either by a military court or even a private inquiry by the committee of the Guards Club. But these failed and on 1 June the case came to court, before jury and the Lord Chief Justice, Lord Coleridge.

The five accused of slander were represented by George Lewis, (the solicitor whom Lady Charles Beresford had approached with Daisy's Brooke's threatening letter and who had shown it to the Prince of Wales) and Sir Charles Russell, who would become Attorney-General for the second time in 1892. Gordon Cumming was represented by the Solicitor-General, Sir Edward Clarke. It was Clarke's conduct of the case which, as the Prince's biographer, Philip Magnus, commented, made it seem to the mass of people 'as though the Prince of Wales were on trial.'[36] Thanks to Clarke he had to attend for six days and only missed the final seventh, when the jury announced their verdict that Gordon-Cumming had indeed cheated and the five accused were not guilty of slander. Sir William's subsequent dismissal from the army and social ostracism were no comfort to the beleaguered Prince. When, the day after the trial ended, Gordon-Cumming married an American heiress, Bertie exploded to his son George; 'Thank God! – the Army and Society are now well rid of such a damned blackguard. The crowning point of infamy is that he, this morning, married an American young lady, Miss Garner (sister of Mme de Breteuil) with money!'[37]

Sir Edward Clarke spared no effort in his condemnation of Gordon-Cumming's accusers, particularly the Prince of Wales. His main thrust, that Gordon-Cumming was sacrificed in an attempt to safeguard the Prince's reputation and conceal any public knowledge that he enjoyed illegal gambling, found a large and receptive audience. There were many calls for the Prince to make a public statement condemning all forms of gambling. Queen Victoria suggested a letter to the Archbishop of Canterbury, Dr Benson, but the Prime Minister Lord Salisbury felt this was not the answer. In letters to both Lord Hartington and Lord Cadogan, senior friends of Bertie's whom the Queen trusted and who were brought in as go-betweens, he gave his reasons. Rebutting a letter from Gladstone suggesting an announcement, Salisbury told Hartington that he felt it was no business of any minister of the Crown to 'make any such pronouncement'. There were clear subjects on which ministers could be expected to give an opinion, 'but the private morals of the Prince of Wales do not come into that scope and we ought not to be questioned about them. If we are questioned we should refuse to discuss them.' He went on to voice equal misgivings about the Prince himself saying anything publicly,

> If he was fortunate in his expressions, he might produce a favourable effect by such an utterance; but it would be exceedingly difficult and the chances are much against him. And it would be an acknowledgement of submission to the spiritual thunders of the Revd Hughes Hughes, which would be a bad precedent for the future.[38]

Eventually, in August 1891, Bertie did exchange a series of letters with the Archbishop, which aired suitable sentiments at the same time as emphasizing his support of racing, condemnation of which he refused to contemplate.

> I have a horror of gambling, and should always do my utmost to discourage others who have an inclination for it, as I consider that gambling, like intemperance, is one of the greatest curses that a country can be afflicted with. Horse-racing may produce gambling, or it may not; but I have always looked upon it as a manly sport which is popular with Englishmen of all classes.[39]

Bertie was fortunate that throughout these proceedings his family and friends supported him wholeheartedly. But many of them admitted in private that errors of judgement had been made throughout. In May 1891 Charles Carrington wrote furiously in his diary:

> I met John Delacour in St James's Street who said Sir William Gordon-Cumming, if he is allowed to retire from the army and was not kicked out, would take his name off all his clubs: would leave England for ever and practically confess, and throw up the sponge – I went and told Francis [Knollys] this; but George Lewis the lawyer cannot resist the splendid advertisement of this miserable baccarat business, and insists on bringing the P of Wales into Court. He said in my presence "the public must not be disappointed". It is deplorable as the scandal of the P of W being implicated in a dirty

gambling row of this sort will do incalculable damage. Coventry and Owen Williams have behaved all thro' like idiots.[40]

Queen Victoria was even more outraged. However, as always when her son was faced with a personal crisis, her support was constantly affirmed with her letters to him and his sister Vicky in Germany, tempered only by fears for his – and the monarchy's – reputation. In the middle of the trial she wrote to Vicky on 8 June:

This horrible Trial drags along, and it is a fearful humiliation to see the future King of this country dragged (and for the second time) through the dirt, just like anyone else, in a Court of Justice. I feel it is a terrible humiliation, and so do all the people. It is very painful and must do his prestige great harm. Oh! if only it is a lesson for the future! It makes me very sad.[41]

Alexandra was similarly supportive. She wrote to her younger son 'Darling Georgie' that only his father's 'good nature' had caused him to become involved and she referred to Sir William as a 'worthless creature' and 'vile snob'.[42] (During the nineteenth century a snob was more akin to a cad rather than having today's meaning of socially ambitious.) But the situation placed strain on their relations through the summer of 1891, running concurrently as it did with the more testing problem of Daisy Brooke. It was not in Alexandra's nature to confront her husband when she was unhappy. Instead she tended to remove herself. During the autumn of 1891 her usual absence from England was extended. She accompanied Bertie to Cowes and then, as was customary, left to visit her family in Denmark shortly after he had departed for Homburg. But as public discussion of Tranby Croft quietened down, rumours circulating in society about the continuing Beresford scandal upset her enormously. Instead of returning to England as planned on 13 October, at the last minute she went to Lividia, in the Crimea, to stay with her sister and the Tsar, and to celebrate their silver wedding. As a result, she was away for Bertie's fiftieth birthday on 9 November, which had already been marred by the fire at Sandringham on 31 October.

Popular moralizing about the Prince of Wales's involvement in illegal gambling combined with widespread disapproval of his liaison with Daisy Brooke to put his reputation at its lowest level. While he was prepared to be seen to make amends over the baccarat case, his conduct regarding Daisy Brooke more often than not was insensitive. In July 1891 Charles Carrington travelled by boat to South Africa with the Marquess of Stafford (who would succeed his father as Duke of Sutherland a year later). Also on the boat was a certain General Booth. Comments by both the general and Lord Stafford made depressing listening for the ever-loyal Carrington. Booth was forthright as Carrington wrote to his wife (using the nickname by which he invariably referred to the Prince of Wales in letters to her):

> His ideas of poor Tum are simply awful, and his description of the estimation in which he is held by the religious portion of the lower classes is rather alarming . . . Everyone has a notion that a Brooke divorce case is only a question of weeks, and I have been perhaps useful in disillusioning Booth's mind on that score; but it is very sad to hear such opinions openly expressed when one thinks what a power Tum might be in the country. Stafford has been very outspoken about 'Daisy'. He and Lady Stafford were induced to go to the opera with Lady Brooke on the distinct understanding that Tum was not to be there; of course, in he walked, and Strathy took his wife away. This infuriated Tum who abused and cut her last year, but it is alright now. This is all very sad and, of course, gets repeated . . . The feeling against him is evidently much stronger than one had any idea of, and I can't help feeling apprehensive.[43]

The Princess of Wales's deliberate absence from her husband was ended by crisis when Prince George fell seriously ill with typhoid only days after his father's birthday. He recovered after spending six weeks in bed, but relief at his safety was overtaken by the death of his older brother, the Duke of Clarence. Such family blows served to heal the rift between Bertie and his wife – who could never maintain a position of anger with him for very long. They also produced public sympathy which helped to dispel his unpopularity. But Tranby Croft and Daisy Brooke together made for the most disapproved of episode in Bertie's life and because of the fall in his public esteem that they brought about, provided a salutary lesson.

CHAPTER SEVEN

TOWARDS THE THRONE

Almost exactly a year after the Duke of Clarence's death the Princess of Wales was stricken by the death of her closest male friend, Oliver Montagu. Montagu, only forty-eight when he died, was a younger son of the Earl of Sandwich. He commanded the Royal Horse Guards and was an equerry to the Prince of Wales. His attitude towards the Princess was one of Arthurian chivalry. He never married, instead serving her with dedicated loyalty and affection. She was devoted to him and, after his death, wrote that he was 'the best and truest of men, one to be relied on in every relation of life; faithful, discreet and trustworthy, gentle, kind, just and brave, and noble both in life and death.'[1] As Alexandra's biographer, Georgina Battiscombe, concluded: 'Although they had not been lovers they had been very close to one another'.[2] Every year she sent flowers on the anniversary of his death, to be placed on his grave in the churchyard of Hinchingbroke, the family home in Huntingdonshire.

As both Carrington and Esher recorded separately, his death increased the loneliness which the Princess's deafness, the loss of her son and – to an extent – the behaviour of her husband together contributed. Carrington (who had become Lord Chamberlain in 1892, assuming responsibility for court functions such as levées and afternoon receptions) wrote briefly to his wife, 'Oliver is buried on

Tuesday. The princess goes abroad immediately. Tum does both lev-ées.'³ Esher was less guarded, writing to Millicent Stafford (shortly to become Duchess of Sutherland, whom Esher greatly admired and who was one of his most intimate correspondents), he said:

> I can imagine the profound distress of the Princess of Wales, so isola₁ ₂d, as she is from all human affections. It will probably be a great temptation to her to remain much out of the country. For many years her life can only have been interesting through its relation to him . . . So she will probably turn away with her broken wing and gravitate more to her relations in Russia and Denmark.⁴

During the following year, 1894, Esher's predictions proved accurate when the Prince and Princess of Wales both travelled to Russia. Alexandra went first with their daughters in July, to attend the wedding of her niece, Grand Duchess Xania, the Tsar's eldest daughter, to Grand Duke Alexander Michaelovitch. Alexandra and her daughters returned to England, but another royal Russian wedding seemed imminent after the betrothal of the Tsarevich Nicholas to Bertie's niece Princess Alix of Hesse. This possible match was eclipsed, however, at the end of September, when Tsar Alexander III, aged only forty-nine, became seriously ill. He was taken from St Petersburg to the royal palace at Lividia on the Crimea coast, in the hope of recovery, but he died on 1 November. On 3 November the Prince and Princess of Wales arrived, to comfort her sister, the Russian Empress.

For the next month Bertie was at his most considerate and energetic throughout the exhausting funeral arrangements. He spent his fifty-third birthday travelling on the cortege train which carried the dead Tsar first to Moscow and on to St Petersburg. While his wife consoled her sister he concentrated on establishing friendly relations with his nephew the new Tsar, Nicholas II, and maintaining harmony between the other royal relations who attended the funeral. Throughout the processions in both cities, which lasted for hours, and the successive funeral services, which were equally lengthy, Bertie was reassuringly in attendance on the new young Tsar and won universal admiration. His equerry Arthur Ellis might write with exasperation in a letter to Queen Victoria of 'the thirty-ninth repetition of the same mass', but the Prince offered no such complaints, even when, at the final service before interment he had to kiss the dead Tsar's lips. Nor were there many moments of humour to lighten the oppressive atmosphere of mourning, although Charles Carrington (who was in attendance as the Queen's Lord Chamberlain) could hardly contain his mirth after Bertie and his nephew had bestowed honorary ranks of Colonel on each other; the Scots Greys and 27th Dragoon Regiment of Kiev respectively. Carrington found the Prince proudly trying on the new uniform and was greeted by 'a fat man in a huge shaggy greatcoat looking like a giant polar bear.'[5]

The young Tsar married his cousin Alix on 26 November, a few days after the completion of his father's funeral and on 2 December Bertie left St Petersburg for home, with his son the Duke of York, whose presence had been a boon for his father. The Princess of Wales remained with her sister for a further two months. Carrington wrote before the departure: 'They are all delighted with the Prince of Wales; his sympathy and attendance of these terrible ceremonies have touched their hearts. There is no-one like him when there is any real work to be done. He seems to be made of iron.'[6] Bertie was even more gratified that, for once, his visit appeared to have been appreciated at home, especially when the Prime Minister Lord Rosebery wrote in fulsome terms. After congratulating the Prince on 'the good and patriotic work that you have accomplished since you left England' he went on, 'Never has your royal Highness stood so high in the national esteem as today, for never have you had such an opportunity. That at last has come and has enabled you to justify the highest anticipations.'[7]

Rosebery's optimism was premature, for nothing about Bertie's position was to change to any degree. But he had demonstrated his instinctive skill at capitalizing on personal relations at a time when many in Britain were keen to dissipate the suspicion which had long troubled Britain's relations with Russia. His continued exclusion by the Queen may have been frustrating. But the manner of operating that Bertie established during these years was far better suited to his temperament and way of life than relentless poring over papers and lengthy correspondence with ministers.

Queen Victoria communicated either directly with her ministers or through Ponsonby, and through the network of her family on the continent. She saw no need, and had no desire to cultivate informal personal relations. By contrast, the wide range of friendship and acquaintances that sustained the Prince of Wales's life were to prove invaluable when eventually he succeeded to the throne. They were to be a major influence on the changing style of monarchy which he introduced, as one of his ministers, St John Brodrick, later described.

> In general society the long seclusion of Queen Victorian weighed heavily against the social recognition of men with public achievements to their credit, unless they were actually national heroes. King Edward's catholicity was a real strength to the Crown. All sorts of people came into the social limelight, hitherto reserved for the few. Moreover, his perchant for men of business extinguished the last ember of the early Victorian view that there was some hiatus between aristocracy and trade. But the fiction died hard.[8]

Over the years an array of firm contacts were established to serve different requirements. Congenial ambassadors such as the Russian Baron de Stael, the Austrian Count Mensdorff and the Portuguese Marquis de Soveral became friends. Financial and business advice – and assistance – continued to come from various Rothschilds, as well as the Hungarian Jew, Baron Maurice de Hirsch. Hirsch held huge shooting parties for the Prince on his continental estates and shared his enthusiasm for racing. For his part Bertie gave Hirsch the weight of his social approval. After Hirsch's death in 1896, the executor of his will, Ernest Cassel, came to the fore, and by the time of the Prince's accession had become one of his inner circle of confidants. In addition to his regular travels in Europe, house, dinner and shooting parties, all provided opportunities for the cultivation of personal relations at which Bertie excelled, and for the informal exchange of opinions and gathering of information. By the time he became King the network, at home and overseas, was impressive.

Bertie's success in Russia was in marked contrast to his relations with the other most powerful European monarch, his nephew William II, who had become the German Emperor in 1888 after the premature death of his father, Frederick III. Frederick reigned for only ninety-nine days before his death from cancer. William's succession was viewed with consternation by his mother, Bertie's sister Vicky, even if Bertie himself was characteristically prepared to overlook the constant irritations which had troubled relations with his nephew. At an early stage, however, it was clear that responsibility would not make the young Emperor any more conciliatory, rather the opposite. Now senior in precedence to his uncle, he found a number of opportunities to cause trouble and offence. Bertie's nature was to avoid all such personal confrontations, but at times he found his nephew's antics intolerable. His sentiments were often shared by Queen Victoria who repeatedly found that her authority as grandmother counted for little. In the troubled prelude to William's state visit to England in 1889 she wrote to the Prime Minister, 'The complaint that the Prince of Wales has treated him as a nephew, and not as an Emperor, is really too vulgar and too absurd, as well as untrue, almost to be believed. If he has such notions he had better never come here. The Queen will not swallow this affront.'[9] Relations were temporarily patched up, however; the Emperor did come, and was at his most charming.

The bonhomie between uncle and nephew was superficial and temporary. In May 1891 Bertie wrote to his sister Vicky: 'Willy is a bully, and most bullies, when tackled, are cowards.'[10] Unfortunately, 'tackling' his nephew was out of the question, not least because a few weeks later Bertie's involvement in the Tranby Croft affair provided William with an excuse to send the Queen a swingeing criticism of his uncle's conduct. A few years later the bullying Bertie referred to effectively forced the Prince's retirement from yacht racing, the sport that gave him great satisfaction during the early 1890s. The unbeaten successes which he achieved at Cowes with his yacht *Britannia* from its first season in 1893 were brought to an abrupt end when the German Emperor decided to take up the sport in earnest. In 1896 he produced *Meteor II* a larger version of *Britannia* and designed by the same man, which proved invincible. The competitive Bertie was not prepared to take part in order to be defeated by his nephew. Equally unpalatable, the German Emperor began using the regatta for a tasteless display of German imperial might, arriving in the Solent escorted by either the newest or largest ships in his navy. The following year *Britannia* was sold and, although he and Alexandra continued to attend Cowes, Bertie retired from the sport. 'The regatta at Cowes was once a pleasant holiday for me, but now that the Kaiser has taken command it is nothing but a nuisance, with that perpetual firing of salutes, cheering and other tiresome disturbances.'[11]

The Prince's poor relations with his nephew were a constant irritant at this time. The problem was to become more serious once he became King. A basis of mutual royal trust might have lessened Anglo-German friction. Instead, Bertie's long-suffering efforts at harmony with his nephew – often made with little appetite – were repeatedly fruitless. In the end he was driven to the opinion that William was a liability and beyond any beneficial influence.

As Bertie bowed out of the yachting arena his fortunes on the turf at last moved into the ascendant. His successes around the turn of the century brought him enormous pleasure, and considerable financial reward. In the early years his horses were in the care of John Porter, the leading trainer of the period. But in 1892, the Prince decided to move to Newmarket. The move was prompted by convenience, as Newmarket was midway between London and Sandringham, whereas Porter trained near Newbury, and by his racing manager, Lord Marcus Beresford, who clashed regularly with Porter over the royal horses. (It was typical of the Prince that he did not allow differences with Lord Marcus's brother, Charles, to interfere with their relationship.)

Porter laid the foundation of future successes when in 1885 he bought a mare called Perdita II for the newly established royal stud at Sandringham. At the time Sir Dighton Probyn, the benign Comptroller and Treasurer of the Prince's household for over twenty years before becoming Keeper of the Privy Purse throughout his reign, complained to Porter of the £900 spent on the mare, 'you will ruin the Prince if you go on buying these thoroughbreds.'[12] Considering her offspring won £73,000 in prize money for the Prince of Wales, she was one of the best investments of his life.

The royal horses were now housed in palatial new quarters at Newmarket's Egerton House, and trained by Richard Marsh under the eye of Lord Marcus, with regular visits from their owner. It was the mating of Perdita II with the Duke of Portland's famous sire St Simon which produced the magic touch. Their first son, Florizel II, brought Bertie his first success at Royal Ascot, but higher hopes were invested in his younger brother, Persimmon. As a two-year-old in 1895 he won two major races and was beaten once, by St Frusquin (owned by the Prince's friend Leopold de Rothschild), who was to be his great rival the following year. In 1896 injury prevented Persimmon from running in the first colts' Classic, the 2,000 Guineas at Newmarket, which St Frusquin duly won. But the meeting did give the Prince his first Classic when his filly Thais won the 1,000 Guineas. The scene was set for the Derby at Epsom, for which Leopold de Rothschild's horse was made favourite.

Only days before the race the Carringtons entertained the Prince and Princess of Wales to dinner, attended by Princess Victoria, and Princess Maud with her husband Prince Charles of Denmark. Carrington wrote afterwards that at dinner:

> Lily [Lady Carrington] told the Prince of Wales that she had been on two occasions to see the Derby when her relations' horses were running. Her brother-in-law's (Lord Hastings) horse Melton and her cousin's (Lord Rosebery) Ladas and they both won. He said 'you must come down to see my horse win: it will bring luck and it is certain to come off a third time.' And he asked us to come down with him and to join the royal party.[13]

The Prince's superstitions were well-founded and after one of the most exciting Derbys in history Persimmon beat St Frusquin by a neck. He would have been delighted to know that it was the first Derby recorded on film and he led Persimmon into the winner's enclosure surrounded by what Carrington described as 'an extraordinary ovation'. He went on: 'The Princess of Wales was so overcome with excitement that "she kissed old Sir Henry Keppel on the top of his bald head".'[14] The lucky mascot, Lady Carrington, was given a diamond brooch depicting Persimmon. At Bertie's traditional Derby dinner for members of the Jockey Club the air of celebration persuaded the Earl of Ilchester to attend, overcoming his dislike of the Prince which dated from him being told that Bertie had once called him 'stingy, ugly and stupid'. As a result when someone suggested that Ilchester should invite the Prince to shoot at his Dorset estate, Melbury, he had replied that it was, 'impossible. I am too stingy to entertain the Prince properly, too ugly to take the Princess in to dinner and too stupid to take your hint.'[15]

Persimmon followed the Derby win by capturing the last Classic of the season, the St Leger at Doncaster. In 1897, as a four-year-old, he won the most lucrative race of the calendar, the Eclipse Stakes at Sandown and gave the Prince of Wales the perfect celebration of the Queen's Golden Jubilee by winning the Ascot Gold Cup. George Lambton, perhaps the shrewdest judge of horses of the period, wrote of that day: 'When Persimmon was stripped for the Ascot Gold Cup he stands out in my memory as the most perfectly trained horse I ever saw.'[16] Persimmon won over £35,000 in prize money and added over £100,000 in stud fees as a stallion. He was without question the Prince's best and favourite horse and his statue still adorns the stud yard at Sandringham.

In 1900, three years after Persimmon's retirement his full brother Diamond Jubilee enjoyed an even more successful career, carrying off the coveted Triple Crown of all three colts' Classics, 2,000 Guineas, Derby and St Leger. His victories made the Prince of Wales the leading owner for the only time in his life; earlier in the year his Ambush II won the Grand National and this quartet of wins in one season remains a unique feat. While Persimmon had been temperamental, however, Diamond Jubilee was frighteningly bad-tempered. In all his races he was ridden by his stable lad, Herbert Jones, who was promoted to jockey because he was the only person for whom the horse behaved. On one occasion Diamond Jubilee bit off another unfortunate stable lad's finger.

At the time of Bertie's successes on the Turf his sister Princess Louise, Marchioness of Lorne, was confiding to her mother's doctor, Sir James Reid, that, in her opinion, if the question arose Queen Victoria should abdicate because: 'The people are learning to do without her . . . and she is reducing the Prince of Wales to a nonentity.'[17] The Princess was devoted to her brother and although she was prone to being outspoken, many agreed with her sentiments about his fate in the last years of Victoria's reign.

In 1892 Bertie was invited by Gladstone, who had, aged eighty-three, just embarked on his fourth and final ministry, to serve on a royal commission on the aged poor, which he accepted with enthusiasm. Gladstone's suggestion followed the rejection a year earlier by the then Prime Minister, Lord Salisbury, of Bertie's offer to serve on a similar commission looking into the relations between employers and employees. Salisbury considered the question to be too controversial for royal involvement and the Queen agreed.

The Aged Poor Commission pioneered plans for state provision for those too old to work and unable to support themselves. It saw the first discussion of state pensions which were subsequently introduced during Edward VII's reign in 1908, by Lloyd George as Chancellor of the Exchequer. Most of the meetings were in 1893 and the Prince attended thirty-five out of a total of forty-eight.

Throughout his life Bertie showed a great admiration for Gladstone, in striking contrast to Queen Victoria. The Queen terminated decades of antagonism towards her longest-serving Prime Minister with a final insult in 1894, when he resigned from office for the last time. As was customary, he went to Windsor Castle bearing a letter with his suggested successor; especially pertinent as on this occasion there were two candidates. The leadership could either pass to Sir William Harcourt, Chancellor of the Exchequer and Gladstone's natural political successor, whom the Queen disliked almost as much as the outgoing Prime Minister, or to the Foreign Secretary Lord Rosebery. The Queen did not even open the letter, and had already dispatched her private secretary to formally ask Lord Rosebery whether he would try to form a government. Carrington wrote in his diary, 'If this is true, and it becomes public property when Mr G's life is written the public feeling will be that he has been harshly and unkindly treated.'[18]

When Gladstone died four years later the Prince of Wales insisted, in the face of considerable opposition from the Queen, on acting as one of the pall-bearers at the funeral. According to Lord Esher, there was 'no precedent for a Prince of Wales acting in that capacity to a "subject"'[19] and opposition was only overcome with the greatest difficulty. Such personal gestures, for which Queen Victoria had little time, were a hallmark of Bertie's character and won him both friends and admiration.

When Lord Rosebery's brief tenure of office ended in 1895 and Lord Salisbury once again returned as Prime Minister, the Prince of Wales was offered little information or opportunity for action. And occasionally when he was privy to information from his own sources, it did not always turn out to be an advantage, as was the case over the Jamieson Raid in 1896.

The Prince's son-in-law, the Duke of Fife, was Vice-President of Cecil's Rhodes' British South Africa Company which, through the

1890s, moved rapidly towards open confrontation with the Transvaal Republic over the future of the whole South African subcontinent. Other leading figures in the company were its president, the Duke of Abercorn, and Sir Horace Farquhar, a banking partner of Fife's who later became Edward VII's Master of the Household, but whose business morals were highly questionable. In 1891 Charles Carrington wrote in his diary of his scepticism about the wisdom of a dinner given by Fife in honour of Rhodes who was visiting London. The Prince of Wales headed a group of men of whom Carrington wrote, 'no such collection of people were ever got together in honour of one man.' He went on, 'Abercorn, Fife and Horace Farquhar are only dummies and figure-heads and we may live to see a great disaster or swindle in which the Royal Family were implicated in South Africa.'[20]

His predictions nearly came true. Many years afterwards Francis Knollys told Carrington that he – and the Prince of Wales – had known all about the planned Jamieson Raid before it happened, as had both Fife and Farquhar. In the event, after the initial fiasco and the surrender of the raiders to the Boer President Kruger, only the intervention of the German Emperor and his infamous telegram congratulating Kruger swung public attention and criticism away from those who had instigated the plot.

When the war that Rhodes and Jamieson's action had made inevitable finally broke out in 1899 it cast a deep shadow over the last years of Queen Victoria's reign and over her personally. In the immediately preceding years, her withdrawal from public notwithstanding, most observers marvelled at her continuing power and spirit. Lord Rosebery wrote tellingly: 'Her chief influence lies in her womanhood . . . she is an old lady, with all the foibles and strengths of one.'[21] In his diary Lord Esher described a party followed by a concert in Windsor Castle's Waterloo Chamber in 1898, when he was amazed how she ate everything put in front of her, 'including cheese and a pear after dinner.' After the concert 'mulled port was handed round, which the Queen seemed to like exceedingly.'[22] Such jollity ceased after the outbreak of war and the various setbacks in 1900 made for a sombre year. British unpopularity on the continent forced an unprecedented change in the Queen's schedule when her annual trip to the French Riviera was cancelled. Instead, she visited Ireland for the first time in forty years.

The last years of Queen Victoria's life were also saddened by regular personal losses. In 1895 the loyal Henry Ponsonby died and the following year Charles Carrington bemoaned the death of Prince Henry of Battenberg, married to the Queen's daughter Beatrice: 'Prince Henry's death is a great calamity, as the gloom from which the Queen had emerged seems to be settling down again.'[23] In 1900 the Boer War claimed her grandson, Prince Christian Victor (the son of Princess Helena and her husband Prince Christian of Schleswig-Holstein) and the same year the Prince of Wales's brother, Alfred, Duke of Edinburgh, died of cancer. (His dissolute son, also Alfred, had died the previous year from venereal disease.) Possibly hardest to bear, it was also in 1900 that it became known that her favourite child, Vicky, was suffering from cancer which had killed her husband Frederick and which brought her death only months after Victoria's.

On 18 December 1900 Queen Victoria left Windsor Castle for the last time and travelled to Osborne. Her health had been steadily declining since the summer and now, in her eighty-second year, she had only a month left to live. Nonetheless, duty continued to be her first priority. On 2 January she received Lord Roberts on his return from commanding the army in South Africa and invested him with an earldom and the Garter, despite the fact that Roberts was about to become supreme Commander-in-Chief while Queen Victoria had hoped the post would go to her son, the Duke of Connaught. On the 18 January 1901 the Court Circular announced: 'The Queen has not lately been in her usual health and is unable for the present to take her customary drives.'[24] Edward Hamilton commented in his diary on the news that her two doctors had been dispatched to Osborne: 'They will make as light of the illness as they can – Royalties always pooh-pooh illness'.[25] He also noted that the Queen had lived exactly as long as George III, but that her problem appeared to be a combination of cerebral trouble and digestive power. On the same day the Prince of Wales was summoned from London. He arrived on the 19th with Alexandra who came from Sandringham. The following day he returned to London to meet his nephew from Germany, refusing to allow crisis to interfere with protocol. He greeted the Emperor at Victoria Station wearing the uniform of the Prussian First Dragoon Guards.

Queen Victoria died at 6.30p.m. on 22 January. Her son telegraphed to the Lord Mayor of London, 'My beloved mother, the Queen, has just passed away, surrounded by her children and grandchildren.'[26]

and thence to St George's Chapel. Two days later, following a ceremony attended by the royal family, she was finally laid to rest at Frogmore, beside her husband in the mausoleum she had built nearly forty years earlier. Only after this ceremony did Lord Esher feel able to write in his diary. 'So ends the reign of the Queen – and now I feel for the first time that the new regime – though full of anxieties for England – has begun'.[2]

Many others shared Esher's apprehension. The death of Queen Victoria sharpened the focus on Britain's situation at home and abroad, and the problems which the stability of her continued reign had appeared to subdue. The war in South Africa had made Britain deeply unpopular in Europe at a time when she had no formal allies as a result of Salisbury's foreign policy of 'splendid isolation'. The war itself was destined to drag on until May 1902, exposing shortcomings and deep disagreements in the organization of the armed forces, both military and political. Reform of these problems and the creation of a modern army run by a well-ordered hierarchy of the War Office and generals, became a major – if elusive – issue of the new reign.

The war situation combined with the growing economic might of both Germany and the United States to cast doubts over Britain's prestige and power, both of which had been unquestioned for most people so long as Queen Victoria was alive. At the same time, she handed on to her son a political situation which was far from enviable, but from which her long tenure on the throne had made her immune. The Prime Minister, Lord Salisbury was aged seventy at the time of Edward VII's accession. A year later he handed over leadership of the government to his nephew, Arthur Balfour. Salisbury may not have completely lost his interest in politics, but he certainly had no appetite for assisting his new King into the constitutional position of monarch. While the government was widely criticised, not least because of their stranglehold over legislation by virtue of their insurmountable majority in the House of Lords, their Liberal opponents were in a state of disunity and in no position to mount a challenge for power.

Given the situation, the new King's greatest achievement during the early months of his reign was to dispel any suggestion that the monarchy was in a state of inertia, of uncertainty as to how to follow the achievements of his mother during what Edward Hamilton referred to as: '. . . perhaps the most glorious of all reigns in this country',[3] a phrase with which many contemporaries would have agreed.

Edward VII's determination to move forward, and the political frustrations which were to confront such initiatives throughout his reign, was exemplified by the row over the Protestant Declaration. By ancient tradition, unchanged since the Bill of Rights of 1689 which safeguarded the country's Protestant democracy, before reading his first speech from the throne, the King was duty bound to make a declaration which repudiated Roman Catholicism and included such archaic phrases as: 'the invocation or adoration of the Virgin Mary or any other saint and the sacrifice of the Mass as they are now used in the Church of Rome are superstituous and idolatrous'.[4]

The King regarded the declaration as deeply offensive to his thousands of Roman Catholic subjects. While there was no time to make any changes before his speech, he determined that the necessary alterations would be speedily effected, to ensure that none of his successors had to make a statement of such religious intolerance. For Lord Salisbury and his government, however, it was far from being a matter of pressing importance and they showed little interest in carrying out the King's wishes. When, in June 1901, a newly drafted declaration was drawn up, it was substantially the same as the old one. In a scene that was to be repeated on many occasions through Edward's reign, the Lord Chancellor, Lord Halsbury, deservedly incurred the royal wrath by publishing the new wording before submitting it to the King. The King accused Halsbury of 'bungling incompetence' and the argument rumbled on throughout the summer of 1901. But the King's efforts came to nought as no new declaration was adopted by parliament. It was not until after George V's accession in 1910, that a bill was finally passed through parliament, limiting the declaration to the Protestant intent.

> I do solemnly and sincerely in the presence of God profess, testify, and declare that I am a faithful Protestant, and that I will according to the true intent of the enactments to secure the Protestant succession to the Throne of My realm uphold and maintain such enactments to the best of my power.[5]

From the outset Edward's reign was characterized by energy and habit. Although nearly sixty his energy was phenomenal and well suited to accommodate his peripatetic way of life. Previously this had been largely organized around the calendar of his social life. Now he moulded the pattern of his monarchy to fit harmoniously with his other commitments. He had no intention of making changes except where absolutely necessary, as Philip Magnus concisely illustrated when outlining what became a pattern that only ever varied in detail.

King Edward continued to spend Christmas and New Year at Sandringham through which (as well as through Windsor and Balmoral) guests perpetually flowed. He came to London, for a night, two or three times during January; and he spent one week shooting with the Duke of Devonshire at Chatsworth or, later, with Lord Iveagh at Elveden.

King Edward moved to Buckingham Palace at the end of January in time to open Parliament in State; and through February he entertained guests or went out to dinner, theatre and supper parties every evening without exception. He left England punctually at the beginning of March for two months' holiday in the sun. He liked to spend a week in Paris where he enjoyed strolling incognito on the boulevards, followed by three weeks at Biarritz. He would then cruise for a month in *Victoria and Albert*. He liked to cruise in the Mediterranean, but he loved to improvise and sent explosive telegrams to more than one First Lord of the Admiralty who tried incautiously to induce him to state his plans in advance.

Returning to London at the beginning of May in time to preside over the Season, King Edward again dined out or entertained friends every night. He gave famous and splendid suppers in a private room behind his box at the Royal Opera House, Covent Garden; and he spent every week-end at friends' houses, Sandringham, or in his private quarters at the Jockey Club at Newmarket.

Moving to Windsor Castle for Ascot Races in the middle of June, King Edward paid an official visit (lasting three or four days) every July to some provincial centre, before going, at the end of that month, to stay with the Duke of Richmond for Goodwood Races. He left Goodwood for Cowes to preside over the Regatta at the beginning of August, when he made the royal yacht his headquarters.

Immediately after Cowes, while Queen Alexandra went to join her sister, the Dowager Empress of Russia, in Denmark, King Edward went to Marienbad in Bohemia for a month's cure. His very comfortable suite of rooms at the Hotel Weimar were furnished each year in a different style, but he travelled more simply abroad than Queen Victoria had done . . .

On returning from Marienbad, King Edward liked to spend a few days at Buckingham Palace during the second week of September, before going to stay with the Saviles for Doncaster Races, and then with the Arthur Sassoons in Inverness-shire. Balmoral with its grouse and deer, remained his headquarters through October; and from there he attended the autumn race meetings at Newmarket, using his royal train.

The first week of November was spent at Buckingham Palace; the second at Sandringham; and the last two at Windsor. The first week of December was spent at Sandringham, and thereafter, for an entire fortnight, King Edward indulged in a round of Christmas dinner, theatre and supper parties in London to which he looked forward boyishly, and which he enjoyed thoroughly until his health started to fail.[6]

It was very different from the annual progressions of Queen Victoria in the latter decades of her reign: Windsor, Balmoral, Osborne, and her summer holiday in France. But it illustrated his personality that thrived on change – albeit in an orderly fashion – and his wish to make the monarchy appear lively rather than primarily symbolic. At first some people close to the changes were apprehensive. Lord Esher wrote in February 1901: 'It may be my imagination but the sanctity of the throne has disappeared. The King is King and debonair, and not undignified – but too human.'[7] The humanity was to provide his vital quality, both personally and in its effect on the monarchy.

Lord Esher, who succeeded to his father's title in 1899, had been closely involved with the royal family since 1895 when his friend Lord Rosebery made him Secretary to the Office of Works which controlled repairs and improvements to royal palaces, government buildings and their surroundings, as well as having a role in the organization of state ceremonials. One of Esher's first improvements was to install a lift for Queen Victoria at Windsor. Shortly after his accession Edward VII's gratitude to Esher for all this work was shown in the award of the largely honorary position of Deputy Constable and Governor of Windsor Castle.

Two more different personalities would be hard to imagine than the new King and the man who would become his most privileged adviser and political confidant. Esher, married with children, had enjoyed close personal relationships with other men since his days as an Eton schoolboy; he was intellectual and literary. And yet an easy compatibility grew between the two men. So long as they remained private, the personal lives of the King's friends and close associates did not concern him. He enjoyed the way that Esher fed him titbits of gossip and found his astute, caustic opinions of politicians and others stimulating. There was also a similarity in the way they worked. The King thrived on a busy, varied programme and became frustrated or bored when tied down over a single issue. Throughout his career, Esher declined any job or office that would restrict his freedom and formalize his position. His ambition was for influence, not position, as his biographer, James Lees-Milne pointed out: 'He loved power and he enjoyed exercising it behind the scenes.'[8]

Edward involved Esher closely in the organization of Queen Victoria's funeral. Thereafter, through the first year of the reign the King detailed him to supervise the necessary alterations to the royal homes, especially at Windsor Castle and Buckingham Palace. It was an issue that consumed much of the King's – and at times Queen Alexandra's – energy and enthusiasm. As well as a detailed and frank journal Esher at this time corresponded daily with his son Maurice, with whom he was infatuated, and almost as frequently with close friend Millicent, Duchess of Sutherland. Extracts through 1901 chart the progress of change as well as shedding light on the new monarch. When Esher visited Windsor with the King on 6 February he wrote:

> The Indians – who were there – [Queen Victoria's Munshi] were wandering about like uneasy spirits. No longer immobile and statuesque as of yore . . . Knollys thinks he [the King] will not live much at Windsor. That he would be bored there. He goes back to London tomorrow to reside at present at Marlborough House. Later on he is to occupy Buckingham Palace when he can get rid of his brothers and sisters, now camping there.[9]

By the end of the month the King appears to have found a solution to his family problem.

This afternoon I have two hours with the King at Buckingham Palace. He has settled into inhabiting his father's rooms there, and at Windsor. Rooms that have not been used since 1861. His determination to get rid of the family using his horses and carriages, has been a subject of much worry, and today he had the brilliant and not ungenerous ideal of presenting every member of the family with a carriage and pair and telling them to clear out! It is in reality cheap at the price.[10]

Both the new King and Queen greatly enjoyed their elevated circumstances. And there were immediate changes of atmosphere in the royal palaces. In June 1901 Lord Carrington wrote to Sir Arthur Bigge, who had taken over from Henry Ponsonby as Queen Victoria's private secretary and was made private secretary to the Duke of York at Edward's accession: 'Your report of Windsor Castle under the new reign is interesting. Cigars in the white drawing room – well! I suppose one could get used to it! and HM must smoke and play bridge somewhere.'[11]

But arrangements were often fraught with argument not least because, as Esher wrote, 'Of course, the Queen's obstinacy is so tremendous that there is no moving her by cajolery.'[12] After his wife confessed that she had never seen Queen Victoria's rooms at Buckingham Palace, Edward was quite happy to enjoy showing them to her, and discovering little treasures long concealed by his secretive mother. But Esher told his son that when Alexandra voiced a wish to inhabit the state rooms at Windsor: 'There was a smart difference of opinion. He was very firm and rather cross – to her I mean.'[13] Towards the end of 1901 a stumbling block to the domestic arrangements continued to be Alexandra's unwillingness to leave Marlborough House. 'The King reminds me now and then very firmly of his mother. He has the same way of emphasising speech by bowing his head. However, today he spluttered and swore in a manner wholly unlike Queen Victoria.' The King's frustration was aroused by continuing domestic problems as Esher went on to describe. 'I luckily thought of a compromise – a thing he loves! – and he jumped at it; anything to avoid a row.'[14]

From the first months of his reign Edward VII exuded the blend of bonhomie and grandeur which would be the hallmark of his kingship, distancing it apart from his mother's monarchy and making his well suited to the times. In May 1901 Esher visited Marlborough House after lunch and found the King, 'sitting in his room upstairs with his after luncheon cigar. Looking wonderfully like Henry VIII, only better tempered.'[15] In late October, arrangements at both Windsor and Buckingham Palace were still in disarray, but at times the King was happy to remain oblivious to the chaos.

> On Thursday at Buckingham Palace he looked up everything but my remembrance of him principally is sitting on a turned up table in the middle of the ballroom, surrounded by masses of bedroom furniture, smoking a cigarette and gossiping to me about old Wetherby, the secretary of the Jockey Club who had just retired and talking to me about old Tattersall who – he said – was reported to be the natural son of Sir Robert Peel.[16]

While the King enjoyed a moment's relaxed gossip there were more important things to be dealt with. During 1901 the most pressing was the progress of the war in South Africa – as well as its wider implications both at home and overseas. After the series of British victories in 1900 (such as the relief of both Ladysmith and Mafeking), largely achieved through overwhelming superiority in numbers, it was clear that the Boers could no longer expect to win the war. But 1901 saw them mount a hugely effective campaign of guerrilla warfare that prolonged hostilities until May 1902. The frustration of British troops led to the imprisonment of Boer women and children in open camps that caused outrage amongst European countries. In Britain, public opinion was encouraged by newspaper comment into disbelief that the 350,000 troops under Lord Kitchener could not finally overcome the Boer forces who totalled hardly more than 50,000.

For sixty years Edward had been excluded from either active involvement or any decision-making role in military affairs. Now the issue was at the top of his agenda as the new King and he attacked it with gusto. The problems of the South African campaign raised a host of questions about the army and its administration which were to continue throughout his reign.

During the nineteenth century the army had evolved to be primarily colonial and ceremonial. Most of the campaigns that it undertook,

whether in Egypt or against the Zulus, highlighted deficiencies. But sufficient impetus for reform was not built up until the mass mobilization and logistics of moving large numbers of troops to South Africa, the constantly publicized failures of the war, as well as new unpalatable aspects such as women and children being herded into concentration camps.

St John Brodrick, Secretary of State for War at Edward's accession, was soon introduced to the new King's energy and methods. During the last months of Queen Victoria's reign the flood of new officers being commissioned into the army had not been signed by the sovereign as was the usual custom. Brodrick estimated that there were some 4,000 outstanding; by May 1901 the King had ploughed through almost all and they were passed on to the Secretary of War for his signature. Faced with such a task on top of his other work, Brodrick sat up all one night to complete the work, but his labours prompted a request to the King's private secretary, Francis Knollys, that perhaps a less time-consuming system could be devised. 'Knollys burst out laughing, and said that King Edward, after wrestling manfully with this inordinate demand, had thrown it up and got a stamp, which his private secretary could wield. Needless to say no Secretary of War so far as I know has ever since signed a commission.'[17]

Brodrick also found the royal demands on his time equally onerous. Communications from the King – either direct or through Knollys – confirmed Edward's desire to become actively involved in all aspects of the military: the organization of the war to a speedy conclusion; the discussion of necessary reform of both the army and the War Office; promotions, civilian appointments and decorations; and the increasingly vexed question of the future of the post of Commander-in-Chief.

Some members of parliament both doubted and openly questioned the constitutional propriety of such direct royal activity. During the first year of the reign Sir Henry Campbell-Bannerman, leader of the Liberal opposition in the House of Commons, made it clear to the Government leader, Arthur Balfour that, 'If the name of the Secretary for War were seen so often in the papers as having been in audience at the Palace, he would call attention to it in the House of Commons in relation to the constitutional government of the army.'[18]

Reform of the army would come later in Edward's reign. The damning criticism of the South African War Commission which reported on the conduct and administration of the war, led to the subsequent setting up of the War Office Reconstitution Committee whose proposals set in motion the major reforms such as the appointment of an administrative Army board, the replacement of the individual Commander-in-Chief with a collective General Staff, and extensive reorganization of the military's relationship with the War Office.

As far as the King's relations with Brodrick were concerned, the most significant fact was Lord Esher's presence on both committees. Esher was convinced of the urgent need for army reform, and of his own qualification to be centrally involved in the necessary process. Both the King and the Prime Minister agreed about his suitability. Esher had reservations about Brodrick while the Secretary for War, not unnaturally, had suspicions about the degree to which Esher was privy to vital information, and about his access to and influence over the King; suspicions which developed into open mistrust and condemnation. Brodrick himself described the root of the problem in his memoirs:

> Before long it was clear that by the time any decision had come to the point when the Cabinet could lay it before the Sovereign, the issue had been largely prejudged, on the incomplete premises of an observer who had no official status. In other words Esher, whether intentionally or not, had constituted himself the unofficial adviser of the Crown, and his ambition to control what he termed the 'hornet's nest' from outside became for a moment the ruling passion of his life.[19]

The machiavellian Esher was impervious to such criticisms; privately he rather enjoyed them as they indirectly confirmed his influence. Instead he was happy to report to Maurice in September 1902 that while staying at Balmoral, 'HM confirmed to me at dinner last night that he cannot stand Brodrick. This is confidential – he thinks him useless and a fidget and a muddler.'[20]

Esher's communication of confidential information to his son outraged the Secretary for War, who wrote of the decision to relieve Redvers Buller of his command in South Africa in October 1901:

Even with these limitations Esher's 'Secret Service' sensed him of all that was known at Balmoral, including the King's views as telegraphed by me to the Prime Minister, and the reactions of the Cabinet Committee. He thought himself justified in disclosing to his second son, a cadet at Sandhurst, these intimate official details, before any decision was given or the facts had been circulated to the Cabinet.[21]

But Brodrick was up against a formidable opponent, whose influence with the King and the Prime Minister meant he would inevitably prevail. By 1903 Esher was convinced that Brodrick was an obstacle to his proposed army and War Office reforms and wrote 'It looks as if the opportunity might well be taken to get rid of Brodrick, and I fervently hope this will be the case.'[22] The opportunity came later in the year with the argument over the retention of Lord Roberts as Commander-in-Chief of the army. Esher, the King and the Prime Minister were all for change, and Esher was able to write to Brodrick in August that the time had come for him to resign and give up the fight to retain Robert's position. In the Cabinet reshuffle that autumn Brodrick was moved from the War Office to the India Office.

It was a reflection of Edward's personal qualities that Brodrick, while resenting Esher's influence, left office with nothing but admiration for the King. While the Boer War continued, Brodrick considered that, 'the King's willingness to receive all officers of high rank returning from the front – temporarily or permanently – and his genius for inspiring confidence, was of inestimable value.'[23] Of more concrete importance was Edward VII's active support for reform of the army medical system, which was an immediate and lasting success.

The war in South Africa had shown the system to be painfully inadequate. Much of the impetus for improvement came directly from the King. Medical matters were of abiding interest to him and he knew well a number of the leading surgeons and doctors consulted, such as Sir Alfred Fripp and Sir Frederick Treves. The King supported all initiatives to improve the professional skill of army doctors, and their rank and social standing in relation to serving officers and the success achieved convinced Brodrick that the Army Medical Service was 'the best service of the Allies in the Great War'.[24] He also knew where the credit was due. 'The one great monument to King

Edward's military interest was the reform of the medical system which he pressed forward from the first day of his reign.'[25]

But above any single achievement, it was the King's personal manner which fostered good relations. At dinner at Sandringham or Balmoral he might let off steam about Brodrick or any other cabinet minister. But, unless unreasonably provoked, he was scrupulously courteous and frank in direct communications. When, in 1902, they had been at odds Edward wrote to Brodrick in precisely such a vein: 'You need never fear that I shall not always give you my heartiest support in all matters concerning the reform of the Army, which is so much wanted. But at the same time you must expect my criticisms, and they will doubtless be frequently at variance with your own views.'[26] Such honest reassurance concealed the frustration which Brodrick occasionally caused the King – which Esher so enjoyed recording. It encouraged Brodrick to the opinion that:

> The impetus which King Edward gave to all military progress was of abiding service to this country. If at times his authority, as I have shown elsewhere, was used by others unduly to belittle the existing War Office system, of which he had not sufficient personal experience, the immense advantage of the Army during his short reign is the best tribute to his influence at its head.[27]

In July 1901 Charles Carrington wrote in his diary about the new King: 'He and the Queen are very popular with the public but Society is furious at his taking so much notice of the Jews. Sir Ernest Cassel (who is called Sir Windsor Cassel), George Lewis [the solicitor], Alfred Rothschild etc. are his intimates and people in Society are open-mouthed about it.'[28] Nothing demonstrated the King's disregard for such criticism more than the appointment of his friend the furniture-magnate, Sir John Blundell Maple to be the third member of a commission to review the royal finances, with A. J. Balfour and Sir William Harcourt. Knollys might have been able to greet the trio with the proud assertion: 'For the first time in English history the heir-apparent comes forward to claim his right to the throne unencumbered by a single penny of debt',[29] but as Sydney Lee added: 'It was also authoritatively stated that he had no capital.'[30] His accession removed the income of the Duchy of Cornwall and, six months after

Queen Victoria's death, the grants voted for his children in 1889 ended under the terms of the original agreement.

The King did not inherit any of his mother's private fortune which was divided in her will between her younger children. Queen Victoria considered that his position as King would ensure that he was guaranteed sufficient funds by the government. Edward accepted the decision without complaint, and did the same himself. His eldest son was similarly accommodating when he acceded as George V, but his decision to continue the tradition brought great resentment from his eldest son, Edward VIII, who remarked caustically when his father's will was read: 'Where do I come in?'[31]

Edward VII had no powers to change the arrangement set up by George III that revenues from the Crown estates should be largely surrendered in return for a guaranteed Civil List. But these revenues had grown from £289,248 in 1838, when Queen Victoria came to the throne, to £592,066 in 1901. After the deduction of certain agreed costs this produced a payment to the Exchequer of £479,675. The King felt that as the Civil List had remained unchanged for sixty years, its figures deserved review. In February 1901 Edward Hamilton, a senior official at the Treasury and well-known to the King since his days as Gladstone's private secretary, noted in his diary that he was detained in London on a Sunday by a summons from the King.

Hamilton was of the opinion that savings in past 'great abuses in the Royal Household – waste and extravagance', could go a long way towards providing the extra funds that Edward VII would require compared to what had been voted to his mother in 1837. If this were possible then the Civil List's total need not be greatly increased and anyway, Hamilton argued it was better to take away some of the financial commitments of the Civil List funds than to increase the total.

At Marlborough House Hamilton found both Sir Dighton Probyn and Francis Knollys with the King and wrote afterwards in his diary:

> The King wanted to have a little general talk about the Civil List. He took the bull by the horns at once, and said that in view of the way he intended to do everything he could not see how he could get on with less than half a million. He was given to understand on

good authority that such a sum would not be thought excessive and would be granted without difficulty. I told H.M. that I could not express any opinion . . . He liked the idea of being relieved (if it were possible) of such charges as the payment of income tax, postage and telegraph charges, the 'Queen's premium' charges, and part of any rate of the pension charge. He was quite willing to call upon the great Officers of State to report how abuses could be stopped, salaries reduced, sinecures abolished – in short, how economies – and there is undoubtedly room for them – could be effected.[32]

The Cabinet Committee that studied the Civil List for the Chancellor of the Exchequer decided that the King should be relieved of £20,000 of pensions, postage and telegraph charges, and Queen's premium charges. Income tax, however, they were not prepared to concede. As Hamilton commented: 'This they thought would look bad just at the moment.'[33]

Hamilton was summoned to Marlborough House again ten days after his first visit, during which time the Chancellor, Sir Michael Hicks-Beach, had put his proposed Civil List figures to the King. The King clearly appreciated the delicacy of the situation, and balanced a feeling that the government had been somewhat ungenerous with an understanding of the political implications. Hamilton felt that the King had not clearly understood the full content of the Chancellor's proposal in which substantial savings from Queen Victoria's expenses, such as pensions, when combined with the basic figure of £450,000, made up the 'half a million' the King was looking for. Hamilton wrote afterwards in his diary.

'I had a long and interesting talk with the King who was extremely nice and cordial. He had, he said, sent for me not as an official but as a friend, [and that I was to give him my advice frankly] . . . He did not want to haggle, and he could not haggle. But he must have enough to "do it with" and he must "do it handsomely".' Hamilton then explained how the hidden benefits enhanced the figure and thereafter: 'He owned that the arrangement was better than it looked; and he changes his whole tone towards it.'[34]

A reflection on how far the government were prepared to go to minimize the increase in the actual funds voted to the Civil List by parliament was given by Hicks-Beach's suggestion that the King should charge the Duke of York £20,000 per annum rent for Balmoral. (This would also enable the Duke to justify receiving the same annuity as his father had done.) Edward would not accept the plan, however, and said to Hamilton: 'H.M. could not go and reside at his Scottish seat on the sufferance of his son'.[35] The skilful Hamilton proposed instead that the Duke of York pay £10,000 nominal rent for Abergeldie Castle on the Balmoral estate and for shooting and fishing there, and £10,000 towards the upkeep of Sandringham where he had a house and enjoyed the shooting. This was accepted by the King.

After some more fine tuning, such as increasing the dowry that would be payable to Queen Alexandra after the King's death from £60,000 to £70,000, parliament voted with a minimum of the Radical opposition that traditionally accompanied any discussion of royal finances. The Civil List basic fund was £470,000 which included provision for Queen Alexandra. Additional funds were voted for the King's children: £40,000 per annum for the Duke of York (who was formally appointed Prince of Wales by his father in November 1901). He also received £60,000 per annum income of the Duchy of Cornwall and £10,000 for his Duchess. Edward's three daughters each received £6,000 per annum, on a basis suggested by the King, that the money should be 'pooled' and allocated according to their means and requirements.

For the King, fully aware of the traditionally problematic nature of changes in grants of public funds to the monarchy, an important agreement was for the figures to be lasting for the duration of his reign. They were, although not without an attempt by the Treasury in 1907 to question the arrangements over funding for foreign sovereigns paying state visits to Britain. Lord Knollys, for whom preservation of his master's agreed prerogatives was a crusade, responded with vigour and success and the attempted change was repelled. At the end of the lengthy negotiations in 1901 the King would hardly have been pleased to know that the successes of his racehorses were considered by his advisers to be valid for consideration in the question of his finances – and how much he should be offered in the Civil List. One of Hamilton's last comments at the time was: 'Though the King has not private fortune like Queen Victoria had, he has a valuable asset, which she did not have in "Persimmon" and "Diamond Jubilee", which sires ought before long to bring in £20,000 a year'.[36]

The Civil List agreement combined with the new King's personal desire to cause a whirlwind in the royal household. Ten days after the Civil List became an act of parliament on 25 June 1901 Charles Carrington recorded that: 'The King is cutting down everywhere and selling huge quantities of sherry.'[37] But the changes were not always popular, especially amongst those whose worth was being scrutinized. 'The King is very active and looks into everything, or as some dissatisfied courtiers say, pokes his nose into everything – one court lady told me "the King is getting above himself!" '[38] The pace of change appeared so strong that Esher, fearful that important trappings of the monarchy might be swept away, wrote to the King, 'urging him to adhere to all ceremonial practices and traditions unless they are "ridiculous" '.[39]

Continuity with Queen Victoria's household was, however, retained in many personal instances. Sir Arthur Bigge, who had succeeded Henry Ponsonby as her private secretary in 1895, was made private secretary to the new Prince of Wales, a position Bigge continued to hold after the Prince's accession as George V in 1910. The genial assistant private secretary Frederick Ponsonby was retained in the same position. Ponsonby described with quiet amusement the opposition that greeted his appointment from Francis Knollys, who regarded him as superfluous and suspect as, 'Marlborough House was firmly convinced that Buckingham Palace was hopelessly out of date and that none of Queen Victoria's household were any good.'[40] Knollys eventually had to back down, due to a near-crisis over the royal correspondence.

Initially the King tried to open all of the 400-odd letters he received a day, but after a few weeks he gave in and sorted them by envelope into personal or official and descending order of importance. Once this mound was passed on to the private office for action Knollys and his existing team were unable to keep up. Ponsonby describes how, when the King became aware that letters were going unanswered for over a week, 'he said I was to go down and see Francis Knollys. I was to tell him that I had been appointed to take as much work off his hands as possible and I was to induce him to confine himself to the really important stuff.'[41] Nonetheless, the upshot was that: 'Francis Knollys and Bryant [his chief clerk] looked upon my efforts as an affront to Marlborough House, and that they very much resented my butting in.'[42]

Such teething problems in his household hardly affected Edward, certainly not in comparison to the feeling over one of his major breaks with his mother's reign, the relinquishing of Osborne House. During his Civil List discussions with Edward Hamilton, in February 1901, the King had been adamant that he had to retain the house. Hamilton wrote in his diary:

> The King by the way told me that it was impossible for Him to part with Osborne; for He found that it was one of the Queen's last wishes that, if He did not want to live there himself, His brothers and sisters should have access to the place. Of course they can make the most of this and live upon Him as much as they can.[43]

By December 1901, the King's attitude was shifting. Lord Esher wrote to his son: 'After that we passed to a much more delicate topic, the handing of Osborne to the nation. He cannot afford to keep it – but his family object to giving it up.'[44] Esher's last remark made light of the outrage felt by the King's sisters – as predicted by Edward Hamilton – but efforts were to no avail. Neither Edward nor Alexandra had ever wanted to use the house steeped in memories of his early family life. They were more than happy at Sandringham. A major influence, however, was the King's discovery that the Prince of Wales held a similar view. Safe in the knowledge that he was not depriving his son, the King presented Osborne to the nation. Queen Victoria's own apartments were preserved in privacy, the main wing built by the Prince Consort became a convalescent home for army and navy officers, and the stable complex became a new college for naval cadets.

It was an admirably practical solution, but one which continued to rile in the family for many years and provided the German Emperor with an opportunity for stirring trouble as he did in a letter to his aunt Princess Louise, Duchess of Argyll. Thanking her for her Christmas present at the end of 1906 he went on – in full knowledge of what had been Osborne's fate: 'They recalled to me the many happy times of my childhood spent in dear Osborne!!!, Windsor, Balmoral! . . . Osborne, what became of this heavenly, holy spot so dear to me!'[45]

The new King did not allow his sisters to stand in his way. Indeed, his progress through 1901 exhausted many around him. Lord Esher complained to his son after a late night at Windsor: 'The King plays bridge, and keeps people up till nearly one, which is very trying.'[46] It was a similar story at Sandringham, albeit in the contrastingly relaxed atmosphere that always prevailed at the place Edward considered home.

> It is altogether different here from Windsor. No ceremony at all. Just a country house. After dinner the Queen played 'patience' with Gladys de Grey and Nelly [Esher's wife]. The King sat on the sofa and talked for about half an hour – then the women went to bed – and the King led the way to the billiard room. He sat down to 'bridge' and the rest of us sat and talked . . . I talked to Soveral, who was charming and witty as usual. About one o'clock we went to bed.[47]

No doubt the new King was especially pleased with a journey he had made a few weeks earlier with his racing manager Sir Marcus Beresford, from Sandringham to Newmarket in his new motorcar. Beresford told Esher that they drove 'fifty miles in two-and-a-half hours. Not bad. He says the dust was something perfectly portentous. They were white as millers.'[48] The picture would have greatly appealed to Beresford who was well-known for his sense of humour.

Queen Alexandra was equally purposeful during the early part of the reign. 'She objects to being called Queen Consort. She means to be The Queen'[49] Esher wrote in February 1901 during arrangements for the State Opening of Parliament which was another important revival by the King. A month later, 'I spent the morning with the Queen at Buckingham Palace – she was in tearing spirits and will enjoy her new home once she begins to arrange her rooms.'[50] Towards the end of the year arrangements for the forthcoming coronation assumed major importance for both King and Queen. Esher was centrally involved and he was forever discussing issues with both. The Queen's concerns revolved around appearance – hers and those in attendance. 'The Queen has settled to have four duchesses to stand near her in Westminster Abbey and to arrange her crown. She is to select the four herself "tall and well matched".'[51] A month later he reports a remark made by the Queen to Arthur Ellis. '"I know better than all those milliners and silly antiquaries; I shall wear exactly what I like and so shall my ladies – Basta!" Is she not a little devil of obstinacy. I cannot help admiring her – she will do exactly what she pleases!'[52]

The coronation's date had been set for 26 June 1902 and Edward absorbed himself in all arrangements of what would be the most spectacular ceremonial of his reign. To mark the occasion, and despite the King's initial determination to 'keep the list within the limits adopted at the time of the Diamond Jubilee'[53] a total of over 1,500 new Honours were handed out. Among these were the twelve inaugural members of the King's new Order of Merit which was officially established in June 1902. This prestigious honour was limited to a total of twenty-four members and in the personal gift of the monarch. The King had desired that it would be to 'reward in a special manner officers of the Navy and Army, and Civilians distinguished in Arts, Sciences and Literature'.[54] The Prime Minister, Lord Salisbury, raised what could have been perceived as possible ingratitude by senior military figures, who did not wish their officers to be included in an honour which did not reward specific military service. But it was the King's personal order and such questions were brushed aside.

Days before the event the ceremony and, it seemed, the King's life itself, were suddenly threatened by a critical illness. The King developed acute appendicitis and was in great pain when he arrived at Buckingham Palace from Windsor on 23 June. With the coronation imminent the illness was kept secret, but the King's doctors, Sir Francis Laking and Sir Thomas Barlow, and the surgeon Sir Frederick Treves, had no illusions about the gravity of the situation. They told Edward that the coronation must be postponed indefinitely and that an operation was necessary. He replied that he would 'rather die in the Abbey'. When they told him that would be a dangerous possibility, the King consented to an operation by Treves, to be conducted at Buckingham Palace. Treves operated on 24 June, not a moment too soon as the King was in enormous pain from a large abscess that the surgeon removed. The abscess was on the point of bursting and causing death from blood poisoning.

News of the operation's success and postponement of the coronation were announced simultaneously to a stunned public. As Esher suggested in a letter to his son on 30 June, the King's popular esteem was now unquestioned: 'The King's popularity – his personal popularity – is extraordinary. There is no doubt that, in spite of the Queen's presence, Ascot was a *manqué*'.[55]

Edward possessed rare physical resourcefulness which was proved by the pain he had to endure both before and after the operation, and by Sir Thomas Barlow's opinion that when leaving hospital he was 'a week ahead of an ordinary patient'.[56] The coronation was set for 9 August and the King left London to convalesce aboard the *Victoria and Albert* on the Solent. The successful operation saved his life and had a number of beneficial after-effects. Knollys told Esher that he had seen the King: 'Looking ten years younger. He sleeps eight hours at night without moving, a thing he has been unable to do for years. He recognizes that he has been living too hard, so his illness may – after all – prolong his life. He is far less irritable too – which is a sign of health.'[57] When Esher visited the King aboard the royal yacht he was proudly told of a reduction of eight inches around the royal waist and over two stones in weight. He was also shown that, if subdued, the royal temper had by no means disappeared. The King liked to sit on deck reading in a specially made, enormous deck chair that had wheels but was immobile without assistance.

> Lying on deck the other day he sent his nurse on some errand when a terrific storm came on and he was soused. He shouted for help and no one came. At last Treves thought he heard shouting and arrived on the scene to find the King wet to the skin and using horrible language about everybody. However, he saw the humour of the situation instantly and was none the worse.[58]

The King agreed to the doctors' advice that a shortened coronation ceremony was advisable, but he refused any threat to the dignity of the occasion such as the construction of a ramp up which he could be pushed, rather than having to mount the steps of Westminster Abbey. The European representatives had all assembled in London in June and virtually all had returned to their respective homes by 9 August, while representatives of the colonies had, by and large, stayed on. This only emphasized the occasion as a celebration of the monarchy and its Empire as the London crowds cheered tirelessly and virtually every part of the Empire was represented.

The main anxiety during the actual ceremony was the condition of the eighty-year-old Archbishop of Canterbury, Dr Temple. The King confessed afterwards that at one point he thought the venerable prelate would collapse and that he almost had to catch him when he faltered when kneeling in homage. Charles Carrington wrote in his diary: 'The old archbishop could hardly get through the service, and being as blind as a bat, made several mistakes in his reading, though everything was printed for him in enormous letters. He also put the King's crown on the wrong way round and it had to be taken off and put back the right way.'[59] Carrington could not resist going on to describe the downfall of one of Society's grand dames that caused universal amusement.

The Duchess of Devonshire (or Ponte Vecchio or Old Bridge as she is called from her devotion to that game) was very anxious to get home, and quarrelled with the officials who tried to keep her quiet. However she would have her way, pushed pass the Gentlemen at Arms, who vainly endeavoured to stop her and, being unable to see the steps, went head over heels down them.[60]

CHAPTER NINE

ALICE KEPPEL

'Mrs George Keppel is in high favour'[1] Lord Carrington wrote with disapproval in his diary in July 1901. Similar remarks reoccur in his and other diaries and letters such as Lord Esher's throughout Edward VII's reign. The King's friendship with Alice Keppel was the strongest indication that his character and habits did not change on accession to the throne. Many people championed her cause. But there were plenty of others – including Edward's closest advisers and leading politicians – who considered the relationship a flaw in his monarchy because it lowered public respect for him and his position. Considering how attuned to public opinion Edward would prove to be throughout his reign any arousal of public disapproval was a weakness. Carrington confided such worries to his diary in July 1902, 'Mallett tells me the king is very popular in the City: but that everyone knows about his friendship with Mrs George and people talk of it openly and deplore it.'[2]

The friendship illustrated the particular blend of court, politics and society that the King created around himself. Personally, Alice Keppel encapsulated much that he had always admired in women. She was attractive in a voluptuous, sensual manner in direct contrast to the classical but detached beauty of Alexandra. One of seven sisters in a family of eight children Alice was a natural conversationalist, full of jokes and fond of argument – during which her deep voice, which smoking made progressively more throaty, rose in volume. As was fashionable she wore her thick chestnut hair up, and her most arresting facial feature was piercing, deep blue eyes.

Alice Keppel first met Edward in 1898 when she was aged twenty-nine. Her father, Admiral Sir William Edmonstone, 4th Bart, had served for a time as Naval ADC to Queen Victoria. His daughter moved easily into the Prince of Wales's social circle, some of whose members were already her friends and acquaintances. Her husband, The Hon. George Keppel, was a younger brother of the Earl of Albemarle and from another large family, of ten children. The couple were both admired for their looks and socially well-connected. Nonetheless, Alice's friendship with Edward elevated her beyond all reasonable expectation. Esher may have been characteristically sharp when he wrote shortly after Edward's death that 'When she came into his life twelve years ago she was bankrupt'.[3] But there was more than an element of truth in his assertion. Alice married her handsome, amiable husband in 1891. After following a traditional younger son's path into the army George Keppel was enjoyable company and his looks were widely admired, but he had few prospects and he and his wife were not well off.

Within a short time all this had changed. George Keppel was given employment by Sir Thomas Lipton, the Scottish tea magnate and big-yacht racing friend of the King, while his wife was safeguarded by the Edwardian financier par excellence, Sir Ernest Cassel. Cassel's financial empire was immense by the end of the nineteenth century. It had been built on secure foundations of railway investments and subsequently large foreign loans – including many to various governments. An inscrutable loner, whom some considered taciturn to the point of rudeness, he assumed a position of immense influence through Edward's reign, both as the King's own financial adviser and successful investment manager, and as an informal adviser to the British government. Cassel's association with the King was the most satisfying prize of his life. The relationship was close, but Cassel's lack of humour or interest in gossip and the King's reticence towards the Jewish newcomer precluded it ever being intimate.

Cassel's fortune mounted throughout his life from his early years in Cologne. But at the same time he was plagued by personal sadness.

His wife died of consumption in 1881 after only three years of marriage. Thirty years later, in 1911, their only daughter Maud died of the same disease ten years after she had married Major Wilfred Ashley. After the death of his wife, Cassel's household was run by his sister Bobbie who retained a strong German accent throughout her life and referred to him as her 'bruzzer'. She was also well-known for her spoonerisms, such as her assertion that Cambridge was 'forty miles away as the cock crows.'[4]

Cassel's rise to royal favour with Edward coincided exactly with that of Alice Keppel and they forged a powerful partnership. Cassel was an associate and executor of Baron Hirsch, the Jewish Bavarian who had amassed an immense fortune building the Balkan railway to Constantinople, and who courted Edward's friendship with financial assistance, invitations to slaughter thousands of partridges on his Hungarian estates, and by lavish investment in horseracing in England. Following Hirsch's death in 1896 Cassel first came into contact with Edward in his capacity as Hirsch's executor.

During the next five years the King occasionally sought financial advice from Cassel and shortly after the beginning of the reign the arrangement was formalized. On 7 March 1901 Cassel sent a significant card from his Old Broad Street office which established the King's investment account with him:

> I hereby acknowledge having received from His Majesty the sum of twenty thousand six hundred and eighty five pounds. This sum is deposited with me for the purpose of being invested. The records of this and any future investments I may make on behalf of his Majesty will be kept in an account opened on my books this day entitled Special A.A. Account. E. Cassel.[5]

Cassel applied all his financial acumen to the King's investments. Towards the end of 1902, in spite of the King withdrawing £10,000, within a matter of weeks the account had risen to over £30,000. The King was not a 'sleeping' investor and regularly sent Cassel notes with his thoughts on the markets. Immediately after the signing of the Vereeniging Treaty which ended the Boer War, he wrote in June 1902:

You will doubtless have heard that Peace is signed which is the greatest blessing which has been conferred on this country for a long time! 'Consols' are sure to go up tomorrow. Could you not make a large investment for me? It is to be hoped that the Chancellor of the Exchequer may announce on Wednesday not to put the extra pence on the Income Tax.[6]

As well as organizing the King's finances Cassel was happy to provide a similar service for Alice Keppel. She, in return, was able to give him unwavering support both with the King and society at large. Cassel also proved useful by his willingness to host dinner parties large or small and be told whom to invite by Edward, as demonstrated by a card sent from Marlborough House in 1901. 'My dear Cassel, I have just heard that Mrs K will be back at the end of this week – so if you write to her at Hotel du Rhone, Paris – I think she would probably be able to dine with you on Sunday next and I hope Mrs T may also be able to come.'[7] Such accommodation of the royal will at times lapsed into surprising sycophancy. In April 1902 Cassel wrote proudly to his daughter Maud from the royal yacht, *Victoria and Albert*; 'The King is very well and in the best of humours. Rather pleased with me because I made one or two mistakes in bridge and I can be chaffed mercilessly . . . This is the finest yacht I have ever seen and probably unparalleled anywhere.'[8]

In the early years his increasing favour was deplored by traditional members of society, not least because he lacked the social polish of Edward's other Jewish friends. In July 1900 the Carringtons dined with Albert Sassoon and his wife at their home in Albert Gate. 'A huge dinner for the Prince of Wales – Rosebery, Mensdorff, Edgar and Lady Helen Vincent. Devonshire was twenty minutes late. Israel in force, Reuben Sassoon, Mr and Mrs Leo and Alfred Rothschild, and that awful Sir Ernest Cassel who is in the highest favour, and of course Mr and Mrs George Keppel.'[9] Only weeks after the King's accession Sir Edward Hamilton (whose position as Permanent Chief Secretary to the Treasury gave him regular contact with Cassel through the reign) voiced the concerns of many observers after attending a small dinner given by Cassel for the King. Alice Keppel was one of the few guests and Hamilton wrote afterwards in his diary:

It shows how easy it is to be out in one's calculations. I quite made up my mind that when he came to the Throne, the King would have such a sense of his own dignity and be so determined to play the part of monarch that He would only dine at exceptional houses. But after dining with Cassel of course he can dine anywhere. I much regret it.[10]

Hamilton was steeped in the social priorities of the Victorian period, as were many others. But events soon showed that their criticisms would have little effect. They would have heartily disliked the letter sent by Sir George Lewis to Cassel in 1899, congratulating him on his knighthood; 'I enjoy it all the more because our careers are almost identical – we have worked steadily up from the bottom to the foremost place and I hope it is not egotism to say we both have the fullest confidence of those who know us.'[11]

Only months later Lewis's assertions were confirmed at the highest level when Cassel received a note from the Chancellor of the Exchequer, Sir Michael Hicks-Beach: 'I should like to consult you on some important financial questions now under my consideration, on which your opinion would be of great interest to me.'[12] In 1906 it is Hamilton who, as Treasury Secretary, writes in a similar vein, 'Could you by chance look in here at 5 o'clock this afternoon? You would catch the Chancellor of the Exchequer, and he would be glad of a little general talk with you.'[13]

Cassel maintained an outward diffidence towards parliamentary politics. But, as in the friendship he forged with Alice Keppel, well aware of the benefits it would yield, he was equally shrewd over the politicians he cultivated. In April 1908, Winston Churchill, one of parliament's most outspoken and controversial rising stars, became married. Lord Esher wrote to his son Maurice that after attending a House of Commons debate 'Winston picked me up as I was leaving and I walked to his house in Bolton Street, which is charmingly done. The drawing room is all in oak with books and one picture by Romney which is quite beautiful. The *whole* a gift from Cassel! These financiers always take up with the young rising politicians. It is very astute of them.'[14]

Alice Keppel's rise was as inexorable as Cassel's and equally impervious to criticism or disapproval. In March 1901, after a meeting at

Buckingham Palace, Esher scolded in his diary: 'Then he drove off, I hope not to see Mrs Keppel – but I strongly suspect him.'[15] Immediately after the King's operation, in July 1902, Lord Carrington was both annoyed and concerned that Edward's doctor, Sir Thomas Barlow, knowing his close friendship with the King, should use a visit to air his views. 'Barlow (like many people who cannot mind their own business) then began about "Mrs George" and hoped someone would be patriotic enough to point out the danger the King was running as regards popular opinion.'[16]

The grandee Carrington may have considered it no business of the doctor to speak to him about such matters, but his own feelings were regularly recorded in his diary or letters to his wife. One of the most significant was made on 15 July 1902: 'Mrs George Keppel saw the King yesterday at Buckingham Palace, and remained some time.'[17] Coming as the King was recovering from his operation, and the day before his departure for convalescence aboard his yacht, it was almost certainly the opportunity Mrs Keppel took to acquire the letter from the King which was to cause such a stir at the time of his death. No doubt worried about his condition during his illness and the operation itself, she persuaded Edward to pen a note bidding her to see him in the event of another critical or life-threatening illness. A fortnight later Carrington's disapproval continues: 'Mrs George, Mrs Arthur Paget and Lady Kilmorey have arrived at Cowes; and are staying on board Arthur Morley's yacht. This would be enough to make old Sam Morley turn in his grave.'[18]

By this time, however, Alice Keppel had become an indispensible part of the King's life and its annual progression. She was invariably a fellow guest at shooting parties in January, usually first at Chatsworth then, following the Duke of Devonshire's death in 1908 with Lord Iveagh at his Suffolk home, Elvedon. During the King's spring visit to Biarritz Alice went with her two daughters and stayed as a guest of Ernest Cassel at the palatial Villa Eugenie which Cassel rented each year. Summer weekends were spent at West Dean with Evie and Willie James, racing at Goodwood or, later, with the Grevilles, Ronnie (who died in 1908) and his wife Maggie, the formidable heiress of a Scottish brewer at Polesden Lacey in Surrey. Arthur Morley, Sir Thomas Lipton, or other sailing magnates were happy to provide accommodation on their yachts during the royal visit to Cowes. After

Edward's autumn sojourn to Balmoral he met up with Alice staying with the Sassoons at Tulchan Lodge, just further north on the River Spey, and in October they stayed together with the Saviles at Rufford Abbey for the St Leger meeting at Doncaster. Between these annual fixtures were innumerable evenings in London when she was constantly in attendance.

At times the question of her presence bothered hostesses, especially the more nervous gossip-conscious ones such as Constance Duchess of Westminster. The Duchess was the sister of Lady Randolf Churchill's youthful second husband George Cornwallis-West, described by one contemporary as, 'good-looking fellow; short on brains'[19] and the bird-like Princess Daisy of Pless who twittered her way around English and Continental society and later set down her exploits in breathless memoirs. The Duchess wrote anxiously to the Portuguese Ambassador, the Marquis de Soveral – another constant attendant on the King with the advantage of being close to Queen Alexandra: 'Soveral, will you be very nice and give me your advice? The King and Queen are coming to Eaton Dec. 13th to 17th for three days' shooting. Now, shall I ask Mrs G.K. or not? I want the King to be happy but I don't want to annoy the Queen, so please tell me what would be best.'[20] Sadly, Soveral's reply is not recorded.

The Duchess's concern about the King's happiness hinted at the foundation of Alice's Keppel's success, which Esher further illuminated in July 1905 when he was one of the guests staying with Lord Redesdale at his Gloucestershire home, Batsford Park. He wrote to his son Maurice:

> The King is perfectly happy. His admiration for Mrs K. is almost pathetic. He watches her all day and is never happy when she's talking to someone else. I suppose, like all other human affection, it will cool. But she has wonderful skill and is really fond of him. She is never bored of him and is always good-humoured. So, her hold over him grows. It is a beneficial influence. I must say that I understand her physical charm, although she's not a beauty.[21]

In this instance Esher was well disposed towards Mrs Keppel – not always the case – and his description highlights the weakness towards infatuation which Edward retained throughout his life.

It was a friendship built upon compatibility and companionship rather than one rooted only in passion. This made Alice Keppel increasingly relevant to the King's happiness as he grew older. As Esher said, she was not a great beauty, compared, for instance, to Daisy Brooke (by this time the Countess of Warwick) in her hey-day. By the time of Edward's accession, however, Daisy Warwick's hey-day was not only over, but – despite her continuing beauty – her reputation had left her vulnerable as Esher observed at an evening 'Court' in May 1903.

> Lady Warwick and her girl were there – there was a good deal of interest at the reception they would get. The King gave her a sickly and rather uneasy smile, while the Queen was perfectly icy. I cannot imagine a woman of her position caring to run the risk of such a greeting. It is rather pathetic too when the old intimacy with the King is considered. However, she has only herself to thank. She used to complain of his assiduity and could not make up her mind between him and other people until she had alienated him altogether and then she regretted.[22]

To a great extent Alice Keppel avoided causing any such ripples and the different nature of her relationship with the King was confirmed most emphatically by Queen Alexandra's attitude towards her. Unlike Daisy Warwick, Alice Keppel could never rival the Queen's beauty, which was constantly remarked upon throughout Edward VII's reign. When Lord Carrington was at the Spanish court in Madrid in 1901, as the special envoy to announce Queen Victoria's death, he wrote to the King that the Spanish Queen was very anxious to know about Queen Alexandra's toilette, as she thought Her Majesty always was the best dressed lady in Europe. Secure as Queen, Alexandra was prepared to tolerate Alice Keppel, in order to please her husband, with an attitude described by Esher during Ascot Week in 1908.

> The party at Windsor changed on Saturday. The Westminsters, Londonderrys, Dudleys etc. left and were replaced by Asquiths, Grey, Morley, Mrs Keppel and the Saviles. Several only stayed on. He is always persona gratissima especially to the Queen. And she, although she raises no objection to Mrs K. coming to Sandringham, never likes her advent at Windsor.[23]

The King carried out much of his social and public life without the Queen and it was reasonable for her to expect Alice Keppel not to intrude, or to be forced upon her. The Duchess of Westminster was only one among hosts and hostesses well aware of her feelings. Like his Portuguese counterpart Soveral, the Austrian ambassador, Count Albert Mensdorff was a regular figure in the royal circle. Mensdorff was not one of Alice Keppel's admirers. He is usually credited with naming her 'La Favorita' and was overheard on one occasion caustically referring to Alice's friend, Lady Sarah Wilson, as 'her lady-in-waiting'. In March 1907 he described in his diary an official dinner he had given for the King and Queen at the Austrian embassy, noting with relief: 'Thank God Mrs Keppel had already left (London) so that I could safely express polite regards to her and didn't need to have her, which is never agreeable when the Queen is present.'[24]

When confrontation was likely those around the Queen knew her displeasure would be aroused. At Cowes one year the Prince of Wales reported to his wife that all was quiet but: 'Alas, Mrs K. arrives tomorrow and stops here in a yacht, I am afraid that peace and quiet will not remain.' The Princess of Wales heartily disapproved of the royal favourite and replied: 'What a pity Mrs G.K. is again to the fore. How annoyed Mama will be.'[25]

Queen Alexandra could afford to treat Mrs Keppel with polite disdain and to laugh at the comical sight of her portly husband seated next to the similarly shaped *favorita*, as she did on one occasion as they left for a drive at Sandringham. But lesser people were not able to risk her opposition. As her relationship with the King continued through his reign so her perceived influence grew and at a dinner given for the King by Lord Rosebery in February 1908 Carrington noted: 'Mrs George Keppel, very smart and much toadied to.'[26]

Like most intelligent society ladies, she held strong opinions on politics and its leading figures and was not afraid to air them, even to someone like Carrington, whom she knew was not her most ardent supporter. The Liberal election victory in 1906, ended any aspirations Lord Rosebery might still have held to lead his party again. Shortly afterwards Carrington (whom everyone knew to be Rosebery's cousin and close friend) wrote in his diary that while at Hinchingbrook, Lord Sandwich's home, 'I sat next to Mrs George Keppel at dinner, who remarked: "Three men thought themselves indispensable and all found their level. Randolf Churchill, Curzon of Kedleston, and Rosebery." [27]

Although he did not approve of Alice Keppel and had no need to 'toady' to her, even Carrington realized that on certain occasions it was advisable to accommodate her – and thereby keep the King happy. Six months before the long-heralded fall of Balfour's government and the Liberal triumph of 1906, the Carringtons gave a dinner party for the King at their London house in Princes Gate. Carrington was one of the few Liberal grandees who had remained faithful to the party and had not joined ranks with the Unionists. The evening was both social and political and the guests included Sir Henry Campbell-Bannerman who would lead the new Liberal government, as well as Alice and George Keppel.

The chief purpose of the party was to improve the King's opinion of his future Prime Minister, which to date had been clouded by suspicion. The possibility that Campbell-Bannerman's position within his party might not be secure enough to guarantee the King asking him to form a government increased the need for good relations. Carrington was wise enough to know that Alice Keppel's presence – and more importantly, a positive opinion of Campbell-Bannerman from her – would certainly encourage a favourable outcome, which he appears to have achieved.

> HM was in capital spirits and remained till nearly one o'clock. He played bridge and won £4. After dinner he had a long conversation with CB on foreign politics and the King told me as he went away he was quite satisfied with CB's opinions and declarations. It is satisfactory to know that the King is satisfied with CB as Tweedsmouth told me last week that HM had been very outspoken about his utterances on foreign affairs, and found great fault with him. [28]

Alice Keppel was too skilful to put herself in a position where she could be accused of being manipulative. Nonetheless her eldest brother, who had succeeded their father as Sir Archibald Edmonstone 5th Bart in 1888, was made a member of the King's household in 1907. He had in 1895, married Evie Forbes's first cousin, Ida Forbes. But given the King's enjoyment of conversation it is inconceivable that he did not discuss politics with Alice. During the debate over tariff

reform proposed by the Colonial Secretary Joseph Chamberlain, which split Balfour's government, she was a confirmed anti-Chamberlainite, or 'free fooder' as they were known. On one occasion Edward VII told Balfour that he would never agree to any protectionist tariff on foodstuffs and later, when the Prime Minister suggested Chamberlain to succeed Curzon as Lord Warden of the Cinque Ports the King refused. During the latter years of the reign Esher was certain that Edward's accommodating attitude towards Lloyd-George when the latter was Chancellor of the Exchequer was partly due to Mrs Keppel's support.

All the compliments paid to Alice Keppel regarding her discretion and beneficial influence while Edward was alive pale in comparison to the eulogy that Lord Hardinge of Penshurst set down in his private papers shortly after the King's death. Hardinge was Permanent Under Secretary of State at the Foreign Office at the time and about to become Viceroy of India; he had also been one of the King's inner circle of advising friends throughout the reign and the motive for setting down such a glowing tribute appears not far removed from the 'toadying' that Carrington dismissed.

> I take this opportunity to allude to a delicate matter upon which I am in a position to speak with authority. Everybody knew of the friendship that existed between King Edward and Mrs George Keppel, which was intelligible in view of the lady's good looks, vivacity and cleverness. I used to see a great deal of Mrs Keppel at that time, and I was aware that she had knowledge of what was going on in the political world.
>
> I would here like to pay a tribute to her wonderful discretion, and to the excellent influence which she always exerted upon the King. She never utilized her knowledge to her own advantage, or to that of her friends; and I never heard her repeat an unkind word of anybody. There were one or two occasions when the King was in disagreement with the Foreign Office, and I was able, through her, to advise the King with view to the policy of the Government being accepted. She was very loyal to the King, and patriotic at the same time. It would have been difficult to find any other lady who would have filled the part of friend to King Edward with the same loyalty and discretion.[29]

The King unquestionably took an interest in her opinions, but there is no evidence that she ever offered them unless asked. Instead her presence was primarily calming and enjoyable; helping him win at bridge or, more to the point, ensuring that he was able to lose with good humour. She rarely dissented from the royal will; if she did so, it was over trivial matters as Esher described on one occasion during a party at the James's Sussex home, West Dean.

> There was a regular hump between the King and Mrs K about the motor-drive. He wished her to go, she wished to stay at home. He got his way, but at the price of a freeze. However, she is so good-humoured that it all passed over quickly. She sits next to him at dinner, irrespective of rank! and she has, in fact, to entertain him all day. She never comes down before midday, which is natural – or she would never get five minutes to herself.[30]

Although some contemporaries deplored the effect of the friendship on the King's public reputation at home and abroad, after a time most who moved in their circle agreed with Esher that as the years went by she became increasingly able to keep royal boredom and wrath at bay. Even Carrington was of this mind and wrote in February 1905 of a visit from his Buckinghamshire home to Rosebery's nearby Mentmore, where the King was staying: 'HM is in great spirits and health.' After listing the guests, who included Alice Keppel: 'HM stays till Wednesday which rather disconcerts his hosts. But so long as Mrs George is here he is perfectly happy.'[31]

Carrington and others who worried about the royal reputation still had to endure occasions such as a dinner given by Sir Samuel Evans, a pugnacious Welsh MP who had risen with his friend Lloyd George and in 1908 became Solicitor-General. Carrington complained to his wife afterwards that: 'He was very tonguey about Mrs George Keppel, who is referred to as "our woman"'.[32] Among people with the fiercely held principles of Evans, the King's reputation was undoubtedly diminished by his association with Alice Keppel.

His broader popularity was not affected. Most people saw Mrs Keppel as a source of irreverent amusement, like the cab-driver who found himself with Mrs Keppel as his fare and on being given the destination 'King's Cross' responded: 'Very sorry to hear it ma'am. I hope you will be able to get him round in time.'[33]

CHAPTER TEN

THE KING AND HIS MINISTERS

Despite its brevity Edward VII's reign from 1901 to 1910 witnessed fundamental change for the monarchy. The reasons were political, social, and personal. Political and social change and the King's personality combined with the result that during nine years the constitutional role of the crown was established in a form that it has since retained.

Party politics through the second half of the nineteenth century had been fiercely fought and often acrimonious. Gladstone's Home Rule campaign split the Liberal party and formed the Unionists out of anti-Home Rule Liberals and the Tories. Most significant for the future, among those Unionists were a majority of the land-owning grandees who for over two centuries had maintained the Whig tradition. The resignation of Gladstone for the last time in 1894 was a political watershed. It ended 'the two party close balanced political situation of the Victorian era.'[1]

At the same time Queen Victoria brought the monarch's position into sharp focus by imposing the royal prerogative. Ignoring the retiring statesman's opinion, she asked Lord Rosebery to form a government rather than Gladstone's Chancellor and preferred successor in the Commons, Sir William Harcourt. Her doctor and confidante, Sir James Reid said bluntly to one of the Liberal leaders: 'Queen Victoria thought precious little of your Liberal Government but she considered Rosebery the least dangerous of the lot.'[2] The Queen's antipathy to Harcourt was sharpened by his 1894 budget introducing death duties. Rosebery's government lasted just over a year and was replaced by an alliance of Tories and Unionists.

When Lord Salisbury took office in Rosebery's place it was the first time that the Conservative ranks had been formally joined by the Unionists, whose leaders – the Duke of Devonshire, the Marquess of Lansdowne, Joseph Chamberlain and Henry James – all joined the Cabinet. The government remained in power for ten years and its veneer of continuity disguised forces for change which first surfaced in the resounding Liberal victory of 1906. So many Liberal peers had left the party over Home Rule that Lord Carrington, one of the minority to remain with the party, remembered that they were so few it was difficult to get enough together for the traditional eve of the parliamentary session dinner. Carrington was fiercely critical of Salisbury's government. He considered it to have been 'the most dangerous government in modern times on account of its strength and weakness: the weakness of its policy and the strength of its majority.'[3] Throughout the long period of office the Liberals were at odds with each other. Rosebery and Harcourt were at loggerheads, not least because Rosebery refused to reveal his hand over whether he was still a candidate for the leadership or not.

The ageing Lord Salisbury remained in office until the end of the Boer War in June 1902 and a month later handed over leadership of the government to his nephew A. J. Balfour. The following year the statesman who had been in politics for over half a century died at Hatfield. Never again would either a government or political party be actively led from the House of Lords. Peers would continue to hold key Cabinet positions but the ensuing years established that the real power base lay with the Members of the House of Commons as the elected representatives of the people. In 1905 Edward VII indirectly acknowledged the democratic nature of the position Prime Minister by formally giving it a place in the table of precedence for the first time, fourth after the Archbishop of Canterbury, the Lord Chancellor and the Archbishop of York.

During the early years of her reign Queen Victoria – largely through the dogged and successful interventions of the Prince

Consort – had established the monarchy's constitutional position as one of constant involvement and decision-making. Her unstinting attention to state papers ensured that, as her reign progressed, there were few instances when ministers were able to circumvent her. At the same time, foreign and colonial affairs; European relations, India, Africa and Ireland, and in response to these, military affairs – all areas where the crown's involvement was tacitly accepted – continually dominated the political agenda. They did not diminish during Edward VII's reign. But they were joined by contentious domestic issues; social reform, education, taxation and, finally, the balance of power at Westminster. All were politically charged and steadily shifted the executive focus away from the supposedly impartial crown.

Even if it had been constitutionally acceptable for Edward to maintain the same style of monarchy as his mother, both his own personality and his ministers suggested a different route. The King was always more interested in people than ideas, although Esher's comment early in the reign was unduly harsh: 'I do not believe he ever has an original thought. Probably a man who never ceases talking from eight in the morning until past midnight has no time for thinking.'[4] Memories of the long, agonizing evenings during his youth at White Lodge, Richmond, surrounded by eminent elders, gave him an abiding aversion to pontificating, to which ministers, nervous in the royal presence, were prone. As a result he often gave the impression of either boredom or of not listening and on occasions even his warmest supporters such as Admiral 'Jackie' Fisher were critical of this. In 1904 Fisher complained to Lord Esher, after an audience explaining his ideas for naval reform, that 'The King will not listen to detail and all impressions are evanescent.'[5] In reply Esher, who, with the exception of Francis Knollys, had more interviews with the King than any other person during his reign gave a more accurate assessment.

The King has two plates in his mind. Once receives permanent impressions, generally of persons which leads him to say 'that is Jack F's opinion and it is sure to be right' (upon naval questions and so on). The other receives the impression of *things*, and they are evanescent, but the former is the important factor in dealing with the King, because you can nearly always rely upon his backing you, if your impression is on plate number 1.[6]

Intuition rather than constant study may have been the King's preferred *modus operandi*, but few observers accused him of laziness or neglecting his duties. At first, his activity exhausted most of those around him and in 1903, while staying for a summer weekend at West Dean, Esher wrote, 'The King goes to bed as late as he can, but is up before eight and works away until ten – when we breakfast. He never seems to require rest. Of course he gets through a great deal of work, as he never leaves over anything until next day. All papers and letters of the day are dealt with within twenty-four hours.'[7]

The King's constant movement was another aspect of his desire for activity and influenced his style of monarchy. In April and May 1903 he carried out state visits to Portugal, Gibraltar, Italy, and France. Two days after his return to England he received the Prime Minister, A. J. Balfour, spent the day at Kempton races and held a court at Buckingham Palace in the evening. The next day he saw the Foreign Secretary Lord Lansdowne before returning to Kempton. Two days later he carried out a four-day visit with Queen Alexandra to Edinburgh and Glasgow, where Esher recalled, 'The Queen has created a vast astonishment by her youthful appearance. She does these things so gracefully.'[8]

Even during a major constitutional crisis the political activity was fitted in with the King's movements. Inevitably there were hitches – but remarkably few. In September 1903, when Balfour was faced with a series of Cabinet resignations, the King had recently returned from his annual visit to Marienbad followed by a state visit to Austria, and had gone to Balmoral. Balfour telegraphed to Balmoral for permission to publish the resignations. The King initially agreed, but then cancelled his decision by telegraph the next day on the grounds that Balfour would be at Balmoral at the weekend and, 'It would not look well in the eyes of the world that a matter of such importance should be settled without my having seen the Prime Minister.'[9] The King's intuition was right but too late, as Balfour published after receipt of the first directive. A month later, on 19 October, when the new Cabinet appointments were being made, the King established a record that well illustrated the crown's energetic travels. Sir Almeric Fitzroy (who had to attend as Clerk of the Privy Council) wrote at Wynyard Park, the Marquess of Londonderry's seat in County Durham, where a Council was held to appoint Lord Londonderry the Duke of Devonshire's replacement as President of the Council,

A record has been established today, the King having held two Councils, at 11a.m. and 10.30p.m. respectively, on the same day, more than two hundred and fifty miles apart. Nothing particular distinguished the first [at Balmoral], at which Salisbury received the Privy Seal and was sworn a Privy Councillor. I came down by the King's train at two o'clock from King's Cross, which did the distance to Thorpe Thewles in five minutes under the five hours. Mensdorff and the Duke and Duchess of Devonshire were the only other passengers.

Lord Londonderry and his son met us at the station and on reaching Wynyard we found most of the party lingering over tea in the library. The King told me he would hold the Council immediately after dinner, and was most interested to hear that, as far as we had been able to trace, the last occasion on which a council has been held in a country house belonging to a subject was in October 1625 when Charles I held one at Wilton, the Lord Pembroke of the day being his chamberlain. Lady Londonderry was greatly excited over the event, and was particularly pleased to learn that the King desired the documents connected with the Council to be headed 'At the Court at Wynyard' which is indeed the old style.

The party assembled for dinner at 8.45 including the Duke and Duchess of Devonshire, Lord and Lady Shaftesbury, Lord and Lady Crewe, Mensdorff, Kintore, Walter Long and Lady Doreen, Mrs George Keppel, Lady Helen Stavordale, Castlereagh, Fritz Ponsonby, Seymour Fortesque, and Eddy Hamilton.

After describing the house Fitzroy continued.

Immediately the ladies had left the dining-room the King called to me to say that the Duke of Devonshire would take his old part: 'He will assist at his own funeral,' as His Majesty put it with great good-humour. After the Council three bridge tables were set up, at one of which were the King, the Duchess, Mrs Keppel and Seymour Fortesque, and most of the rest played poker. Fortunately Lady Shaftesbury had other tastes, and I talked to her for more than an hour.'[10]

Two years later, as Balfour's increasingly beleaguered government came to an end the outgoing Prime Minister had to wait before announcing his resignation for the King to return to London from Sandringham, where he had spent his annual visit for Queen Alexandra's birthday. The King remained in London the next day to invite Sir Henry Campbell-Bannerman to form the next government and then left to shoot with Lord Alington at Crichel in Dorset.

At Campbell-Bannerman's resignation in March 1908, the King's itinerant style of monarchy for once caused disapproval. As he left for his annual visit to Biarritz his ageing, ill Prime Minister was failing. While Queen Alexandra sent a bunch of fresh violets she had picked at Windsor, the King urged him not to resign before he returned to England, and continued to do so right up to the day before he telegraphed his acceptance of the resignation on 3 April. Before leaving England Edward had made contingency plans by arranging for Campbell-Bannerman's successor, Asquith, to travel to Biarritz for the kissing of hands – if necessary. Nonetheless, as Knollys wrote candidly to the King: 'The appointment of Prime Minister has for the last 4 or 5 weeks been in complete abeyance',[11] and even the King's most loyal supporters were critical. Carrington wrote in his diary: 'It is perhaps not quite wise in a Sovereign to let people know that in a crisis he is not indispensable, and that events of the greatest importance cannot be satisfactorily settled in his absence. Some people think it is the only blunder of his reign.'[12]

Arthur Balfour was an aristocrat to his languid fingertips, but on his assumption of the Prime Minister's position, the fifty-three-year-old bachelor had few illusions about his intellectual compatibility with his monarch. Recalling the reign in a letter to Lord Lansdowne in 1915 Balfour wrote: 'Now so far as I remember, during the years during which you and I were his ministers he never made an important suggestion of any sort on large questions of policy.'[13]

Balfour was the most admired figure among the constantly self-admiring group the Souls – named by Lord Charles Beresford in 1887 because they were always talking about their souls. They were drawn together by their distaste for the philistine, philandering, sport-loving set who surrounded the Prince of Wales. During his leadership of the House of Commons from 1895 Balfour honed himself into a formidable parliamentarian with near-infallible knowledge of constitutional procedure.

Such a background was not auspicious for future relations with his King. In addition Balfour was a notoriously casual correspondent – to a degree which infuriated Esher and, more particularly the King's secretary Francis Knollys, who suspected deliberate breaches of the royal prerogative in any ministerial lapse. Edward VII however, unlike his mother who corresponded voluminously with her prime ministers, was often irregular and brief in his own official correspondence. Where long documents were required he usually preferred to dictate a draft to be sent by Knollys, or the assistant-secretary, Fritz Ponsonby. It was a habit that Esher, ever conscious of constitutional niceties, deplored as inviting the belittlement of monarchical authority; 'The Queen always wrote her scolding letters to ministers in her own hand – and never by the private secretary.'[14]

Throughout the early years of the reign Balfour firmly rebutted Edward's attempts to activate the monarch's claim to see Cabinet papers concerning issues still under discussion. Involving the monarch in Cabinet discussion may not have been either practical or desirable. But to supply tardy information of Cabinet meetings and, even worse, present agreed Cabinet decision for royal approval in the form of a *fait accompli*, were practices of which both Balfour's government and, more especially his Liberal successors, were guilty. Balfour complained of being unable to capture the King's attention for any length of time. For his part, the King remonstrated to either Knollys or Esher, that he could not get anything out of Balfour when they discussed an issue. Correspondence shows that Edward – whatever he might say in private – was in the main scrupulously polite and encouraging towards Balfour and regularly took the opportunity to offer his congratulations on a parliamentary or political achievement. In February 1902, when Balfour's parliamentary skill was largely responsible for the passing of the new Education Act, Knollys wrote: 'I am desired by the King to congratulate you on your success and on the way in which the measure has been handled throughout.'[15]

Later the same year a seemingly minor incident over making the Shah of Persia a Knight of the Garter, exposed the problematic relations between Edward and Balfour's government. Courting of the Shah was a priority of British diplomacy in order to counter Russian ambitions towards Persia and the possibility of the unreliable and corrupt Shah responding to Russian overtures. Early in 1902 the fuse of the coming crisis was lit by Sir Arthur Hardinge, British Minister in Teheran, who assured the Shah that if he accepted the government's invitation to England later that year, the King would confer on him the Garter. The King had a low opinion of the Shah. In 1873 Queen Victoria had bestowed the Garter on his father, but Lord Rosebery, during his period as Prime Minister, had persuaded Queen Victoria that the nation's most distinguished Christian order should no longer be offered to non-Christians.

The Foreign Secretary who was the King's principal adversary in the row over the Shah's garter was the fifth Marquess of Lansdowne, one of the last aristocratic political grandees. His family owned thousands of acres around their English seat, Bowood in Wiltshire, in Scotland, and even more around Derreen in County Kerry. Lansdowne House was one of London's most elegant houses. In March 1903 Esher described visiting Lansdowne at the Foreign Office: 'In his beautiful rooms hung with splendid portraits by Raeburn, and that wonderful group of Scottish writers and liberals who were contemporaries but not friends of Scott's.[16] For Lansdowne the Foreign Office came towards the end of a career which emulated his statesmen forebears and included periods as Governor-General of Canada, Viceroy of India and Secretary for War.

Before inheriting the marquessate when aged only twenty-one he had held the subsidiary title of Lord Clanmaurice and was for the rest of his life known by his friends as Clan. Quiet, courteous and reserved, he was happiest fishing on his Scottish estates and a sense of duty rather than enjoyment of position and power was responsible for his political career. Not naturally forceful, as Foreign Secretary he came up against a king with an intense, active interest in foreign affairs. Not one to court royal favour Lansdowne was also sensitive to what he regarded as intrusions into his authority. As result, conflict with the King was always possible, and blew up most seriously over the Shah's Garter.

After the King had told Lansdowne of his opposition to the idea, correspondence makes it clear that ministers considered that Edward would give way in order to support government policy. They saw that he had no alternative. In June Hardinge sent Lansdowne a long memorandum discussing all the reasons why the honour should be offered. The King, increasingly bothered by his developing appendicitis, was not inclined to give in. With the Shah's visit scheduled for August now imminent, Hardinge forced Lansdowne's hand in a memo of 19 July when he threatened to resign if the Garter was not given. He ended by accusing the King of obduracy: 'So long as he was well all went beautifully and we were on the eve of seeing a great British success in Persia – now the whole thing is a ghastly muddle.'[17]

After the Shah's arrival in England on 18 August Edward VII interrupted his convalescent cruise to entertain the visitor aboard the *Victoria and Albert* at Portsmouth. Lansdowne took his chance to present a memorandum whereby the statutes of the Order of the Garter could be revised for it to be given to a non-Christian. This memorandum became the central issue in the argument. Afterwards Lansdowne maintained that the King had given his assent to the changes and that they could be put in motion in time for the Garter to be conferred before the Shah left England. Edward protested vigorously and his feelings were relayed to Lansdowne in a letter from Knollys in August. The King regretted that he was unable to alter his decisions for reasons already known. Knollys went on:

> To give it, HM would be yielding to the Persians and, unless given personally by me, it loses its whole importance. It would moreover necessitate my giving it to the Sultan who has just sent me the highest order, and also the emperors of China and Japan. It must be explained to the Grand Vizier, that Queen Victoria gave it to the Shah's father as it was the first time a Persian sovereign had visited England. I consented the other day to consider any proposal to alter the statutes, and I never intended that these alterations should be rushed through to meet the present difficulty, or that the Shah should know anything about it. I cannot have my hand forced.[18]

Lansdowne was faced with an increasingly irate King, but also a thoroughly indignant Shah – who refused the offer of a miniature of Edward VII surrounded by diamonds and a selection of orders for members of his suite. Thus frustrated on both sides, the Foreign Secretary persisted and ordered designs for a suitably changed Garter star from the crown jewellers Garrards, drawings for which he sent to the King. The royal response was understandably furious.

When Lord Lansdowne threw up the hasty memorandum of Portsmouth during the Shah's visit last week the King consented to give it his fullest consideration, and nothing more . . . It is unheard of, one sovereign being dictated to by another what order should be conferred upon him. The Shah ought to have been satisfied with the miniature in diamonds which the King thought would please him, and which he conferred upon him personally . . . The Shah forces himself upon the King when he knew his visit here this year was most inconvenient on account of the Coronation, and since by the King's serious illness – and he leaves this country in a huff like a spoilt child, because he cannot get what he wants. It cannot be helped. Lord Lansdowne states that a determined effort should be made to strengthen our hold in Persia. In this the King concurs. But we should not have lost the hold which Russia now possesses if the government of the day had kept its eyes open, and had had more competent representatives at Teheran to maintain its interest and that of our country.[19]

A few days later Lansdowne wrote indignantly to Major General Sir Arthur Ellis, Comptroller in the Lord Chamberlain's department, who despite being a royal servant for many years, never felt himself bound to courtesy towards the monarchy. When in St Petersburg in 1894 for the funeral of the Tsar, as the Prince of Wales's equerry, he had written to Francis Knollys: 'That old tiresome woman at Windsor Castle telegraphs hungry for more letters and I have written at great length, the feeblest platitudes nine times.'[20] Now, on holiday at the Empire Hotel in Buxton, he encouraged Lansdowne's irritation with the King, telling him of a letter he has received from Knollys aboard the royal yacht, describing the royal rage.

What you will do I cannot think – but this I am sure of, that to get the thing settled it will require the written pressure of a 'Cabinet Question' . . . I won't weary you with the infantile arguments in the letter just received, but it is manifest that he doesn't take in the very elementary part of the matter – nor does he deem to realize that having given his word he cannot go back.[21]

With the King's recent operation in mind Ellis ends the letter: 'It is all more than tiresome and it seems to me that the situation demands the necessity of what Treves calls "a major operation" with you to give the anaesthetic and Balfour the knife – Inshallah!'[22]

Although offered lightheartedly, Ellis's advice was taken up. By the end of August Lansdowne told Balfour he would resign. 'If the King is obdurate there is, so far as I can see, one way out for me and that will be "out" in the most literal sense of the word.'[23] Initially Balfour attempted to smooth over the situation replying, 'Any real quarrel with HM on this subject must somehow be avoided. Important as it is, it would not bear a public discussion. I am sure he is anxious not to embarrass you, but I think he has not thoroughly understood what the position is.'[24] After Knollys wrote directly to Balfour, however, continuing the King's robust stance with accusations that Lansdowne had tried to force his hand, that Hardinge had behaved very badly and that 'to give way would show great weakness on his part',[25] Balfour sent the letter to the Duke of Devonshire with his own thoughts:

My dear Devonshire, would you mind considering the enclosed documents and then having a talk with me about them. I think the position a very grave one. Please note that a. none of my colleagues so far as I know, are aware of what has been going on – and that *he* [Lansdowne], has not seen Knollys' letter of *yesterday*. I feel convinced that if he does see it, he will resign at once.[26]

The argument was now no longer about the Shah's Garter, but basic constitutional principle, as Devonshire made clear in his reply. In June he told Lansdowne that the King's reservations would have to be respected. But now he advised Balfour: 'The King is evidently irritated and I dare say would lose Lansdowne without much regret, but can we sacrifice him? My own impression is that if we stand by him, the King will give in.'[27]

Thus advised Balfour wrote to Knollys in November when an understanding tone is mixed with clear threats regarding the possible resignation of Lansdowne. 'If he resigned, could the matter stop there – in these days of government solidarity?'[28]

In the context of the monarch's relations with the Cabinet it was a significant position and Edward VII would find himself threatened with such 'government solidarity' on a number of occasions in the future. It also forced the King to give in. Considering that the affair had blown up during his serious illness, that he had been coerced if not blatantly misrepresented by Lansdowne, the tone of his reply, sent through Knollys, was magnanimous.

> My dear Balfour, in sending the accompanying answer to your memo you may like to hear that the King has really been most reasonable and sensible about the whole matter, and the line which you took up and the arguments which you used were undoubtedly the best and most judicious. He was extremely kind in all he said about you, and he knows you feel for him in the position in which he is placed – he is sore with Lansdowne but not so much though as I think I expected, and he is angry with Hardinge.

Knollys's memo continues:

> It is hardly necessary for me to tell you that it is very far from his wish to place the government in a difficulty with a foreign power and least of all with Russia, with whom our relations are complicated and troublesome. You assure His Majesty that such would be the case were the Shah not now to be given the Garter, and from patriotic motives, therefore, and a high sense of duty, he consents, though with the greatest reluctance, to confer it upon him.'[29]

The row over the Shah's Garter was a single instance where confrontation arose between the King and his ministers. But by 1903, when the Colonial Secretary, Joseph Chamberlain's vigorous promotion of protectionist tariffs was dividing the Conservatives, the continuing instability of Balfour's administration continually worked against satisfactory relations between the monarchy and the government. Chamberlain's supporters were committed to his vehemently expressed proposals to safeguard Britain's manufacturing industries and agriculture. His opponents accused him of deliberately destroying the government and of abandoning free trade, the foundationstone of Victorian economic philosophy and success. Lord Carrington had always viewed Chamberlain with grave mistrust. After the Jamieson Raid in 1896, when Chamberlain was also Colonial

Secretary, Carrington noted in his diary that: 'He knew all about what was contemplated, though he lied like a thief saying he was quite ignorant of the whole transaction.'[30] At the end of 1903 Carrington closed his diary in dispair: 'So ends a year of turmoil and strife – caused by the impetuosity of an arrogant, unscrupulous and ambitious man – Mr. G. [Gladstone] distrusted him and showed it, and Chamberlain who began life as a Birmingham radical and republican mayor is now the wrecker of the Tory party who dare not avoid protection.[31]

By this time Balfour's attempts to steer a middle course had failed. While rejecting the imposition of a tariff he would consider it if similar protectionist measures by other countries made this necessary. Chamberlain resigned and shortly afterwards the threat of departure from free trade brought the same action from the Chancellor Charles Ritchie, the Secretary for India Lord George Hamilton, and the Secretary for Scotland Lord Balfour of Burleigh. They were joined three weeks later by the Duke of Devonshire. Carrington's comments came in the light of this political instability which Esher also deplored. He wrote to his son Maurice in October 1903:

> Arthur Balfour will have to assert his authority in political matters. It is dangerous for the King and may be dangerous for the monarchy to let the present state develop. HM must rule, but he must not govern. Hitherto the distinction has saved the crown, and placed it above party conflict. It is the duty of Arthur Balfour to check the departure taken by HM: so different from the line of the Queen. It should not be hard to do, if Arthur is firm, for the King is the most reasonable of men when he's talked to straight.[32]

Esher had good reason to write in this vein. As part of the Cabinet reshuffle that the resignations prompted, the King and Balfour had both told Esher that he should join the government as Secretary of State for War. They considered it a natural formalising of Esher's close involvement in the army and War Office reform that was such a major issue, and one in which the King was unfailingly interested. Esher, however, had no intention of giving up his freedom of action and position as the King's confidante – a position greatly resented by ministers. Esher's decision aroused initial anger in the King, but he soon accepted it. Within a few weeks he suggested to Balfour that Esher should head a committee to advise on reform of the War Office and on 7 November 1903 the War Office Reconstitution Committee was publicly announced, consisting of Esher, Admiral Sir John Fisher and Sir George Clarke.

Sir George Clarke, an ardent imperialist, had been secretary of the Colonial Defence Committee before becoming Governor of Victoria in 1890. Jackie Fisher was at the time Commander of the Fleet at Portsmouth and Second Sea Lord. With the encouragement of Lord Selbourne, the First Lord of the Admiralty, he had already shown his zeal and skill in naval reform which he would extend from 1904 when he was appointed First Sea Lord.

Esher and Fisher together ensured that the King was closely involved with the workings of the Committee which reported to parliament early in 1904. It recommended the appointment of an Army Board (similar to the Admiralty Board), and a General Staff to replace the Commander-in-Chief as administrative head of the army. The Committee proposed a new position of Inspector-General as the most senior military individual. Finally, the War Office would be radically decentralized and the Committee of Imperial Defence given a permanent secretariat, with Sir George Clarke as the first Secretary.

Esher's consummate skill in handling King and Prime Minister ensured favourable opinions from both. His eagerness for the abolition of Commander-in-Chief's position was prompted by his desire to remove Lord Roberts, the incumbent since 1901. Esher certainly influenced the King against Roberts and wrote to his son Maurice in March 1903 about an interview with Edward:

> He made me sit down, and he talked – as he so often does – with the greatest freedom – his relations with the C-in-C are not friendly. Lord Roberts has mismanaged him and the King chafes under the little man's ignorance of the English army, and his persistence in pushing all his Indian friends in to high military posts.[33]

A year later Esher had the satisfaction of engineering Roberts' departure and the King's brother, the Duke of Connaught, became the first Inspector-General.

The Committee's work marked a new departure for the army, but it

was largely counter-productive politically. The appointment of a non-government committee was seen as weak and dangerous; Esher's position was resented and suspected by those in parliament and outside. On a personal level, when Esher refused the post as Secretary for War the man appointed was H. O. Arnold-Foster whose relations with the King were even less satisfactory that those of his predecessor, St John Brodrick. In fact they were probably the worst of any of Edward's ministers.

Arnold-Foster's unhappy predicament illustrated the political dangers that could arise from Esher's position. The resentment he caused was encapsulated by Lord Salisbury (son of the Prime Minister), writing to his cousin Balfour:

> I suspect A-F has again made a mess of it, but I think Esher's relations with the King are in the highest degree unsatisfactory. He ought either to be a responsible minister and defend his views in Parliament or (at the very most) he should confide himself to intensely confidential communication with yourself.[34]

Arnold-Foster had his own plans for reform of the War Office, but they were inevitably threatened by Esher's committee's work. In addition the Secretary for War's progress often was not assisted by his manner, as Balfour hinted in July 1904 when he wrote to Esher about Arnold-Foster: 'He is at once unconsciously inconsiderate of other's feelings and unduly sensitive to his own – a rather unfortunate combination.'[35] Suspicion that his views were not given a fair chance by the King because of Esher's influence made Arnold-Foster dilatory in communication with the monarch, with unfortunate results. In November 1904, when Arnold-Foster sent an important army order to the King, Esher wrote to Balfour's private secretary, Jack Sanders:

> Why oh why does our dear and silly A-F submit that Army Order to the King after it has been approved finally by the Army Council? In spite of all our efforts to induce him to send early copies of his projects privately to Knollys. Here we are, all trying to help him, and he goes and hurls this document, full of things the King hates, at H.M.'s head. He is really too foolish.[36]

The King's relations with Arnold-Foster deteriorated right up until Balfour resigned on 4 December 1905. The government's last months were fraught with trouble: the continuing fiscal row over tariff reform; the struggle in India between the Viceroy Lord Curzon and the Indian Army's Commander-in-Chief Lord Kitchener, which culminated in Curzon's resignation after he had made ever-mounting accusations of disloyalty against Balfour and most of the Cabinet; and problems in Ireland which led to the resignation in March 1905 of the Irish Secretary Balfour's fellow-Soul and friend, George Wyndham.

These political problems deeply concerned the King. But his constitutional involvement through much of 1905 threatened to be of a more serious nature. There was uncertainty over whom he should ask to form a Liberal government in the event of Balfour's resignation; Henry Campbell-Bannerman, the party's leader in the House of Commons since the retirement of Sir William Harcourt in 1899; Lord Rosebery who had continued in his position of maverick self-imposed isolation; or Lord Spencer, a friend of the King and the leader of the rump of Liberal peers in the House of Lords. Predictably, Esher was closely involved, discussing the issue with both the King and Balfour. He recorded his views in different letters to his son. On 20 June 1904 he had written after a long talk with Balfour, which covered the possible fall of his government:

> We then discussed the possible action of the King and he agreed that it was most important that on the first occasion during his reign, when the King was called upon to use his prerogative to form a new Administration – his action should be strictly constitutional and according to precedent. Arthur Balfour has no doubt that the King should send for Campbell-Bannerman and not for Lord Spencer: on the grounds that the former is the recognised leader of the Liberal party, while the latter is only the leader of about 20 peers and that the question as to whether CB could or would form a government is not one that in its primary stage should concern the sovereign.[37]

Balfour was of the opinion that the King should not be given the chance to make a choice over his Prime Minister. But in March 1905 Esher was concerned that the King might be persuaded to send for

Campbell-Bannerman and Spencer together and ask their advice, which would be a disastrous subjection of the royal prerogative. A few months later, he need not have worried. The King was better aware than any of his advisers of the necessary course of action and in the event the 69-year-old Campbell-Bannerman overcame all the obstacles to forming a government with a sufficient presence of Liberal Imperialists – in particular their leading trio of H. H. Asquith, R. B. Haldane and Sir Edward Grey, to balance the more Radical majority of the party. In contrast to their inclusion, the exclusion of Lord Rosebery ended his real political influence.

Perhaps not surprisingly, the Liberals' assumption of office was not achieved without a surfeit of manoeuvring. They had been out of office for a decade and the complexity of their various internal groupings – Liberal Imperialists and sympathizers with Rosebery, Campbell-Bannerman supporters, die-hard Radicals and others – made hard bargaining a strong likelihood. Less expected was the degree to which the monarchy was drawn in to a potentially dangerous constitutional position from which the King distanced himself with skill.

Francis Knollys was both a lifelong Liberal and concerned that what he considered the true values of his political creed could be submerged under a Radical wave. In the autumn of 1905 the triumvirate of Haldane, Asquith and Grey sought his – and through him the King's – support for their plan that Campbell-Bannerman should be forced to go to the House of Lords and leave Asquith as Leader of the House of Commons. Given his sympathies, Knollys' response was more than might have been expected from the monarch's private secretary. On 12 September Haldane wrote a letter to Knollys which Campbell-Bannerman's biographer, John Wilson, considered with some justification, to be 'grossly improper for a politician who had never held office, still less been a member of any Cabinet, to address to the Private Secretary to the Sovereign'.[38] The letter outlined the determination of the trio for Campbell-Bannerman to go to the Lords – a move without which they would not join his government. It also itemised the offices they each preferred; Asquith to be Leader of the House and Chancellor, Grey Foreign Secretary and Haldane himself Lord Chancellor. Among many references to the self-sacrifices that each of the three would be making to take such senior office, Haldane did add the caveat that, 'the only thing that could affect the decision which our conference this week brought us to, is the thought that it could in any way embarrass the King.'[39]

The reply from Knollys was full of encouragement.

Many thanks for your important and interesting letter . . . which I presume you will not object to my showing confidentially to the King . . . In the event of his sending for Sir H. C-Bannerman my belief is that he will strongly urge him to go to the House of Lords as Prime Minister, partly because he will think that Asquith would be the best man to lead the H of Commons, and partly because he would fear that Sir H.C.B. being a weak or at all events not a strong man like Asquith, would be inclined to give way to pressure from the extreme left, whereas were he in the House of Lords he would not be liable to this pressure to the same extent.[40]

Here Knollys was clearly voicing his own concerns, but he went on to take up Haldane's guarded offer:

If Sir H.C.B. declined to act on the King's suggestion and you and your friends refused to join the Government, H.M. would be placed in an awkward position. A cabinet of which Sir H.C.B. was the head, without the moderates, would, it appears to me, be disastrous both for the Country and the party . . . what the King would desire would be the presence of a restraining influence in the Cabinet . . . men like yourself, Asquith and Sir E. Grey.[41]

A fortnight later Haldane was invited to Balmoral.

Haldane's actions would appear to confirm Campbell-Bannerman's laconic description of his colleague: 'Haldane always prefers the back-stairs; but it does not matter for the clatter can be heard all over the house.'[42] When the time came he handled the situation with skill and resolution that the trio did not expect. He did not return to London from the Continent until 12 November and the next day scored his first victory over Asquith. As part of the overall plan between himself, Haldane and Grey, Asquith visited Campbell-Bannerman with the intention of persuading him to go to the Lords. Instead, he was told by Campbell-Bannerman that the Lords was 'a place for which I have

neither liking, training nor ambition'.[43] When offered the post of Chancellor and asked to discuss how other Cabinet positions would be filled, Asquith was disarmed.

On 5 December, when Campbell-Bannerman was summoned to Buckingham Palace, the King did indeed suggest that he went to the House of Lords: 'We are not as young as we were Sir Henry!'[44] But the King's suggestion would have come without the intervention of Haldane and, when Campbell-Bannerman stated a preference to stay in the Commons, even if at some future date the move was possible, the King happily concurred and showed no inclination to press the matter. Despite repeated efforts by the self-effacing new Prime Minister, the flow of royal conversation prevented his effecting the ritual kissing of hands, but Edward VII – if he had noticed – was unperturbed when he reported the interview to his son from Crichel. 'At 10.15 I had a long interview with Sir H. Campbell-Bannerman who undertook to form a Government but up till now nothing is settled and he has many difficulties finding the right people – nothing could be nicer or more courteous than he was.'[45]

Edward had thoughtfully given Campbell-Bannerman a full week to fill his government, for which his new Prime Minister was grateful. He used the time to good advantage. Press opinions encouraged those who still thought he might be persuaded to move to the Lords and Asquith had a last go at the suggestion. But when given a deadline to make up his mind over joining the government as Chancellor, he agreed. Before the week was out Haldane and Grey were stirred by memories of their assurances not to put the King in a difficult position. Apparently, Haldane's friend Lady Horner reminded him of their pledge and when he went to see Grey, although he repeated his resolution not to take office he was not completely secure in his position. 'Was it quite so clear from the ethical standpoint that we had fully considered the necessities of the King and the Nation?'[46] With these feelings to the fore both men capitulated into high office, Grey to become Foreign Secretary and Haldane Secretary for War.

The King's involvement in these political negotiations was effected with discretion. His acceptance of Campbell-Bannerman was influenced by his gaining a far better knowledge of a man he had viewed with great suspicion since Campbell-Bannerman's inflammatory speeches condemning the conduct of the Boer War. Edward's improved opinions came about during their mutual sojourns at Marienbad. Campbell-Bannerman and his wife had been visiting the German spa town since the 1870s, and he first met the King there in 1904. The following year, during the twilight weeks of Balfour's government, the King had time to form a personal opinion of his future Prime Minister. He found him surprisingly likeable. Fritz Ponsonby, who was in attendance remembered:

> Apparently the King thought he would be prosy and heavy, but found to his surprise that he was quite light in hand with a dry sense of humour. He told several amusing stories and was very good company. After this a sort of friendship sprang up between the two and the King seemed to like the straightforward way he had of stating his convictions without fearing that his opinions might be distasteful to His Majesty.[47]

The following year both men greatly enjoyed Campbell-Bannerman's joke over a newspaper photograph showing them in earnest conversation above the caption 'Is it Peace or War.' Campbell-Bannerman told his private secretary, 'Would you like to know what the King was saying to me? He wanted my opinion whether halibut is better baked or boiled'.[48]

At the time of his resignation, Balfour had gambled by not asking for an immediate general election, in the hope that a few weeks in office would expose the Liberal party's weaknesses and differences. The election was held in January 1906 and told a very different story. Balfour and a number of senior colleagues lost their seats as the Liberals were swept to power. They took 377 seats giving them an overall majority of 87 over 157 Unionists, 83 Irish Nationalists and 53 Labour members, whose influence was recognized by the appointment of John Burns to the Cabinet. When Campbell-Bannerman suggested that Burns might become First Commissioner of Works, Knollys complained to Esher: 'It would be an insult to the King, to propose Burns for the post of First Commissioner of Works, though of course he would make no objection to his occupying some other office . . . If he is not actually a Republican, he is very nearly one.'[49] Burns became President of the Local Government Board, and caused consternation at Buckingham Palace when he arrived for the ceremony of receiving his seals of office in a navy blue 'reefer' jacket instead of the customary morning coat. He did later assume the dignity of office and wear knee-breeches which Esher called 'a revelation' and, in testament to the personal friendliness and courtesy which smoothed the King's relations with his ministers, remarked: 'Me and 'im get on first-rate together.'[50]

Knollys bemoaned the radical changes that appeared inevitable when he wrote to Esher in March: 'The old idea that the House of Commons was an assemblage of "gentlemen" has quite passed away.'[51] There were a few comforting faces in the government such as Charles Carrington, whose long loyalty to Campbell-Bannerman was rewarded with a Cabinet post as President of the Board of Agriculture, but they were outnumbered by those new to office and from the Radical wing of the party, such as David Lloyd George who became President of the Board of Trade.

Unfortunately, the informal friendship between King and Prime Minister struck up at Marienbad, hardly helped overcome Edward's immediate and mounting frustration at Campbell-Bannerman's insufficient Cabinet reports and general failure to keep the King well informed. The King was left furiously minuting the brief documents he was sent with remarks such as: 'I should hardly have thought it worth P.M.'s while to send me enclosed account of C. Council which virtually gives none at all.'[52] Knollys wrote constant rebukes, but to little or no avail. On one occasion in 1907 he complained to Esher that the paucity of information was making a fool of the King. But Esher blamed both Campbell-Bannerman and the King himself for his failure to correspond regularly and personally with his Prime Minister – as Queen Victoria had done. Dismissing Campbell-Bannerman with characteristic brusqueness: 'No one can make a silk purse out of a sow's ear, and CB is too old not to be incurable. The indolence of age is upon him,' Esher outlined his real fears.

I don't for a moment believe that he wishes to leave the King in the dark, but he cannot bring himself to write. It thoroughly bores him. His contempt for precedent, the fact that he had no long apprenticeship in government, and the fact that the King never, never writes to him direct, all tend to make him perfunctory. The result is sad, both in the interests of tradition and of the monarchy. In the interests of both the practices which were availed under the Queen should be adhered to, because the position of Sovereign should be altogether independent of the personality of the monarch, if the monarchy is to stand. The King's personality is the great factor nowadays. And this is a stumbling block in the way of his successors. His office should be as sacred as his person and CB is lowering the former.[53]

Esher was guided by his deep-rooted respect for constitutional tradition and the practices conducted by Queen Victoria, which instinctively led him to prefer the institution to the personality of the monarchy. But the personal element which Edward brought to his position enabled the monarchy to assume reality to the vast mass of people beyond the politicians and limited few who were in direct contact with the crown.

Frustrated by his Prime Minister's tardy communications, Edward was kept better informed by some members of the Liberal Cabinet, notably Haldane who as Secretary for War assumed a position of regular contact with the King. As the new administration got into its stride, however and, as widely expected, began tabling important motions for social reform, the King was often more concerned with the retention of dignity than the detail of policy. Edward made this priority and attempts to safeguard it an important function of the crown. He might privately deplore some of the government's more radical proposals but he accepted that real opposition to them was constitutionally impossible. But he expected his ministers to show respect for their own position and for the crown and did not hesitate to criticize when they failed to do so. John Burns first incurred royal displeasure when he called for the abolition of the House of Lords during the 1906 election and when Campbell-Bannerman himself spoke during the 1907 debate of a Women's Enfranchisement Bill, the King complained: 'It would have been more dignified if the P.M. had not spoken on the Bill – or backed it up. But he appears to wish to stand well with everyone!'[54]

Far more serious were a number of speeches by Lloyd George over the Education Bill, introduced in 1906. His initial attacks on the House of Lords were deplored by the King and at one stage Knollys threatened Campbell-Bannerman:

Mr Lloyd George is very anxious that the King and Queen should go to Cardiff next summer to open some new Docks there, and they have given a half consent that they would do so, but the King says that nothing will induce him to visit Cardiff unless Mr Lloyd George learns how to behave with propriety as a Cabinet Minister holding an important office.[55]

When, a few months later, Lloyd George inquired in a speech: 'whether the country was to be governed by the King and his Peers or by the King and his people' Knollys furiously reprimanded the Prime Minister:

> The King sees it as useless to attempt to prevent Mr Lloyd George from attacking, as Cabinet Minister, the House of Lords, though His Majesty has more than once protested to you against it . . . But His Majesty feels he has a right, and it is one which he intends to insist, that Mr Lloyd George shall not introduce the Sovereign's name into these violent tirades of his; and he asks you, as Prime Minister, to take the necessary steps to prevent a repetition of this violation of constitutional propriety and good taste.[56]

In addition to such confrontations with ministers, the political temperature throughout Campbell-Bannerman's government was high. The King used his experience wisely by taking every opportunity to advise restraint. When the Prime Minister complained that Lord Milner's maiden speech in the House of Lords, denouncing the government's plan to give the Transvaal self-rule, was 'intemperate' the King commented: 'I cannot consider Ld Milner's speech in H of Lds ws "intemperate". If it was what were Mr W. S. Churchill's speeches in the H of Commons'.[57] (Churchill, an Under-Secretary for the Colonies, had introduced the bill in the Commons and denounced Milner in forthright terms, to the extent that the King wrote to the Prince of Wales, 'As for Mr Churchill he is almost more of a cad in office than he was in opposition.'[58])

Ever since the Liberals' election victory their sights were clearly focused on the House of Lords, its huge in-built Conservative majority, and its continuing power to veto legislation. The introduction of the Education Bill in April 1906 announced the assault on the upper

House's privileges by the Commons. The details of the bill did not excite the King. But the greater struggle that it initiated was to exercise, exhaust and depress him at intervals for the rest of his reign. In the past politicians would neither have dared nor, in the main, considered it necessary to ask Lloyd George's question as to whether the King and the peers or the King and the people governed the country. Now many wished to make it an issue. In the circumstances, it was the personal esteem that the King had built up which helped repudiate Esher's warning that the monarchy's unimpaired reputation was at an end.

CHAPTER ELEVEN

ROYAL DIPLOMAT

W hen Prince of Wales, travel on the Continent had been an abiding pleasure for Edward. As King purpose was added to the pleasure with lasting effect on the status of the monarchy. Both during and after his reign ministers were usually quick to minimize any official influence that he had on the course or success of government foreign policy. Balfour dismissed the King's supposed central role in the discussions that led to the formation of the Entente Cordiale with France as 'a foolish piece of gossip'. Far more relevant than any such influence, however, was the immense respect that the King commanded abroad – which grew through his reign – and the effect that his personal diplomacy had on opinions of the monarchy, its status and its activities, both at home and abroad. Even Balfour appreciated the weight that the monarchy carried overseas, as he showed shortly after the death of Queen Victoria, when he urged the new King not to cancel a planned tour of Australia by his son the Duke of York. 'A great Commonwealth is being brought into existence, after infinite trouble and with the fairest prospect of success. Its citizens know little and care little for British ministries and British party politics. But they know and care for the Empire of which they are members and for the Sovereign who rules it.'[1]

Edward VII's reign began with England deeply unpopular in virtually every European country on account of the Boer War. The

German Emperor made the most of the situation and in both Germany and France in particular, the press did the same. In March 1902 Francis Knollys wrote to the Foreign Secretary Lord Lansdowne:

> My dear Lansdowne, would you kindly look at the enclosed. I suppose there is nothing to be done in order to stop these disgusting caricatures. Sir E. Monson [British ambassador in Paris] told me that the French government were powerless unless he lodged a formal complaint followed by prosecution. Lascalles [Sir Frank, the ambassador in Berlin] said the same thing to me when he was last in London in regard to the German caricatures, and that he considered the King was in too exalted a position to make it worthwhile taking notice of them.[2]

Unpopularity fuelled criticism by the European powers who resented Britain's imperial strength and the accompanying detachment from continental affairs which Lord Salisbury's government had pursued for nearly a decade.

When Lord Carrington travelled to Paris, Madrid and Lisbon as one of the King's special ambassadors to announce the death of Queen Victoria and the accession, in March 1901, he was immediately made aware of the degree of personal distinction afforded Edward. Summoned to the Foreign Office by Lansdowne, he was told that he would find the French very stiff and difficult; and that there were several serious difficulties between the two countries. On the contrary, Carrington discovered once he arrived in Paris that his reception was very different from what he had been led to expect from newspaper accounts. 'He and Sir Edward Monson were both wrong as nothing could have been more courteous as President Loubet and all his Ministers – and the President charged me with the most friendly assurances to the King.'[3]

Edward wasted no time after his accession before suggesting the kind of discreet diplomacy which he continued throughout his reign. Often such efforts led to nothing, at other times they gave an edge to government relations which was applauded by his ministers. In March 1901 Russian expansionist aggression along her Manchurian border with China was threatening the settlement of the dispute

A family group at Alexandra's home in Denmark. At the back the Princesses Louise and Victoria stand between their cousins Prince Nicholas and the Crown Prince Constantine of Greece. In front Alexandra's mother, Queen Louise of Denmark sits between her two younger grandchildren from Greece. Alexandra sits next to her sister-in-law, with their father King Christian of Denmark next to them and Princess Maud on the right.

ABOVE Queen Victoria and Princess Louise at Abergeldie in 1890, photographed by the Princess of Wales.

LEFT The marriage of Princess Louise to the Duke of Fife in 1889.

ABOVE The Princess of Wales in 1896 with her two-year-old grandson, Prince Edward, the future King Edward VIII.

LEFT A family group in 1895. At the back, left to right: the Duke of Fife and his wife, the Prince of Wales, the Duchess of York, Princess Maud and Prince Carl of Denmark. The Duke of York holds Prince Edward of York with his mother, the Princess of Wales beside him and Princess Victoria next to her.

LEFT A photograph taken at Balmoral during Tsar Nicholas's visit to Britain in 1896. Queen Victoria looks at her great-granddaughter Grand Duchess Olga, who is held by her mother the Empress Alexandra.

ABOVE The indulgent grandfather: the Prince of Wales in 1898 with his two eldest grandchildren, Princess Louise's daughters Lady Alexandra and Lady Maud Duff.

ABOVE AND LEFT King Edward VII and Queen Alexandra in their coronation robes, 1902.

RIGHT The tombstone of the King's terrier Jack, in the garden of the Viceregal Lodge, Dublin, where he died during the King's visit in 1903.

HERE : LIES

"JACK"

KING : EDWARD'S
FAVOVRITE : IRISH : TERRIER

WHO : ONLY : LIVED : TWELVE : HOVRS
AFTER : REACHING : HIS : NATIVE : LAND
HE : DIED : AT : THE : VICEREGAL : LODGE
ON
JVLY : 21 : 1903

ABOVE Alice Keppel in 1906, when she was aged thirty-seven.

BELOW A large gathering at Windsor in 1907, during a visit by the Kaiser (standing third from the left).

ABOVE The royal yacht *Alexandra*, on which the King sailed to Reval, Russia, in 1908.

LEFT The Marquis de Soveral, the Portuguese ambassador and friend of both the King and Queen; an amusing and eloquent raconteur.

The King and the Tsar at Reval, June 1908.

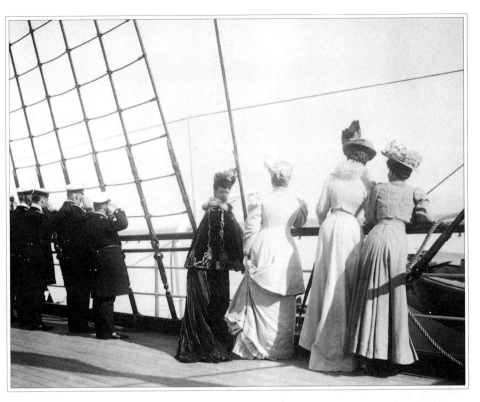

ABOVE On board the Imperial Russian yacht *Standart*, during the Reval meeting of 1908. The Dowager Empress of Russia is looking round. Next to her is Queen Olga of Greece, then Princess Victoria and then Grand Duchess Olga.

BELOW Visits to England's cities and towns were annual events during King Edward's reign and were greeted with tumultuous welcomes, as here in Birmingham in 1909.

LEFT The King shooting at Sandringham.

LEFT The King and Queen Alexandra.

OPPOSITE ABOVE King Edward VII's lying-in-state at Westminster Hall, May 1910.

OPPOSITE BELOW King Edward VII's funeral procession approaches St George's Chapel, Windsor, May 1910.

ABOVE The King's sitting room at Buckingham Palace. Among the many photographs is one of Admiral Jackie Fisher, in the foreground on the left of the desk.

BELOW The King's bedroom, 'with the hats hanging on the pegs, as he loved them to be'.

which involved the other Great Powers, such as Britain who had interests in the Far East. The King suggested that he might write a personal letter direct to the Tsar. Lansdowne replied that he had been unable to see Lord Salisbury, but had spoken to Balfour and other colleagues who agreed with him: 'That such a communication might have an excellent effect at the present time. A little consideration and confidence might remove all these difficulties and YM [Your Majesty] would indeed do a great service to both countries if you could bring them together upon this point.'[4]

A few months later, in August 1901 the King travelled to Germany for the funeral of his sister Vicky who, after much suffering, died from cancer. Edward went on to visit the Kaiser at the royal palace of Wilhelmshöhe. The meeting did nothing to further the possibility of an Anglo-German agreement and the King left with relief for Marienbad, from where he travelled on to join Queen Alexandra with her family in Copenhagen. Here he enjoyed far more cordial relations with his other ruling nephew, Tsar Nicholas, who was visiting with his mother. Edward scored a notable success with the Russian Foreign Minister, Count Lamsdorff. On returning to St Petersburg Lamsdorff reported the meeting with such enthusiasm to the British Ambassador, Sir Charles Hardinge that the latter was moved to write to Sir Thomas Sanderson at the Foreign Office:

> Lamsdorff told me – and others – that he had been immensely flattered at having an audience of the King at Copenhagen, who had been charming to him, and he was most enthusiastic in his admiration for the Queen whom he had seen there for the first time. He compared our King most favourably with the Emperor William, whom evidently he did not get on with, and I should not be surprised if his views were the reflection of his Imperial master's.[5]

The King would have been most satisfied with the second half of Hardinge's report.

Such personal successes notwithstanding, Anglo-Russian relations did not improve. The Manchurian situation dragged on and Russian suspicion of British friendship with Japan became outright hostility in January 1902 when the two countries signed the Anglo-Japanese agreement. The agreement marked the end of an era for British policy by formally allying her with another great power, although not to the extent of active support in any confrontations that might arise. The alliance also recognized the two nation's compatibility as naval, maritime powers and came at a time when Lord Lansdowne had decided that, for the time being at least, the possibility of any formal agreement with Germany was impossible. British public opinion would not tolerate it and German attitudes were not conducive to harmony. The King made a special break during his New Year holiday at Sandringham to travel to London and meet Marquis Ito who led the Japanese delegation to sign the agreement. Later that year he viewed with far less relish the prospect of a visit from his German nephew to Sandringham over his birthday in November. As the Kaiser departed the King muttered to those around him: 'Thank God he's gone.'[6]

1903 witnessed Edward VII's first major diplomatic initiative when, in April and May, he made a series of state visits to Portugal, Italy and, most important, France. Queen Victoria had made one official visit during her whole reign, to Paris in 1855; thereafter her successive summer holidays had been private, the size of her retinue notwithstanding. The personal nature of the King's visits were emphasized when he informed Lord Lansdowne that he intended to break with the usual practice of being attended by a Cabinet minister and instead take with him Sir Charles Hardinge, who had recently returned from the St Petersburg embassy and was about to become Assistant Under-Secretary of State for Foreign Affairs.

Hardinge's wife was one of Queen Alexandra's ladies-in-waiting and a long-standing friend; the King had admired Hardinge's work in St Petersburg and at his earlier post in Teheran. The close rapport that the two men established during the 1903 tour had important repercussions. At the time it said a lot for Hardinge's ambition and diplomatic skill that he was prepared to go against his Foreign Office seniors including Lord Lansdowne and emerge successful. His later rise to become the Foreign Office's head as Permanent Under-Secretary in 1906 gave the King a key ally and central source of advice and information.

The first part of the tour was planned as a Mediterranean cruise with stops at successive ports, ending at Naples. The King intended to travel on to Rome and then to go overland to Paris. Lansdowne had been extremely put out by the King's decision to take Hardinge instead of a Cabinet minister whom Balfour and he would have suggested. He was also lukewarm about both the wisdom of a visit to France and any possible beneficial outcome. With his confrontation with the King over the Shah of Persia's Garter still fresh in the memory, however, his protests were muted and he gave official agreement from the government for the King to inform President Loubet that he would be happy to visit Paris on his return journey. At the end of March Edward, delighted to have got his way and confident that the final arrangements to go to Paris would fall into place, embarked at Portsmouth for Lisbon, surrounded by mounds of luggage.

The quantity of baggage was necessary because to overlook even the smallest detail of diplomatic protocol was anathema to the King. On arrival at Lisbon he was dressed as a Colonel of a Portuguese cavalry regiment, so as to please his host and distant cousin, the King Don Carlos, despite the fact that, as Fritz Ponsonby wrote with amusement, it was, 'a uniform that certainly was not becoming to a stout man as the coat was very short and showed an immense expanse of breeches.'[7] On a par with wearing the right uniform was distributing the right honours and the King happily wrote home to his son, that he had given out 'a good many Victorian Orders, including Grand Crosses.'[8]

The five-day visit to Portugal was arranged by the King's friend Soveral. Resident in London as Portugal's ambassador, Soveral accompanied Edward from England and tried to ensure familiar comforts for the whole party such as whisky and soda in their rooms and tea in the morning. But he could not do anything about some of the accommodation. Ponsonby described his as 'magnificently ugly and not comfortable as we understand comfort.'[9] Such disadvantages did not affect the King, however, who thoroughly enjoyed himself – and his reception – during days of constant activity, much of which he organized himself at the last minute. As well as the usual state banquet and visit to the opera and various receptions there was a pigeon shooting competition and a visit to a bull-fight (where, unlike Spain, the bull was not killed). As they left Lisbon Ponsonby noted: 'What struck me most during this first State visit abroad was that the King himself made all the arrangements and supervised every detail.'[10] Ponsonby would have perhaps been less surprised if he had appreciated the combination of reasons; the King's obsessive attention to detail, his enjoyment of making last-minute additions to a programme, and the long years when he had never been allowed to do what he wanted.

At Gibraltar, where the King lived aboard the royal yacht, he promoted the governor, Sir George White, to the rank of Field Marshal, largely in recognition of his having been the hero of the siege of Ladysmith. He also finally confirmed his visit to Paris and threw Balfour and the government into consternation by reviving the idea of visiting the Pope while in Rome. Edward had originally left England accepting Balfour's advice that a visit would upset Protestants and possibly jeopardize the fate of the sensitive Irish Land Bill. Meanwhile, British Roman Catholics had been upset in 1901 that the Vatican was not included in the round of official visits to European courts announcing Edward VII's accession. Now, their lay leader, the Duke of Norfolk, stressed to Balfour the disappointment they would feel if the King visited Rome without a request to see the Pope.

Ponsonby told Francis Knollys that the King's desire to see the 93-year-old pontiff Leo XIII was prompted 'mainly by curiosity'.[11] There followed an exchange of telegraphs between the King, and Balfour and the Foreign Office in which the King was presented with the alternatives, but no official advice beyond the suggestion that if the King insisted, it should be a private visit. Fuming at what he considered deliberate (and characteristic) vacillating by Balfour, Edward pressed ahead and the meeting was formally arranged when the Duke of Norfolk gained the necessary invitation from the Vatican; for the King to have requested a visit would have been unacceptable to the government.

These negotiations took place while the King was at sea between Gibraltar and Malta, where Edward's visit was the first by a British sovereign. From Malta he sailed on towards Naples, the journey disrupted only slightly by bad weather and the unexpected eruption of the volcano Stromboli as the *Victoria and Albert* was passing. As he approached Naples the King had telegraphed ahead to say that he would arrive incognito; as Ponsonby remarked, 'rather absurd as no other human being in the world would come with eight battleships, four cruisers, four destroyers and a dispatch vessel'.[12] In Naples where he toured the city's slums Hardinge wrote home to his wife that he had had to remonstrate with the King about taking unnecessary risks in public by going without due protection or to unsuitable places and although the King was polite, such warnings were rarely heeded. Officialdom returned on arrival in Rome, where his host was King

Victor Emmanuel III who, like most Italians, was delighted that Edward was visiting his country on his first state tour. They were equally delighted with his impromptu speech without notes at the state banquet and with his mark of respect for the struggles that unified Italy when he stopped, during a tour of the city, at the Porte Pia.

The visit to the Vatican was the last major event of Edward's stay in Rome. His satisfaction at having won his meeting was rewarded by the Pope's charming and friendly reception. The timeliness was emphasized two months later when the Pope died and the visit was a success in that it satisfied Roman Catholics at home without causing Protestant outrage.

Edward's visit to Paris was a personal triumph and only ministerial churlishness suggested afterwards that it had a negligible influence on the signing of the Entente with France in 1904. He arrived by train from Dijon where he had been met by the British ambassador in Paris, Sir Edmund Monson. Prior to the King's arrival there was already a spirit of goodwill in many important quarters, not least in the enthusiasm of President Loubet and his Foreign Minister, Delcassé. During the arrangements for the visit, Loubet had told Monson that, 'a visit from the King in the present temper of France would do an amount of good which is probably not realized in England.'[13] Reporting his conversation in a letter to Lansdowne, Monson went on to describe that the President had stressed how popular the King had always been with all classes of people in Paris and that, 'He could not lay too much stress on the influence which the King's presence in Paris would have on friendly relations between the two peoples. His Majesty's visit here would be the seal of the rapidly strengthening cordiality and would be universally regarded as such.'[14] Monson himself appears to have been confident that the visit would be a success. His German counterpart, Count von Radolin, whose country was monitoring the King's progress through Europe with intense scrutiny, expressed the same view to the German Chancellor, Count von Bülow. He wrote on 20 April that, despite the efforts of the French nationalist press: 'From my own observations I have gained the impression that the journey of King Edward will lead to a détente in the up-to-now not very favourable relations between France and England.'[15] He did qualify his opinion by saying he did not think that the reception would be as enthusiastic as that given to the Russian Tsar, in which he was proved wrong.

Part of the King's success resulted, characteristically, from his energy. Although his progress from Lisbon had been comfortable and stately, it had also been busy, but in Paris he filled his two-and-a-half days to the utmost. As he made his first progress through the city, attended by the French President, there were audible shouts of 'Vive les Boers' and 'Vive Fashoda' – the latter reverse of French imperial fortunes definitely more widely felt than the war in South Africa. But the Parisians had turned out in force to witness the arrival and there were enough cheers for Edward VII to smile constantly and wave in courteous acknowledgement. His first speech was sincere in his expression of happiness at once more being in Paris and well received when he continued:

> The days of conflict between out two countries are, I trust, happily over, and I hope the future historians, in alluding to Anglo-French relations in the present century, may be able to record only a friendly rivalry in the field of commercial and industrial developments, and that in the future, as in the past, England and France may be regarded as the champions and pioneers of peaceful progress and civilisation and as the homes of all that is best and noblest in literature, art and science.[16]

The most accomplished of charmers had begun well.

After dinner at the British embassy he carried on in the evening. Attending a performance of *L'Autre Danger* by the Comédie Française with President Loubet and his wife, the King was in expansive good humour by the interval. Much to the consternation of the French police, he insisted on strolling informally, hardly incognito, among the other theatre-goers. The King's memory for faces was usually infallible and proved so to good effect. Spotting the French actress Jeanne Granier, he advanced towards her with the greeting, 'Ah, mademoiselle! I remember how I applauded you in London. You personified there all the grace, all the ésprit of France.'[17] Heard by those around him, the royal gallantry was broadcast abroad to universal approval and the King rounded off the evening by inviting the whole cast to his box to thank them all personally.

The next day a review of 18,000 troops at Vincennes in the morning was followed by attending the races at Longchamps in the afternoon.

In between, returning from Vincennes, the King stopped at the Hotel de Ville and replied to a cordial official welcome by saying that in Paris he always felt, 'just as though I am at home.'[18] He was hugely flattered that the programme at Longchamp was organized in his honour: the main race the Prix Persimmon, was named after his Derby-winner. Enjoyment turned to celebration with a victory by one of Persimmon's offspring and another by a horse called John Bull. No amount of bonhomie could force the King to endure boring women however, and he found himself seated between Madame Loubet and the Governor of Paris's wife, both of whom were distinctly matronly in appearance, after two races he felt he had done his duty and hissed at Fritz Ponsonby: 'You must get me out of this. Go to the Jockey Club and ask someone to send me an invitation to come and see the new wing they have built or anything that will get me out of this.'[19] The resourceful Ponsonby was successful.

By this time any antagonism from the Parisian crowds had been dispelled and they appeared in increasing numbers to wave and cheer enthusiastically. On the final evening there was a state banquet at the Elysée Palace, where once again Edward VII spoke without notes in faultless French. The reception was all the more cordial because he followed the President who, according to Ponsonby with his eye for the ridiculous, 'had pinned his speech to one of the candlesticks in front of him, which necessitated his leaning forward to read it. The result was that only a certain number of people near him could hear what he said.'[20] The grand finale was a formal visit to the opera and when the King left after midnight for the carriage-drive back to the embassy it seemed that the crowds were still as large as during the day.

The whole tour of five weeks, and the final weekend in Paris in particular, showed Edward VII at his most effective. Regardless of the effect on Britain's official foreign policy it was accorded at the time or later by his ministers, the visit added immeasurably to the prestige of his monarchy. Widely reported in the home press it showed the King to his British subjects, affably and inexhaustibly presenting a national as well as a personal presence that could not fail to stand the country in good stead. It also put the King on a secure footing with his ministers over his diplomatic activities. One verdict that deserves attention was that of Sir Eyre Crowe, whose successive memoranda as senior clerk at the Foreign Office carried considerable weight among civil servants, diplomats and politicians alike. In 1907 he noted for the Foreign Secretary, Sir Edward Grey, that only a marked improvement in French confidence of British goodwill enabled the Entente to be signed in April 1904 and that: 'It was natural to believe that such confidence could not be forced, but that it might slowly emerge by a process of gradual evolution. That it declared itself with unexpected rapidity and unmistakable emphasis was without doubt due to the initiative and tactful perseverence of the King.'[21]

The return state visit made by President Loubet and Delcassé to England in July was equally successfully and later in the year Lord Lansdowne was able to produce early drafts of a proposed agreement. Edward had no qualms about making changes to the Foreign Secretary's terminology and points of emphasis, many of which were accommodated. In the light of the King's contribution to the feeling of goodwill that underwrote the accord, it was tactless in the extreme of the Prime Minister to cause a confrontation. While the King was in Copenhagen with the Queen's family, the agreement was signed in London on 8 April 1904 and on the 14 April Balfour told the House of Commons that parliamentary assent would be necessary to consent to a small cessation to territory in Africa, as part of the agreed terms. Balfour was well aware that in the past authority over such cessations had rested traditionally with the crown, but he either did not think it necessary or lacked the courtesy to inform the King of what he proposed to say. Edward was quick to respond with a protest through Knollys and *The Times* thundered an accusation of unconstitutional action at Balfour. The Prime Minister, for all his apparent casualness, was well prepared. Replying to the King that he was acting on the guidance of both the Foreign Office and Law Officers he later cited Knollys the precedent when parliamentary consent had been required for the cessation of Heligoland to Germany in 1890.

Such royal prerogatives were no longer realistic in the turbulent politics of parliamentary democracy. The possibility of a future decision being made solely by the King and leading to a crisis, would undermine the monarchy's authority and status. But if it was Balfour's intention to thus safeguard the crown, his manner and timing in using a specific event to revoke an established principle was hardly tactful. The King was understandably upset and complained that Balfour had treated him with 'scant courtesy in every respect'.[22]

The previous year the Prime Minister had, for once, been fulsome in his praises after the King and Queen Alexandra returned from a twelve-day state visit to Ireland. They arrived in Ireland the day the Irish Land Purchase Bill – encouraging Irish landlords to let tenants buy their land – received its third reading in the House of Commons. After the King's return Esher was moved to send him congratulations and wrote to his son that: 'After centuries of ill-feeling he has – for the first time – made an impression on both nations and drawn them together. The attitude of the Catholic bishops and priests is a revolution, and if the King perseveres, he might bring about the participation of Ireland.'[23] Balfour himself sent, 'his warmest congratulations on the success of Your Majesty's visit to Ireland. No such event has occurred in the history of the Monarchy: a history which so far as Ireland is concerned has been little diversified by any gleam of brightness.'[24] Lord Lansdowne, who owned thousands of acres around his Irish estate Derreen in County Kerry, was able to write at first-hand that: 'It is impossible to exaggerate the effect produced upon the simple people of this glen by the kindness of your Majesty's demeanour; they refer to it constantly and always in terms of goodwill and admiration.'[25]

Esher's hope that the King would persevere with Ireland was not in vain. He returned the following year with Queen Alexandra for nine days; and again in 1907. After the first of these trips he was put out by the lavish display by the Viceroy, the Earl of Dudley, who was estimated to spend £30,000 per annum of his own money living in suitable style at the Viceregal Lodge. Esher, who thought the position of Viceroy should be abolished wrote with glee: 'He did not enjoy Eddie's [Dudley] display when he visited Ireland no more than Louis XIV did the fêtes of his Finance Minister. Sovereigns do not like being outshone and Eddie has seventy-two servants in gorgeous livery and twelve A.D.C.'s; the King only has six equerries!'[26] By 1907 the situation was rather different; Lord Dudley had been replaced by the Marquess of Aberdeen, who had held the position previously for one year in 1886 and gone on to be Governor-General of Canada. While he was in Canada it had been rumoured that Lord Aberdeen, along with his wife and family, made a custom of dining once a week with his household in the servants' hall and Queen Victoria demanded of her Prime Minister, Lord Rosebery, that he investigate the alleged irregularity. Despite Lady Aberdeen's assurances at that time, it was perhaps not surprising her husband's invitation for the royal visit to Ireland should be qualified by the mention that there might be difficulty in accommodating the royal guests at the Viceregal Lodge; so the King, Queen Alexandra and Princess Victoria stayed aboard the royal yacht.

Inevitably, the French Entente put potential strain on Anglo-German relations. In England, large sections of the press constantly encouraged people to air anti-German sentiments. Although Esher was a friend of George Buckle, the editor of *The Times*, in 1903 he wrote:

> He is absurdly hostile to the German Emperor. It is an almost childish prejudice: dangerous in the editor of *The Times*. The King met him at dinner the other night and remonstrated, but it produced no effect. These journalists are so influenced by small considerations. I believe the trouble originated in Bülow not being over civil to *The Times* correspondent in Berlin.[27]

In June 1904 the King, by now increasingly weary of the German Emperor's behaviour and frequent outbursts against Britain and himself, decided to offer the courtesy of a visit and acquiesced when his nephew suggested that they should meet at the port of Kiel – in order that he might show off some of his new navy. As in the past, personal cordiality was maintained but with no longer-term effect. Nine months later, in March 1905, the Emperor decided it was time to assert German authority in Europe and, at the same time, test Anglo-French resolve. The Entente had agreed that France should be responsible for Morocco, still independent and a country of economic importance, but with a teetering Sultan. The wily Sultan appealed to Germany, and during his annual Mediterranean cruise the German Emperor stopped at Tangiers, where he announced his country's growing interests in Morocco and their intention to defend them.

For Edward, who was also cruising in the Mediterranean, it was more than he could bear. He wrote to Lansdowne that his nephew's action was: 'The most mischievous and uncalled for event which the German Emperor has ever been engaged in since he came to the Throne.'[28] No doubt the Foreign Secretary heartily concurred, but – perhaps amused at the thought of the two monarchs sailing in close proximity to each other – he wrote in more laconic style to Lord Salisbury: 'I hope King Edward will not happen to meet the Emperor, who seems to me unworthy of avuncular encouragement at this moment. The French would not like a public kissing on both cheeks just now – a judicious spanking would – but I won't pursue the subject.'[29]

The outcome of the Emperor's intervention was indeed serious. When the Sultan of Morocco – at Germany's suggestion – asked the interested powers to attend a conference to discuss Morocco's future, the French government refused, feeling there was little to discuss. By this time French public opinion, fuelled by a familiar combination of outrage and fear of Germany, was running dangerously high and when the German ambassador in Paris announced that the two countries could not possibly hope to get on any better while Delcassé, the Foreign Minister, remained in office, he resigned in the ensuing storm. The conference took place, in Algeciras, in January 1906 and in the meantime the King was left contemplating his nephew's behaviour with frustration and anger.

His anger never lasted long, however, and he soon returned to a patient, conciliatory line when communicating with the Emperor. But the King's trust of his nephew would never recover and was influential in his support of the naval reforms of Jackie Fisher, who had become First Sea Lord in 1904. At the same time, the King appointed Fisher his principal naval A.D.C. Edward admired the crusading zeal with which Jackie Fisher approached his task and enjoyed his company, even if at the time he was forced to remonstrate against the Admiral's more outrageous suggestions. The King called Fisher mad when the Admiral enthusiastically advocated that the German fleet in Kiel should be 'Copenhagened', and labelled him a socialist when he suggested cadets' education at Dartmouth and Osborne might be free in order to attract a greater variety of candidates. But the King soon grasped that behind Fisher's unconventional outbursts lay the energy and tactical ability to transform the navy.

At the head of naval opposition to Fisher's reforms was Admiral Lord Charles Beresford. The King had had his differences with Beresford in the past and still referring to him in private as 'a gas-bag' and 'suffering from a not unusual complaint "a swollen head"'.[30] But while supporting Fisher the King was careful to avoid being partisan. As over army reform, public opinion favouring improvements in the navy was qualified by a desire to see cuts in naval expense. Fisher was happy to carry out vigorous reductions and scrapping of old vessels in order to have sufficient funds to modernize; in particular to initiate a programme of building Dreadnoughts that could compete with those of the expanding German navy.

But Fisher paid scant respect to ministers. In addition Beresford, who was Commander-in-Chief first of the Mediterranean Fleet and from 1907, the Channel Fleet, regularly proved a formidable adversary, his popular image and condemnation of radical change attracting wide support among naval officers. Without the King's support which was needed on many occasions, such as when Fisher launched an attack against Haldane and his War Ministry – the First Sea Lord would not have survived, let alone carried through his reforms. Early in his period of First Sea Lord, Fisher told the King in typically blunt language that he would resign if expected to work with a First Lord of the Admiralty. Partly as a result, neither of the successive First Lords, Lord Cawdor or Lord Tweedmouth, held authority over him. But nor were they able to support him against his opponents. Cawdor was a partial invalid when he took office, and Tweedmouth declined rapidly during his period in office due to the brain disease which killed him in 1909. And although the King's support enabled the reforms to go through and the first Dreadnoughts to be built, he could not prevent the ever-worsening rift with Beresford, which intensified after he was forced to resign at the end of 1908. Fisher himself resigned in January 1910, but by then his work was done.

Edward VII's involvement in Europe affairs, momentous or trivial, political or social, revolved around the twin annual fixtures of his spring visit to Biarritz and autumn visit to Marienbad. At both places he stayed amidst deep if unostentatious comfort at the Hotel du Palais and the Hotel Weimar respectively. While he did not expect those around him to attain the same standards, he did feel they should be accommodated in style fitting their station. In 1906, when the new Prime Minister Campbell-Bannerman and his wife returned to their regular if modest rooms at the Hotel Klinger the King wondered: 'I don't know whether this old barrack is a fit abode for the British Prime Minister.'[31]

Although he was often forced to fit in a visit to his neighbouring German nephew while either en route to or returning from

Marienbad, he preferred to travel in the opposite direction to see the ageing Austrian Emperor Franz Joseph, whom he had first met in Vienna in 1862 and whose company he invariably enjoyed. In 1907, when the King visited both German then Austrian Emperors in succession on his way to Marienbad, Charles Hardinge – by now a fixture on most of the King's European tours – was struck by the very different atmospheres, which he described in his report to the Foreign Secretary Sir Edward Grey.

> Although the King was outwardly on the best of terms with the German Emperor, and laughed and joked with him, I could not help noticing that there was no real intimacy between them ... On the other hand the relations between the King and the Emperor of Austria appeared to me to be of the most friendly and intimate character. They seemed to delight in each other's company and were practically inseparable.[32]

During the early years of his visits to Marienbad, from the late-1890s, the company was raffish to a degree which the Campbell-Bannermans – upright Scots – found burdensome, if at times amusing.

> We have now seen a new realization of the true saying that wheresoever the eagle is there will the carcasses be gathered together. Whether on account of the Prince's presence or not, the English & American society here contained an extraordinary number of tainted ladies – including five divorcées and about ten others of various degrees of doubtfulness. The decent people were almost in a minority & we thought of wearing our marriage certificates as a sort of order outside our coats.[33]

But growing prestige brought an increase in sobriety and in later years the King loved the richly cosmopolitan attendance at Marienbad and was never one to complain about the presence of a few colourful rogues. On one visit Ponsonby noted a selection of 'bearded and ringleted Polish Jews'.[34] He did, however complain about the attentions of the crowds, but as Campbell-Bannerman rightly pointed out in response to one such remonstration, 'It would not be agreeable to you Sir, if they did not take any notice at all.'[35]

The King's visits to Biarritz were, by comparison, private. They followed an unchanging pattern of work before lunch and in the afternoon a tour in one of his claret-coloured cars which drove from England ahead of the royal progress by train, under the care of his chauffeur-engineer Stamper. Friends staying nearby might be entertained and Alice Keppel was always installed in splendour with Ernest Cassel at his villa. But at the end of each visit they parted company when the King usually embarked on a cruise aboard the *Victoria and Albert* with Queen Alexandra, with the long-suffering Princess Victoria in attendance. The trials of the Princess's position and chronic sea-sickness were relieved by her enthusiasm for photography.

Other than the cruises and visits to Copenhagen, almost all of the King's European travel was done without the Queen, who loved the royal yacht and her family home but otherwise was steadily less inclined to leave Sandringham. How different things might have been, however, was suggested in February 1907 when the King took her to Paris for a week's private visit. The Queen's excitement was boundless and, among her adventures, she ate in a public restaurant for the first time in her life. Esher wrote to his son after their return:

> The Queen had not been there for eighteen years. She walked about the Rue de la Paix with Lady Gosford and delighted in all the shops. She thought everything very cheap and bought up half the town. At the reception she was at her very best and created the most favourable impression possible. The Parisians have never seen anyone like her. The King and Queen were Darby and Joan and have not got on so well together for years.[36]

Two years earlier, in 1905 Queen Alexandra had been able to share her husband's family pride when, thanks to a large degree to his diplomatic lobbying, their son-in-law Prince Christian of Denmark, married to their youngest daughter Maud, was accepted by Norway as their king. Norway had terminated the union which effectively subjected her to Sweden, and Prince Christian was elected King Haakon VII. Three years later Queen Alexandra accompanied the King when they visited their son-in-law and daughter's new court as part of a triangular journey that also took in Copenhagen and Sweden. The last stop was the most sensitive as Swedish feelings towards England had been distinctly cool since the accession of Haakon VII, but both King Gustav, the Stockholm court and inhabitants warmed to the King and Queen and the visit improved relations by removing Swedish suspicions.

Despite Edward's reassuring approaches to the Russian Tsar, improvement in the two nations' relations was slow in coming. It was delayed by the war between Russia and Japan in 1904 and 1905, during which England agreement with Japan was a cause of contention, and by the accidental sinking of some British fishing boats in the North Sea by the Russian navy. Over this incident the King was more sensible than some of his ministers, who hoped to capitalize on British antipathy to Russia. Shooting with the King at Lord Burham's estate, Hall Barn, Charles Carrington recorded afterwards that the King had 'referred to the anxious time he went through over the Russian shelling of our fishing fleet. He saw at once that it was a mistake and not a question of War; but he seems to have a good deal of trouble in keeping Ministers quiet.'[37] The situation was not helped by the machinations of the German Emperor, who viewed any Anglo-Russian agreement with horror.

But the increasing Anglo-French links and, after Russia's mortifying and ruinous defeat by the Japanese, a recession in English fears of Russian expansionist ambitions, allowed the signing of the Anglo-Russian convention in August 1907, which Charles Hardinge loyally described as 'the triumph of King Edward's policy of which the Anglo-French Entente was the first step'.[38]

The following year, the King demonstrated his influence and independence by carrying off the first visit by a British sovereign to Russia, in the face of public opposition and raucous condemnation by some MPs. The Labour member Kier Hardie was ruled out of order by the Speaker for accusing the King of condoning atrocities, when he spoke in the House of Commons supporting a motion that criticized the government for supporting the King's visit. The motion was defeated by 225 to 59 votes, but Edward was incensed by Kier Hardie's suggestion and he was one of three MPs struck off by the King from the list of invitations for a garden party at Windsor for Members of Parliament. The three members' vigorous complaints that the King's action was an insult to their constituents attracted considerable publicity in the press, much of it critical of Edward's action.

The publicity was not surprising considering that the Tsar's auto-cratic regime was roundly condemned by many in Britain. But in the light of the recent agreement the Prime Minister Asquith and his Foreign Secretary Grey were both certain the visit would be benefi-cial. The King's view was that loyalty from one monarch to another could not be destroyed by the faults of a regime. In addition, not only was the family tie strong, involving both himself and the Queen, but he considered it his duty to help and advise his weak young nephew the Tsar in the hope of a more equable style of monarchy in Russia. Once the government's support was guaranteed his agreement was never in doubt.

Although official, the family nature of the visit was stressed and Queen Alexandra was one of the party, with Princess Victoria. Among the entourage were Charles Hardinge as Minister in Attendance, Jackie Fisher as First Sea Lord, Sir John French as Inspector General of the armed forces, Sir Arthur Nicholson (Britain's ambassador in St Petersburg who was returning after leave in England) and Count Beckendorf, the Russian ambassador in London. Among the King's personal suite was Alice Keppel's brother Sir George Edmonstone, whom the King had appointed his Groom-in-Waiting in 1907.

Off the Baltic town of Reval (renamed Tallin), the royal yacht *Victoria and Albert* was met by its two Russian counterparts, the *Standart* and the *Polar Star*, bearing the entire Russian royal family, and among the rest of their party, Stolypin the Prime Minister and Isvolsky the Foreign Minister. No one set foot on land for fear of attack by anarchists but this did nothing to dampen the spirit of the family party. Jackie Fisher had been especially delighted to be included in the trip by the King even more so when he heard that Queen Alexandra had thoughtfully cabled to her sister, the Dowager Empress, asking that the Tsar's younger sister, the Grand Duchess Olga might be included in the Russian party. Fisher, who adored dancing, had met her at Carlsbad when he had taught her to waltz. Now he delighted the assembled party by once again persuading her to partner him accompanied by the royal yacht's band, although at one point the King was moved to remind Fisher: 'Try and remember you're not a midshipman'.[39]

The highpoint of the family celebrations came when Edward made his nephew an Admiral of the Fleet. The decision was spontaneous, as

Hardinge recalled that at lunch on board the *Standart* on the second day the King passed him his menu on which he had written a note in pencil asking his opinion of the idea. Hardinge concurred with enthusiasm and the honour was announced that evening after dinner when the guns of the British escort ships fired an admiral's salute. The Tsar was thrilled, but the British government was not. Asquith wrote frostily to Knollys informing him that the King had no right to confer such an honour without the full prior agreement of the First Lord of the Admiralty, Reginald McKenna who was, apparently, much put out. On the King's instructions Knollys sent a mollifying reply couched in suitably polite terms and stressing that the King had no idea he was acting unconstitutionally. The letter's postscript, however, kept the Prime Minister alert to the King's readiness to voice his disapproval of what he considered actions unbefitting his ministers: 'PS. The King deplores the attitude taken by Mr Asquith on the Women's Suffrage Bill'.[40]

At the same time a degree of more official ice was broken. Hardinge wrote afterwards that he spent most of the two days in long conversations with Stolypin and Ivolsky discussing foreign affairs. On the journey from England Edward had closely questioned Sir Arthur Nicolson about different aspects of Russian politics, and of the economy such as agriculture. The preparation paid off as both Stolypin and Ivolsky were highly impressed by the King's interest and ability to discuss affairs in their country. Before he left England Edward had been lobbied by the Rothschilds to press the question of the persecution of Russian Jews and whether the Russian government intended to cease the perpetuation of pogroms. Such a request put the King in a potentially awkward situation and a letter from Francis Knollys to Lord Rothschild made it clear that it would be constitutionally impossible for the King to raise such a delicate political matter without the full agreement of Hardinge and Sir Arthur Nicholson. The matter was raised, both by the King and Nicolson, but to Rothschild's annoyance Stolypin's answer reply did not go beyond vague assurances.

Another, contrastingly self-interested, request came from Sir Ernest Cassel for the King to support a Russian loan that the financier was keen to float. No doubt the plan was keenly promoted when the King dined with Cassel the night before he departed for Reval. Hardinge and everyone else who heard of Cassel's request viewed it as a gross abuse of his friendship with the King, and strongly suggested that the King should disregard it. At such times Edward's generosity towards his friends extended to weakness and although he did not raise the loan with his nephew, he did mention that he would be grateful for him to receive Cassel if Sir Ernest visited St Petersburg. The tangible results of the Reval meeting, such as the formation in October 1908 of the Anglo-Russian Chamber of Commerce, were minimal. But it undoubtedly created a mood of diplomatic warmth that encouraged later progress in a manner that Edward achieved on repeated occasions. The trip confirmed how Edward was honing what he established as a style of royal state visit that would enjoy lasting success. Seeking political objectives was not a major priority, and was not within the constitutional authority of the crown. Instead the prestige of the monarchy and Edward's personal reputation abroad were employed on behalf of the nation to further an atmosphere of goodwill, within which specific objectives could be easily sought. The King demonstrated how, if so minded, the monarch was in a unique position to further such an atmosphere and while the true value of his actions may not have been fully appreciated by his own ministers, a similar course would constantly be reiterated by future advisers to the crown.

When Nicholas II – ever sensitive to being patronized by his elders – confessed to his genial, reassuring uncle that he felt infinitely happier than with his contemporary, the German Emperor, when they had met the previous year, he pinpointed the personal ease that Edward brought to his diplomatic activities. The main negative result was the reaction of Edward's other royal nephew and Germany, for whom the Reval meeting caused an outbreak of personal and national paranoia.

CHAPTER TWELVE

PEACE AND UNREST

When cancer claimed the German Emperor's mother Vicky a few months after the death of Queen Victoria she was the fourth of Edward VII's brothers and sisters to predecease him. Of the remaining four, the Duke of Connaught and three sisters, his relationship with the two younger princesses, Helena and Beatrice, was amiable – on his part – but distant. Nonetheless, after his death, Lenchen (as Helena was always called), whose marriage to Prince Christian of Schleswig-Holstein-Sonderburg-Austenburg had caused lasting affront to the Danish Alexandra, wrote tenderly to Lord Esher: 'You known what he was to me, the best, the kindest, the dearest of Brothers.'[1]

With his third sister, Louise who was closest to him in age of all the surviving family members, he had more in common. They both enjoyed gossip and, when Prince of Wales, he brought her home Turkish cigarettes from Constantinople which she smoked in secret. Louise's personal life was often difficult. Her relations with her sisters Helena and Beatrice were stormy and her marriage to the Marquess of Lorne was strained, with regular assertions of his homosexuality and her own affairs. In one instance during the 1890s her sisters accused her of enticing Beatrice's husband, Prince Henry of Battenberg, into an affair. Despite their friendship she was always slightly frightened of her brother and his way of life. When her husband inherited the dukedom of Argyll from his father in 1900 Invereray Castle became their Scottish home. But Louise never allowed her brother to stay with them. She wrote afterwards that she was embarrassed because: 'They were economising. When Mama had visited there were seventy servants, now four.'[2]

Louise was outspoken and she let her temper get the better of her over the design and site of the memorial to Queen Victoria. Being not only a daughter but a sculptor she was furious when she was not invited to join the committee choosing the memorial. She wanted it to be placed in Green Park, not – as decided by the committee – in front of Buckingham Palace where, in her opinion, it would only 'be a rallying place for the mob'.[3] She vented her anger on her brother to such an extent that two years later he – who loathed rows and particularly ones that rumbled on – complained sadly to Esher that he had not seen Louise for nine months. Esher noted afterwards: 'Of course his good nature would like to make it up but he cannot move in the matter. He said he would like me to call on her: and tell her that if she apologizes he will bury the subject and never mention it again.'[4]

The King's contact was most regular with his only surviving brother, Arthur, Duke of Connaught. The Duke enjoyed the military career that the King had hankered after but never been allowed, but jealousy was not in the King's nature. Only when the Duke had been given command of the Guards brigade in Wolseley's army sent to Egypt in 1882, and Edward's own offer of service was rejected, did he feel envious. In 1895 he strenuously promoted his brother's claim to succeed the Duke of Cambridge as Commander-in-Chief, against Wolseley who was eventually given the post. As recommended by Lord Esher's committee, the Commander-in-Chief's position was abolished in 1904. The King was delighted when his brother was offered what became the army's senior active post, Inspector-General. The only difference arose in 1907, following the appointment of the Duke as Field Marshal Commanding-in-Chief and High Commissioner in the Mediterranean. His station in Malta was boring and the Duke thought that militarily the command was useless. When he returned home on leave at the end of May 1908 the King expressed his annoyance to Esher that his brother was taking too long a holiday and idling about in London boudoirs.

The situation became more serious the following year when the Duke not only gave up the command but announced he wanted to publish a statement explaining his reasons for doing so. Both the King and his government were firmly opposed, not least because the Secretary for War, Haldane, would have been faced with awkward questions in the House of Commons. During some fierce exchanges the Duke and his excitable Prussian wife, Louise, had accused the King of sending them to Malta because of their popularity in England, which was nonsense. The Duke's resignation ended his active military career.

Soon after – as always – the King's annoyance subsided. Justifying himself by saying that the Duke was his only surviving brother and had been their mother's favourite, the King was felt to have given in by Esher who grumbled to his son: 'He has been "got at" on his tender side as I always told you would be the case. He is now sorry for his brother and thinks Haldane might let him back on the selection board. It is very tiresome and I do not want to be mixed up in this family affair.'[5] But Haldane threatened to resign if the Duke was reappointed as President of the War Office Selection Board and the King had to give way. Two years later the Duke was sent to Ottawa as Governor-General of Canada.

Edward experienced no such differences with his son. Recalling his own total exclusion from affairs of state by Queen Victoria, he went out of his way to interest and involve the Prince of Wales. Shortly after his accession he set up a desk next to his own at Windsor so that his son could study state papers with him. They were constantly together through the year; always for the family occasions at Sandringham, for the summer in London – where the Prince and his family moved into Marlborough House – and the Derby, Royal Ascot, Goodwood and Cowes. Throughout the winter they met at shooting parties when the Prince of Wales without fail outshone his father. Other than his shooting prowess, however, he lived quite contentedly in his father's expansive and affectionate shadow.

The King's relations with his three daughters were not as close. The eldest, Princess Louise, Duchess of Fife, to whom her father gave the traditional but discretionary title of Princess Royal in 1905, was happily married and devoted to her two daughters, named after her mother and sister, Alexandra and Maud. Extremely shy she was determined to keep her family life private. The prospect of either public attention or unwarranted advice from members of her family were equally distasteful to her. As a result she remained increasingly at her Scottish home, Mar Lodge. The fact that it was only a short drive from Balmoral by no means guaranteed regular visits when her parents and family were in residence.

After the death of her husband in 1912 Louise became ever more reclusive; but in 1923, six years before her death, she was subjected to unpleasant publicity and financial crisis, thanks to her husband's business partner, Lord Farquhar. When Fife had rearranged his family's estates before his marriage, the business and investments were handled by Horace Farquhar, who became trustee of the estates. His friendship with Fife combined with his wealth to propel him into Edwardian society. He was made a peer in 1898 and the splendour of his dinners in London were confirmed by many. Edward VII made him Master of his Household and George V was to follow suit with further offices. Farquhar's estate at Castle Rising – conveniently close to Sandringham – was noted for its partridge shooting.

Neither Edward nor his son gave any indication that they mistrusted Farquhar. But his questionable business ethics were condemned by Lord Carrington in 1907.

A Siberian gold-mining company has been formed by some Jew speculators. Francis Knollys, Lord Stanley, Lord Howe, Sir West Ridgeway and others accepted directorships and the shares were rushed up to £16. They have gone down with a rattle and Farquhar is said to have netted £70,000. He is supposed to have secured all those names, and the papers are open-mouthed at this scandal. It is deplorable that the King's private secretary and the Queen's Lord Chamberlain should have been "let in" and mixed up in affair like this.[6]

When Farquhar died he supposedly left a substantial estate, much of which he bountifully directed towards Louise's daughters. But his estate proved to be overshadowed by debts. Worse, £80,000 had disappeared from the Fife Trusts. The Princess Royal, as his co-trustee, was legally bound to find the money, some of which she raised by selling nearly fifty family paintings. It was a cruel legacy for the most unworldly and retiring of women.

From 1905, when her husband was offered the throne of Norway in 1905 the youngest daughter Maud led a busier life than either of her two sisters. Despite living her married life first in Denmark and then Norway, she never gave up her beloved home in England, Appleton on the Sandringham estate. Before her husband's accession she gained agreement from the Norwegians that she would continue to spend much of each winter there. Most resembling her mother in her irrepressible, girlish sense of humour, she was the most contented of the three daughters; certainly in comparison to the intelligent Princess Victoria, who by the time of her father's accession was almost resigned to her fate as an unmarried maid. Frustration at her enforced role as her mother's companion, which was to become steadily more of a burden, increased the sharpness of her tongue, much of which was directed against her sister-in-law, May, the Princess of Wales. Comments such as: 'Now do try to talk to May at dinner, though one knows she is dreadfully dull'[7] were unfair but regular. Esher was one of her intimates and in 1903 he recorded a conversation, and his conclusions – both sympathetic and flippant.

> Princess Victoria told me that she feared she would have to be an old maid, as nothing would induce her to marry a foreigner, and she was not allowed to marry an Englishman. She asked whether I thought if she married an Englishman it would 'shake the monarchy to its foundations!' For a woman like her, not over fond of society and wishful to be loved, royalty is a hard trade. If she cannot marry, she might perhaps find a lover on the quiet, but she must make haste, as the years pass quickly.[8]

There is no evidence that she ever did.

In March 1902 Lord Carrington wrote critically in his diary that when the King had embarked on a yachting cruise and the Queen had gone to Copenhagen with Princess Victoria:

> The Prince and Princess of Wales have been fagged to go to Copenhagen as well; to their great annoyance and dismay as the journey will cost at least £600. This is another proof of how entirely the P of W is under his father and mother's thumb. He consults the king about everything – even as to whether his footmen are to wear black or red liveries.[9]

215

This was not surprising. The Prince of Wales inherited his father's meticulous interest in clothes and personal appearance, and continued to follow his example even after Edward's death. A footman's correct attire was almost as important for the King as his own, and his appearance was a matter of the utmost significance. His enjoyment of uniforms derived more from the frustration of his ambitions for an active military career than from vanity. When he squeezed himself into a foreign uniform whose cut did not suit his short stature and broad girth, he felt it would be an affront to his host to dress otherwise.

The King's influence on British dress was more lasting, in particular in his adaption of rigidly formal Victorian attire into a wardrobe that made concessions to practicality without any loss of smartness. The short jacket that he wore for the first time during his visit to India as Prince of Wales was the forerunner of the modern dinner jacket, and he made it acceptable to wear a lightweight tweed suit at Goodwood races. Clothes were the main foundation of the King's appearance, but there was always an array of accessories; hats, spats, gloves and canes, watchchains, cigarette cases, tie-pins and button-holes. If the quantity of jewelled rings that he sometimes wore were not to everyone's taste, and the raised heels of his boots to give extra height looked faintly ridiculous, there was never an occasion when Edward's appearance was not immaculate.

The Prince of Wales's deference to his father was confirmed on one occasion in a remark he made to Esher who noted afterwards: 'He likes living near the King yet, he says, all his life he has been rather afraid of him. He never has had any secrets from him, and he never found the King other than most helpful and affectionate: yet he has always feared him'.[10] With other people, however, the Prince was not quite so submissive as Lord Carrington suggested. He voiced strong, often contentious, opinions in the bluff manner he had acquired as a naval officer. Esher warned: 'His outspokenness will always get him into trouble'.[11] At times it did. He told Winston Churchill – whose discretion could never be counted on – that Asquith was not quite a gentleman, shortly before he took office as Prime Minister.

It would not have occurred to the King that he ever frightened his son. He liked to have him by his side as often as possible. Dismayed at their separation when the Prince of Wales set off for Australia in 1901, he – and Queen Alexandra – found some comfort in being left in charge of their four grandchildren: Edward aged seven, Albert (who became George VI) aged six, Mary aged four, and the infant Henry. The three elder children were indulged ceaselessly and the state apartments were accorded scant respect. Esher described an occasion at Windsor when, 'tea was brought in and after tea the children romped in the Waterloo Gallery, which has been polished for the ball and we had to drag them along the slippery floor by their heels, a source of endless joy both to them and to the Queen who looked on.'[12] No wonder that on their return from Australia the parents – who had already protested when the boys' governess was deliberately left behind in London during a visit to Sandringham – were told by Princess Victoria: 'I do hope you will think them well and not spoilt though I think they are.'[13]

The Prince of Wales shared his father's love of Sandringham. In striking contrast to the more expansive scale of life at the main house, he and his family lived in modest discomfort at York Cottage on one edge of the gardens. Successive guests confirmed that Sandringham remained the country house it had always been and did not become a palace. The ceremonial of Windsor and Buckingham Palace was not allowed to intrude. During a summer visit early on in Edward's reign Esher wrote: 'Life here is very simple – The King walks about just like any other country gentleman.'[14]

When walking about the King was usually planning changes. He loved modernity and mechanical devices and Sandringham was where he indulged himself. He was immensely proud of the electric light which he installed instead of the existing gas. The improvements were paid for by the prize money and stud fees of his adored Persimmon. Persimmon's Yard of palatial stables was built at Wolferton Farm and the Persimmon range of conservatories was constructed the length of the huge walled garden; three hundred yards of solid teak and glass. 'All Persimmon' the King would say proudly with a sweep of the arm as he escorted guests for the traditional Sunday tour. When the great horse died in 1908 the King commissioned Fabergé to make him a solid silver model. It was not the first time the Russian craftsman – or in this instance his son, Nikolai – had provided work for Sandringham. Between 1905 and 1906 he spent six months in residence making a series of models of the various prize-winning farm animals.

A golf course, Queen Alexandra's beach house at Snettisham and new organs for the churches on the estates at Sandringham and West Newton were all added during Edward's reign, but serious disruption was caused by a storm in 1908 after which, Esher recalled, 'The place was unrecognizable.'[15] Reginald Blomfield, the fashionable architect and garden-designer, was called in to advise on necessary alterations, in particular the re-siting of the Norwich gates – the loyal city's wedding present to Edward and Alexandra. They had opened onto a stately avenue of limes leading to the north front of the house, but most of the trees were blown down. It was decided to carry out the costly exercise of moving the gates nearly two hundred yards further from the house. This involved diverting the passing public road – and extending the perimeter wall on either side to take in a sweep of the neighbouring Dersingham woods. The walled boundary around the grounds has remained unchanged ever since, and Edward's successors have been grateful for the privacy that his expensive alterations guaranteed.

After the Derby and other victories in 1900 by the King's horse, Diamond Jubilee, the King's fortunes on the turf declined and during the next seven years he won less in prize money than Diamond Jubilee's total of £30,000 in one year. This did not, however, diminish his enjoyment of attending race meetings and his presence added to the popular image of the monarchy and the prestige of racing itself. But to make up for the lack of success, in 1907 Lord Marcus Beresford arranged to lease some yearlings from Colonel Hall Walker's Tully Stud in Ireland. Among the group was a promising colt called Minoru. Two years later the horse gave Edward his third victory in the Derby, the only time in history that the race has been won by the reigning monarch. The King led in his winner to the most tumultuous reception ever seen at Epsom, on what would prove to be his last appearance at the meeting.

As undimmed as his enjoyment of racing was the King's enthusiasm for shooting which he retained until the end of his life. At Sandringham the best of the season was the excellent partridge shooting. Later there were parties for the three main periods of residence through the winter; the King's birthday in November, Queen Alexandra's at the beginning of December, Christmas and the New Year. Lunch on these occasions usually took place in a splendid marquee erected at a suitable site and the King was in his element, organizing the sport and entertainment for his guests and chaffing them about their relative proficiency or lack of it. When he in turn was a guest, comfort, rather than the most challenging sport, was usually the order of the day. This was certainly the case when he shot with Edward Lawson (whom he elevated to being Lord Burnham in 1903), the shrewd and wealthy proprietor of the *Daily Telegraph*. The shooting at Burnham's Hall Barn in Buckinghamshire was not always the most demanding. In 1904 after a visit by the King Carrington noted: 'they shot about 600 pheasants – all very low'.[16] But Edward loved the scale of Burnham's hospitality, described by Carrington when the King went in January 1909. 'Burnham gave his annual feast to the King at Hall Barn. We have the usually enormous lunch in the usual tent and the King did well eating turtle soup, Irish stew, cold truffled turkey, mince pie and paté de foie gras – seven guns killed 2,000 pheasants.'[17]

As Carrington suggested when he said 'the King did well', although Edward VII's enjoyment of food hardly diminished, his capacity did. When Esher was summoned by a telegram from Knollys to breakfast with the King in January 1910 the repast was relatively modest, but the smooth efficiency was unchanged.

> I got to Buckingham Palace at five to ten and went up to the Indian Room. A page asked me if I would take tea or coffee! At ten precisely the King's door opened and he came in with his terriers. We went into the room overlooking the Mall. There was a small table, two places laid. All the breakfast was on the table in front of the King. His tea near him, my coffee near me. He served and the pages and the footmen left the room. He asked me if I would have some fish. There were three dishes – fish, omelette and bacon. When he had finished the fish he rang the bell and the servants changed the plates. Same ceremony repeated after the omelette. Then marmalade and he asked me if I would smoke. He sat there until just after eleven. We talked all the time, army, government reconstruction, gossip.[18]

The King loved gossiping with Esher and other members of his close circle such as Soveral and Charles Carrington and often surprised his audience with his relevations. Winston Churchill's engagement and subsequent marriage in 1908 attracted considerable public attention but the King was able to enlighten Esher on the bridegroom and bride's backgrounds. Having announced on one occasion that only his intervention persuaded the Duke and Duchess of Marlborough to allow their son Randolf to marry the American Jennie Jerome, he later continued:

> The King spoke very appreciately of Mrs Winston and told me what I had never heard, that she was dear old Redesdale's daughter. Lady Helen Campbell is also one of Redesdale's children! 'He did not do so badly' I said. 'No' said the King, 'did you ever hear of Lipton who was asked whether he intended to get married and said, 'Ah nay, but I am just a freelance!' This with a broad accent.[19]

At Buckingham Palace these talks took place in the King's room, in competition with the shrieking of his four canaries, and with the terriers, Jack and Caesar, growling at visitors who ventured too close to their royal master. After Jack's demise in 1903 Caesar's ascendancy was unchallenged, confirmed by his collar inscribed, 'I am Caesar, the King's dog'.

In the middle years of his reign Edward's health – or more specifically his susceptibility to bronchitis and severe coughing – was a constant source of concern to those around him, especially during the winter. It was rare for the King to cancel a dinner party or any other social occasion but in March 1905 Esher noted:

> The King has been rather unwell for four days. One of his lungs has been a little affected and he has had a very bad cough. As he cannot eat much or smoke, he is very uncomfortable . . . He has got a big dinner party tomorrow night which he is not going to attend. He remains in London until the end of the month when he goes to Knowsley [the Earl of Derby's home in Lancashire] for the Grand National.[20]

At the end of 1905, during a bad spell of the fog that was such a regular curse to London through successive winters, Esher noted with concern: 'His staying in London in such weather is really dangerous for its affects his breathing,'[21] and, the following day: 'The King was far from well, he feels the fog oppression severely.'[22]

Coughing, shortage of breath and the other health problems which bothered the King made him intensely irritable. But as his reign progressed he became increasingly determined that they would not interfere with his crowded schedule. An extract from his own diary for one week at the end of June 1906, illustrates the pace at which he led his life.

MONDAY 25 [JUNE].
Morning.
Arrive in London 12.30.
Pces Edward and George of Wales 2.30.
D of Connaught 3.
Visit D and Dss of Connaught at Clarence House 6.30.
Evening.
Dine with Mr and Mrs G. Cavendish Bentinck at Whitehall Gardens 8.30.

TUESDAY 26.
Morning.
Sir H. Campbell-Bannerman 11.15.
Present new Colours to 3rd Batt: Gren: Gds in Buck: Palace
    Gardens 12.
Rt Hon: [R.B.] Haldane 1.
Pss Royal and 2 girls [Alexandra and Maud] & D. of Fife & Pces
Edward and Albert [of Wales] to luncheon – 1.45.
D. of Connaught 3.15.
Sir E. Grey 7.30.
Evening.
Dine with Duke & Duchess of Westminster at Grosvenor House
    8.30.

WEDNESDAY 27.
Morning.
Sir S. McDonnell & Mr Rivers 11.30.
Visit the Cheremetoff Blue Sèvre at Mr Wertheimer's in Bond
    Street 12.
Sir D. Probyn 4.

Evening.
Attend British Canadian Festival Concert at The Queen's Hall by the
London Symphony Orchestra & a Chorus of 250 voices – 9.30.

THURSDAY 28.
Morning.
Leave St Pancras Station 9.20.
Arrive at Derby 11.55.
Drive to R. Agricultural Show & on the way rec[eive]: Address fr.
the Mayor. Lunch in R. Pavilion 1.30.
Leave Derby 3.30.
Arrive London 6.5.
Evening.
3rd Court at Buckingham Palace 10.30.

FRIDAY 29.
Morning.
The King's Birthday officially kept. (Owning to heavy rain
Birthday Parade & Trooping of the Colour at Horse Guards at 11
could not take place).
Pss. Xtian [sister, Princess Helena, who married Prince Christian]
11.45.
Duke of Connaught 12.10.
Motor to Hampton Court Palace & visit Rooms & Gardens
2.45.
Sit to Mr Cope R.A. for picture at his Studio Little Hampton
House 5.
Evening.
Dine with Sir Edward and Lady Sassoon at 25 Park Lane 8.30.

SATURDAY 30.
Morning.
Privy Council at Buck: Palace Lords Crewe, Ripon, & Selfton & Mr
R. Causton 11.15.
Attend Concert at Albert Hall by Vienna Philarmonic society 12.
Dss of Sparta & Ct. A. Mensdorff to luncheon 1.45.
Leave Kings X Station 4.
Arrive at Huntingdon 5.15.

Drive to Hinchingbrooke & stay on a visit to Ld. Sandwich.
Evening.
Dinner Hinchingbrooke 8.30.

SUNDAY 1. Morning Service at All Saints' Church at Huntingdon 11.
Visit Orphan Home for little boys (Waifs and Strays) 12.15.
At 4 motor to Ramsey Abbey & visit Ld and Lady de Ramsey.
Return to Hinchingbrooke 6.15. Play Croquet.
Evening.
Dinner.[23]

Bronchitis and the accompanying coughs were not the only worries.
In December 1908 Carrington wrote in his diary:

> The King's health is not very satisfactory. He did not go to the
> Ilchesters, but to stay with the Sassoons at Brighton. [Sassoon luxury
> and the sea air were a welcome combination.] He has suffered torture
> from neuralgia in the head and was nearly out of his mind with pain
> – poor man – he also has a perpetual tickling in the throat. His tem-
> perature is below normal in the morning and above it at night.
> Laking told Bill [Carrington's brother] he dare not give him strong
> opiates because of his heart. It is very sad, as in the '60s his strength
> was prodigious and he thought he would live to be a hundred.[24]

Escape from the English winter and London's fog was a pressing
reason for the King's prompt departure for Biarritz each year at the
end of February. He insisted on being in London at the end of
January to carry out the State Opening of Parliament. Queen Victoria
had only carried out this ceremonial seven times between 1861 and
1886, and then never during the last twenty-five years of her reign. Its
revival confirmed the extent to which Edward emphasized and
enjoyed the ceremonial aspects of monarchy.

But by the end of February he was usually heartily relieved to be
away. In 1907 he wrote kindly to his Prime Minister Campbell-
Bannerman in 1907: 'I only wish you could have come here, as the
weather since twelve days is perfectly glorious and the warm sun is
tempered by the bracing sea breezes. I felt far from well when I
arrived, but after a few days lost my bronchial cough thanks to this
climate.'[25] The following year Doctor Laking's insistence that the King

leave for Biarritz as promptly as possible and try to stay there for six weeks was partially responsible for the short crisis that arose over Campbell-Bannerman's resignation and Edward's failure to return to London for the kissing of hands with his new Prime Minister, Asquith.

As the King grew older his tendency to worry, at times to the extent of deep and prolonged depression, became worse. And there was increasingly more for him to worry about, as the events of 1908 demonstrated, both before and after the changeover from Campbell-Bannerman to Asquith.

The year began badly with a row into which the German Emperor intervened, to his uncle's extreme annoyance. Concerns at the pace of German shipbuilding led to the formation in Britain of the Imperial Maritime League who criticized the economies being forced on the navy – ignoring the increased efficiency and modernizing that accompanied them. They blamed Fisher and vigorously campaigned for his removal. Therefore, they invited Lord Esher to join their council, in the hope that the presence of such a shrewd and influential strategist would assist their cause. Esher was quick to refuse the offer, but gave the league permission to publish his letter of refusal. In Esher's letter one passage ran: 'that every German from the Emperor down to the last man wished for the downfall of Sir John Fisher.'[26]

On 6 February the letter was published in *The Times* and aroused indignant outrage in Germany. The German Emperor's response was characteristically unconventional. He sent a personal letter to Lord Tweedmouth, First Lord of the Admiralty. This was followed by a letter to his uncle in which he explained why he saw fit to write to Tweedmouth, a step bound to be seen in Britain as unwarranted interference. The letter to Tweedmouth explained that the rumours being put about in Britain could have deplorable results, and that the German navy was built for self-defence not aggression against any one country. The Emperor continued in sarcastic vein about Esher: 'I am at a loss to tell whether the supervision of the foundations and drains of the Royal palaces is apt to qualify somebody for the judgement of naval affairs in general', denouncing what Esher had said as 'balderdash'.[27] To Edward he wrote calmly:

Dearest Uncle, the very animated discussion in the British press about naval matters have [sic] interested me very much. But I have detected some uneasiness about the German Naval Programme, which is unfounded, arising as it does from misconceptions. I therefore took the liberty to write to Lord Tweedmouth and to give him the information necessary to enable him to see clearly. With best love to Aunt and cousins, ever your devoted nephew, Willy.[28]

The calm imperial tones and protestations of family affection only served to increase Edward's anger and he blamed all those involved, including Esher. 'The King is very much disturbed. He is angry with the German Emperor, and annoyed with Fisher and me! It is very natural. He hates a fuss . . . he wrote me a letter of "regret" that I had used imprudent expressions.' Esher went on confidently to say 'this will blow over' (which it did) and to conclude: 'The fact will remain that the Emperor has once more intervened in the domestic affairs of another power.'[29]

Flattered at receiving a letter from the German Emperor, Tweedmouth's personal reply, revealing details of the British Naval Estimates, only made the situation worse and extended the debate in the press.

The King's mood was exacerbated by the affair blowing up just as he heard that King Carlos of Portugal and his son the Duke of Braganza had both been assassinated. Having enjoyed his visit to Portugal in 1903, Edward had entertained the Portuguese royal family at Windsor towards the end of 1907, when Esher remembered the young Duke as, 'such a jolly boy, who I took over the castle'.[30] The assassinations were carried out by left-wing extremists protesting against the dictatorial government by Senhor Franco, whom King Carlos had installed in 1907 in an attempt to end the country's chronic political instability. Edward's outrage at the murders was mixed with gloomy thoughts on the acceptable conduct of monarchs. He agreed with his eminent doctor, Sir Felix Semon that the assassinations were, 'horrible – horrible', but went on immediately: 'But I'll tell you something: a constitutional monarch must not do such things.'[31] Edward marked his respect by attending a Requiem mass, thereby becoming the first English monarch since the Reformation officially to attend a Roman Catholic service. This briefly outraged ardent Protestants, whom the King ignored. The following year he bestowed the Garter on Carlos's young successor, his second son King Manoel. But the assassinations had evidenced the widespread feelings against a monarch and Manoel reigned only until 1910 when Portugal declared itself a republic.

The visits to the Scandinavian Baltic and to Reval during the summer of 1908 were enjoyable successes for the King, but his autumn visit to Marienbad heralded some unpleasant surprises. On the way to Marienbad he followed a testing visit to his nephew at Friedrischof Castle with a far more enjoyable stay with the Austrian Emperor Franz Joseph at Ischl. Therefore he was mortified to hear in early-October that Austria had formally annexed the states of Bosnia and Herzegovina.

The two states nominally belonged to Ottoman Turkey, but they had been for many years effectively run by Austria. Serious unrest in Turkey prompted the annexation, organized by Austria's ambitious and unscrupulous Foreign Minister, Baron Aloys von Aehrenthal. The action was in flagrant breach of the terms of the Berlin Agreement of 1878 which had established conditions for stability in the Balkans. Such a destabilizing move was bad enough for Edward, for whom European peace was an increasing preoccupation. But he was mortified that the Austrian Emperor had said nothing of his country's intentions when they were together at Ischl.

At the same meeting Aehrenthal had assured Sir Charles Hardinge that Austria's response to recent developments in Turkey would be entirely peaceful. Aehrenthal also lied directly to Sir Edward Goschen, the British Ambassador in Vienna, about the second major development caused by Turkey's crisis, Bulgaria declaring unilateral independence from her Turkish overlords. When Goschen raised this possibility Aehrenthal assured the ambassador that there was: 'No truth at all. There is not a word about it in our reports from Sofia'.[32] Two days before the Austrian annexation Prince Ferdinand of Bulgaria announced his country's independence.

Count Mensdorff, the suave Austrian ambassador in London, had long been on cordial social terms with his cousin the King. But the Bosnian crisis ended Edward's friendliness and any inclination on his part to discuss serious matters with the ambassador. On 3 October Mensdorff gave Hardinge a letter from Aehenthal, coolly announcing the annexation of Bosnia and Herzegovina: at the same time told him that he had a similar, personal letter from the Emperor Franz Joseph, for Edward VII, who was at Balmoral. Hardinge was therefore able to forewarn the King of what lay in store when Mensdorff duly arrived at Balmoral for a brief and frosty visit. Lord Redesdale wrote afterwards:

No one who was there can forget how terribly he was upset. Never did I see him so moved. He had paid the Emperor of Austria a visit at Ischl less than two months before. The meeting had been friendly and affectionate . . . The two sovereigns and their two statesmen had discussed the Eastern question – especially the Balkan difficulties – with the utmost apparent intimacy, and the King left Ischl in the full assurance that there was no cloud on the horizon. Now, without a word of warning, all was changed.[33]

Inevitably the German Emperor entered the arena, taking the declared independence of Bulgaria as the excuse for criticizing his uncle. 'I consider that the whole of the action in Bulgaria is due to King Edward VII, who was informed of it at Marienbad'[34] he wrote inaccurately to Bülow at the beginning of October.

By the end of the month the Emperor had administered two further blows to relations with his uncle and between Germany and Britain, with the publication of two newspaper interviews, one in England in the *Daily Telegraph*, the second in America, in the *New York World*. The first confined itself to patronizing remarks about Britain's lack of trust in Germany and his own central role in planning the successful end of the Boer War. The second contained offensive remarks about Edward which – with the rest of the interview given to the *World's* correspondent William Bayard Hale – were vigorously denied by German officials. Denials notwithstanding, the damage was done. The King wrote despondently to his son: 'I always suspected that he hated me and now I know it.'[35] He wrote in similar vein to Francis Knollys, going on to say that in contrast to his nephew's sentiments: 'I have always been kind and nice to him. As regards my visit to Berlin there is no hurry to settle anything at present. The Foreign Office to gain their own object will not care a pin what humiliation I have to put up with.'[36] After such a period it was hardly surprising that the King wrote to Charles Hardinge: 'We are certainly living in critical times, but yet I hope that peace may be maintained – but only because Europe is *afraid* to go to war.'[37]

CHAPTER THIRTEEN

MONARCHY IN DEMOCRACY

In 1908 Lord Esher wrote in his journal; 'We all live in a whirl of magazine literature and restaurant crowds. Electricity gets between us and the stars.'[1] This may seem strange from the increasingly magazine and restaurant dominated decades that have followed, but Esher was not alone when he hankered for the stern values of the Victorian era. Shrewd though he was, Esher looked back to Victoria's monarchy with a nostalgia that strongly influenced his views on the crown's changing image and constitutional position. Together he and Lord Knollys bemoaned what they considered to be the unwarranted erosion of the royal prerogative, and encouraged the King to resist pressure from his ministers. Queen Victoria's monarchy was built on her active constitutional position and longevity never diminished her tenacity. Esher deplored the prominence of the King's personality, fearing that it overshadowed the crown's mystery.

In 1907, discussing Campbell-Bannerman's failure to supply the King with sufficient Cabinet information prior to a decision being taken, Esher argued that the situation would inevitably pose a dangerous threat to royal authority.

> No one can, in this instance, say anything to the PM. The King himself, if he would do it, could write direct and ask whether certain

statements are true, and if so why he was not informed before any decision was taken . . . It is a matter of extreme delicacy. According to ancient usage which has prevailed for sixty years, the fullest statement, supported by reasons, should have been placed before the King, anterior to any final cabinet decision. As it is, the King will know nothing until the decisions of the cabinet are irrevocable because to upset them would mean a change of ministers. The practice which now governs the relations between the King and his ministers, if allowed to continue, must inevitably end in weakening the authority of the crown and the lowering of standards of safety in foreign and home affairs, but especially the former, when the necessity of having to explain the reason to the sovereign imposes upon a government and a minister.[2]

Esher's backward glances to the precedent of 'ancient usage' were out of touch with political reality. Edward VII was experiencing the strengthening of Cabinet government in which consultation with the monarchy was increasingly seen as unwarranted royal interference. Past Cabinets, not least those during the decade of government under Salisbury and Balfour, had been dominated by aristocrats whose social self-assurance was transferred to their politics. As the Liberal victory of 1906 announced many other changes, it heralded a shift in Cabinet construction. In future the holders of key positions would be members of the House of Commons, not the Lords. In Asquith's government that followed in 1908 the change was most pronounced in the appointment of Lloyd George as Chancellor.

Asquith confirmed this development in his reason given to the King for the replacement of Lord Tweedmouth as First Lord of the Admiralty by Reginald McKenna. The Prime Minister argued it was vital to have the heads of 'the great spending departments' in the House of Commons not the House of Lords. Liberal politics throughout their term of office was a juggling act between fulfilling requirements of national security by carrying through army and navy reforms and modernizing the services; and living up to electoral guarantees to reduce the service budgets and spend more on social reforms. In this situation, the service ministers needed to be in the House of Commons to best put their case to the Treasury. The willingness of the House of Lords to reject government legislation encouraged the removal of key Cabinet members from their benches.

The changes were often used to advantage by the King, as in his relationship with John Morley. When he was made Secretary for India, as he was not without vanity, Morley's relations with his monarch were a source of great self-satisfaction. Far more surprising was the manner in which Morley became a productive contact for the King. Despite having been claustrophobically surrounded by intelligent men during his youth, Edward retained throughout his life a fascinated and uncompetitive admiration for some men of learning. Morley was also self-made, the son of a Lancashire doctor and some three years older than the King. He became a distinguished lawyer and historian whom Edward enthusiastically promoted for the position of Regius Professor of History at Oxford when it became vacant in 1902. When Balfour turned the application down with the charming dismissal that Morley – a fervent admirer of Gladstone, whose biography he wrote – 'treats history from a point of view which is certainly not in harmony with the general sentiments of the nation,'[3] the King was able to compensate Morley the same year by making him a founder member of his Order of Merit.

Morley did incur considerable royal opposition to the reforms in India that he carried through in partnership with the Viceroy, the Earl of Minto, a Liberal peer in the old Whig tradition. The reforms intended to diminish the widespread unrest in India. In the King's opinion, however, one issue, the appointment of an Indian native to the Viceroy's ruling council would have the opposite effect. Edward eventually gave his consent, while continuing to register his opposition.

The disagreement did not impair his personal relations with Morley. The King enjoyed the minister's pride in his Lancashire origins which also struck Lord Esher when he visited Morley at his modest Wimbledon villa in December 1906. Esher had been friends with Morley for some years, but this was apparently his first visit to the house, called Flowermead. He wrote to his son that there were just 'two servant maids and a plain wrinkled old wife. Memories of some Lancashire village in which he was born, hovering about him still . . . What then is the secret? Why has power been given by his fellow-countrymen to this man, who has inherited neither position nor wealth?'[4] Rare in nineteenth-century politics, such men of modest origins were increasingly filling the House of Commons during Edward VII's reign.

The King's relations with the Liberal Foreign Secretary Sir Edward Grey were consistently more cordial and constructive than they had been with Lord Lansdowne. Grey was a sensitive country gentlemen, renowned for the high principles which had made him the last of the group to be won over to join Campbell-Bannerman's government in 1906. A friend once said of Grey that if you told him to sign something he should not or you would shoot him, he would reply 'shoot'. Lloyd George added: 'yes, but if you said, "Sign or I'll shoot your pet squirrel", he would sign immediately.'[5] High-minded though he was, Grey did not lack an eye for expediency. In 1908, when the government supported an application from Morocco for a £500,000 loan, Grey approached Sir Ernest Cassel, whose condition was that he be given the Grand Cross of the Bath – the highest rank of that order. Honours were of no significance to Grey and he happily acquiesced with the arrangement. When he was offered the Grand Cross of the Royal Victorian Order he politely refused.

Whereas Lansdowne had often found himself in confrontation with the King over foreign policy Grey saw the potential value of royal diplomacy. By 1908 the Entente with France was firmly established despite the occasional misgivings of the French Prime Minister, Clemenceau, and some of his compatriots. France, however, was formally allied with Russia. Dislike of the Russian autocracy was strong amongst Liberals and fervent in the Radical ranks of the party. As a result negotiations with both France and Russia were a delicate subject. Grey appreciated that in this light the King's personal relationship with the Tsar, his interest in the situation, and visits to Russia, could be put to good effect. Grey supported the meeting at Reval with enthusiasm.

His opinions of Germany were similarly in tune with the King's. In Grey's view the Emperor's behaviour was instrumental in German hostility towards Britain and the cause of increasing public excitement in both countries about the naval programmes. Despite never being himself party to nationalist hysteria, Grey had few illusions about national security. In 1909 a serious Cabinet row developed over the ordering of new Dreadnought battleships. Lloyd George and Winston

Churchill argued for four only; McKenna the First Lord wanted six and threatened to resign if overruled. A vociferous public – encouraged by the Tory opposition – joined in the music-hall chorus 'we want eight and we won't wait.' Grey agreed, and sensing that Asquith was wavering, told him he would resign if the guarantee for eight – four immediately and four to follow – was not given.

In August 1908, when Edward set out to meet his German nephew on his way to Marienbad, he went armed with two memoranda from Grey, discussing the problem of naval competition to varying degrees of detail. The drafts discussed the possibility of a mutual reduction in armament expenditure – especially on the construction of new warships – arguing that the necessary British shipbuilding could only be publicly justified by stressing the need to keep pace with Germany. In an atmosphere fuelled by partisan discussion in the press, this would inevitably further damage Anglo–German relations. Charles Hardinge, who as usual accompanied the King, wrote with pride about the Foreign Secretary's decision to entrust Edward with the memoranda:

> This was really a very interesting innovation, since for the first time in history the British Government briefed the King to act as their spokesman in an interview with the Head of a Foreign State, and it serves as an indisputable proof of the confidence they felt in the wisdom and tact of the Sovereign in dealing with such matters.[6]

Hardinge was puffing up the royal feathers but there is no doubt that Grey felt there was a chance that the private visit might reap some benefit for the government and British people. The King's reaction was typical. Initially he was put out, noting: 'This is, I believe, the first occasion on which the Sovereign has received instructions from his Government!'[7] But more than anything he was irritated by Grey's apparent indecision. The Foreign Secretary's accompanying note vaguely suggested that the King should make up his mind which – if either – memorandum should be consulted, depending on the Kaiser's mood and the atmosphere of their conversation. The King hated indecision, especially in potentially delicate situations. He expected his ministers, if they wished him to do something, to be clear in their requirements. Too often, if there was ambiguity, he found that it worked to his disadvantage. Once over this initial irritation, however, he was happy to do his best. In fact, the opportunity to broach the armaments question did not arise, and Hardinge may not have been so enthusiastic about the scheme if he had known in advance that it would fall to him, in the course of his discussions with the Emperor on Anglo-German relations in general, to bring up the thorny problem.

The second matter of concern at the 1908 meeting was the appointment of a new ambassador in Berlin to replace Sir Frank Lascelles, who had held the position since 1895. Lascelles' friendship with the German Emperor had been patient, but at times too accommodating for British policy to be promoted robustly. A suitable replacement was a delicate matter and Grey consulted the King closely. The first candidate, Fairfax Cartwright was eventually deemed unsuitable and while the Foreign Office seemed temporarily unable to produce a replacement the Kaiser voiced his wish for a political grandee such as Curzon or Rosebery. These were out of the question, but during the meeting the King was able to gain from his nephew a favourable opinion on the appointment of Sir Edward Goschen. Goschen's lack of enthusiasm for the posting was overcome by Edward and he moved to Berlin from Vienna in November 1908.

Throughout his reign, Edward had successfully resisted government pressure to be accompanied by a Cabinet minister on his foreign tours. But the events of the 1908 meeting with the German Emperor and the shifting political balance at home carried sufficient weight for him to accept the Marquess of Crewe, the Colonial Secretary, as his Minister in Attendance when he made what proved the final state visit of his life, to Berlin in February 1909. It was the first visit to the city by a British sovereign for two hundred years. Crewe, Lord Rosebery's son-in-law, was for the King one of the most congenial members of Asquith's Cabinet. Edward had little appetite for the visit, Queen Alexandra who accompanied him, even less. Despite the lack of enthusiasm, the King put an end to his nephew's regular complaint that his uncle saw fit to visit the other European capitals but not his. In a generally strained atmosphere, the most disturbing moment came when Edward, wearing a tight Prussian uniform and smoking a cigar, fainted after a fit of coughing. By the time he left for Biarritz shortly after returning to England from Berlin he was both unwell and exhausted.

In March 1904 the popular press reported with warm approval that the King had met Mr Lloyd George at dinner with Lord Tweedmouth. (They had in fact met socially two years earlier, with Grey.) It was a splendid affair held at Brook House on Park Lane, the house which Tweedmouth would shortly sell to Sir Ernest Cassel. The *Morning Leader* reported:

> For months and years Mr Lloyd George has been the target of the 'slings and arrows' of outrageous Jingoes and now the King has met this terrible person at dinner! It is only another incidence of the supreme tact and foresight of the King. The incident will be gratefully remembered by the vast number of people to whom court functions as a rule possess no interest. More than all, it shows the King is determined to be, not the head of a clique or a class or a Party, but the sovereign of a strong and united nation.[8]

Despite the loyal rhetoric, and rumours that Alice Keppel championed Lloyd-George's cause to the King, personal curiosity – partly inherited from his mother – was probably the main impetus for the King agreeing to meet the Radical member. But, as demonstrated by the constant whipping up of anti-German sentiment throughout the reign, the popular press had become a force for democracy. For the first time, the manner in which the cheap newspapers reported the activities of the monarch influenced popular attitudes.

By the beginning of Edward's reign the circulation of the halfpenny *Daily Mail* was half a million, ten times that of *The Times*. The *Daily Mail* was founded in 1896 by Alfred Harmsworth who became Lord Northcliffe in 1904 and, more significantly, became owner of *The Times* in 1908. Both papers were imperialist Tory in their editorials, refecting the views of their proprietor. Whether Tory or Radical the politics of the *Daily Mail*, the *Daily Express* (founded in 1900), and the *Daily Mirror* (found in 1903) were secondary to the fact that they brought the affairs of the world to an enormous and previously uninformed readership.

From the newspapers' inception their proprietors appreciated that royalty sold newspapers, as Lord Northcliffe pointed out to Francis Knollys in 1908. Following a polite assurance that his – and other editors – were happy to be guided as to what could and could not be published about the monarch he wrote, 'The King has become such an immense personality in England that, as you may have noticed, the space devoted to the movements of Royalty has quintupled since His Majesty came to the Throne, and our difficulties have increased in proportion.'[9]

The difficulties that Northcliffe alluded to were ensuring that royal privacy was preserved, for instance when the King was on holiday in Biarritz. But Edward's constant activity within Britain provided ample material for newspapers and his popular image was buoyed up accordingly. To the average reader the King's personality became inextricably bound up with the public duties that he carried out. Each summer he made visits to major towns and cities. These excursions showed the King at work to thousands of people for whom the constitutional activities of the monarchy meant little or nothing.

Reviews of Territorial Army battalions became fixtures of local significance on the King's annual agenda. The reforms which produced the Territorial and Reserve Forces Act in 1907 caused the King so much annoyance that at one moment in the privacy of Sandringham he burst out that their architect, the War Minister Haldane, was 'a damned radical liar and a German professor'.[10] But the opportunity to inspect and present colours to different battalions around the country greatly reduced the royal indignation.

These, like all his other duties, were carried out with an unflagging energy. There was, however, another more serious and enlightened motivation. From as early as the 1870s, when Queen Victoria's reclusiveness caused him concern for the prestige of the crown, Edward was driven by a conviction that the monarchy should be visible and active, more than just a constitutional figurehead. Now, as King, he was given ample opportunity to apply his beliefs. His sentiments struck a chord at a time of rapidly maturing social democracy. Public appreciation of his appearances demonstrated where much future activity of the monarch would lie.

On his public engagements the King excelled at showing interest, asking questions and putting nervous officials at their ease. He was proud of British technical progress and enjoyed being asked to mark such advances. In 1890 he had been delighted when invited to open the first underground railway in London, from the City to Stockwell. At times, however, enthusiasm for an idea was later tempered by expediency. When plans were first mooted in the 1880s for a Channel Tunnel he had been enthusiastic. But when a bill promoting the scheme was introduced into parliament in 1907 he joined the ranks of its opponents. Jackie Fisher argued forcefully against the idea on the grounds of security and the King agreed. He was even more robust in his opposition to the women's suffrage movement. When the Prime Minister Campbell-Bannerman wrote an article in the *Nation* supporting the Women's Franchise Bill the King was extremely annoyed. The government's official opposition to the Channel Tunnel Bill gave him the opportunity to write in trenchant terms from Biarritz:

> I rejoice to see you 'put your foot down' regarding the Channel Tunnel Bill when the matter was put forward in the House of Commons. I only wish you could have done the same regarding Female Suffrage. The conduct of the so-called 'Suffragettes' has really been so outrageous and does their cause (for which I have no sympathy) much harm.[11]

Progress in medicine and the improvement of hospitals were long-established priorities for the King, and his initiative produced impressive results that were warmly applauded by the public. The deaths of his sister Vicky and her husband from cancer roused his sympathetic interest in the disease and throughout his reign he supported any opportunity to promote the search for a cure. After his surgeon Sir Frederick Treves had visited – at the King's suggestion – the Radium Institute in Paris, Edward wrote warmly to say:

> Many thanks for your most interesting letter. Your visit to the Radium Institute in Paris must have been of the greatest value to you. We must indeed endeavour to have one in London, and we can I hope count on the generosity of *one* individual you are in communication with [Sir Ernest Cassel], and I know my present host [Lord Iveagh] would gladly also assist.[12]

Some contemporaries criticized the 'bevy of Jews' in Edward VII's circle, but he was extremely successfully in persuading them to part with large sums for one or other of his chosen causes. Lord Carrington described such an occasion in June 1896. 'Dined at the

Guy's Hospital dinner. – P. of Wales in the chair. J. B. Robinson and A. Belt of South Africa [both diamond magnates] were at the royal table. Both gave £5,000 for the charity! The total amount announced by the Chairman as collected was £160,000, an enormous sum.'[13]

The following year London hospitals were the Prince's chosen method of permanently marking Queen Victoria's Diamond Jubilee. In 1887 he had supported the foundation of the Imperial Institute similarly to mark the Silver Jubilee. But the success of the Prince of Wales's Hospital Fund for London – which became the King Edward's Hospital Fund – far outstripped that of the Institute. During his reign its income increased from £50,000 per annum to over £150,000, making a great contribution to London's hospitals at a time when the health service was still voluntary.

Queen Alexandra shared his interest. Her main concerns were the nursing services and the Red Cross, and the London Hospital, which she referred to as 'my hospital' and which often benefitted from her compulsive generosity. The hospital's chairman, Sir Sydney Holland (who became Lord Knutsford), recalled being summoned to see the Queen at Buckingham Palace on one occasion, when she carefully produced from beneath the cushion of her sofa a cheque for £1,000 and the same amount in cash as a gift for the hospital funds. The money was concealed from Sir Dighton Probyn, who attempted to exercise some control over her munificence.

Inefficiency always infuriated the King. It hampered the progress of one of his most treasured projects, the Midhurst Sanitorium to treat tuberculosis. At the turn of the century tuberculosis was still probably Britain's most virulent fatal disease. Sir Ernest Cassel had marked Edward's accession with a cheque for £200,000 for the King to put towards a cause of his choice. Edward's choice was tactful, as Cassel's wife had died of the disease, but it was also prompted by the example he had seen at the Falkenstein Sanatorium in Germany when visiting his dying sister Vicky. He set out his ideas to Sir Felix Semon who was to be on the Midhurst committee.

What we require is a Sanatorium for the poorer middle classes. Rich people can avail themselves of private sanatoria, the really poor ought to be provided for by municipalities and institutions of public benevolence, but between these two classes there is a stratum of educated yet indigent patients, such as clergymen, teachers, governesses, clerks, young officers, persons skilled in art, etc. They cannot afford the big sums charged by private sanatoria, whilst they are too proud or too bashful to avail themselves of public charity. These people hitherto have not all been provided for, and my Sanatorium is principally meant to take care of them.[14]

But progress was slow, blighted by administrative muddle so that at one stage the exasperated monarch berated Semon: 'I will tell you something: you doctors are nearly as bad as the lawyers, and God knows that will say a great deal!'[15] Eventually, in June 1906, he was able officially to open the Sanatorium.

Another hospital project that the King championed was the Hospital for Officers wounded in the Boer War, set up by Agnes Keyser in 1898 at her home in Grosvenor Crescent. The King met Miss Keyser that year and she became a friend for the rest of his life. At the end of the Boer War he persuaded her to continue the hospital's work and name it the King Edward Hospital for Officers. Again he enlisted the support of wealthy acquaintances. Twenty-four men, including the King and the Prince of Wales, guaranteed £100 a year for ten years. 'Sister Agnes' as Miss Keyser became known lived to be ninety.

These activities gave the monarchy a visible role beyond the constitutional one which Esher so championed. As the constitutional position changed with diminishing royal prerogatives, they provided a powerful identity for the King. Politicians questioned the royal prerogative with increasing confidence and the King's skill lay in his acceptance that concessions had to be made in areas of real importance – while refusing to give way over lesser matters, such as control over the censorship of plays. Although frustrating at the time – and offensive when handled tactlessly by ministers – the steady reduction of the monarchy's constitutional profile was an important part of its safeguarding for the future. The shift from the crown's constitutional action along well-defined lines, each guaranteed by the royal prerogative, to a less formalized position, demanded a deft touch which Edward VII's experience and character together made possible.

His experience also gave him an insight into how best to approach the social legislation of the Liberal government, whose proposals were destined to bring the confrontation between Lords and Commons towards the end of the reign. The animosity had smouldered for years, fuelled by Liberal resentment that the huge majority of Tory and Unionists peers in the Lords could emasculate Liberal policy. The creation of peers to redress the balance had been suggested since the latter years of the nineteenth century by Liberals, including Lord Carrington who wrote in his diary in July 1899: 'I met Rosebery in the street and had a talk with him. I recommended the creation of one hundred and fifty peers and suggested that the idea should be ventilated. He poo-pooed it saying the Queen would never consent, etc: but seemed afterwards to think there might be something in it.'[16]

The introduction of the Liberal Education Bill in 1906 produced the first clash. Balfour's Act of 1902 had revolutionized the education system, but it had infuriated the large Nonconformist population – Liberals to a man – by providing support from taxation for Anglican and Roman Catholic church schools. The 1906 bill sought to appease them by abandoning denominational religious instruction; the upshot was outrage from Anglican bishops, Roman Catholics and Tory peers. the King did not agree with the bill's suggested changes, but was more concerned by the confrontational atmosphere it produced. Having passed three readings in the Commons it was savaged by a series of amendments in the Lords. In November the King brought Campbell-Bannerman and the Archbishop of Canterbury together to attempt to resolve the deadlock, but to no avail. Edward made it clear to both sides that he fervently hoped for compromise and a joint conference was chaired by the Archbishop. The government was represented by Campbell-Bannerman, Augustine Birrell the Education Secretary who had drafted the bill and Lord Crewe who was Lord President of the Council. Balfour, Lord Lansdowne (who led the Tories in the House of Lords) and Lord Cawdor represented the opposition. Neither side was in the mood for compromise and no agreement was reached. On 19 December the Lords voted heavily to uphold their amendments and as the parliamentary session came to an end Campbell-Bannerman issued a clear warning: 'I say with conviction that a way must be found, by which the will of the people, expressed through their elected representatives, will be made to prevail.'[17]

Campbell-Bannerman died before his claim was put to the test, but under his successor, Asquith, the Liberals continued along their chosen legislative path, introducing bills which they knew were likely to be either changed out of recognition or rejected by the Lords. Asquith's attitude towards the role of the King was equivocal. At times of real crisis he was grateful for Edward's offers of mediation and he occasionally appreciated the difficult path the King steered. But more often he was dismissive, to the point of contempt, of the King's reasonable requests to be consulted. In July 1908, Winston Churchill, whom Asquith had brought into his Cabinet as President of the Board of Trade, sent him a letter from the King requesting to see a copy of the army scheme Churchill was loudly advocating in partnership with Lloyd George and in opposition to the proposals of the Secretary for War, Haldane. Asquith returned it with a note saying: 'I return this. I have replied to Knollys in the sense in which you suggested. It is, in any case, an impertinent request. These people have no right to interfere in any way in our deliberations.'[18]

In the same year Edward was given an opportunity to reflect on the Whig precedessors to Asquith and Churchill's modern style of Liberal politics by the death of his old friend the Duke of Devonshire. When the Duke died peacefully at Cannes aged seventy-four a link with the King's past, stretching back some forty years, was broken. An original member of the 'Marlborough House set', the Duke was one of Edward's most regular and munificent hosts. Through the reign until the Duke's death Chatsworth was the annual scene of a visit by the King and Queen in January. Devonshire was one of a number of old friends to die during the King's reign, so that in 1910, despite Edward being no great age, Lord Carrington estimated that from the old Marlborough House set, only he and Charles Beresford outlived the King.

When the Duke was still the Marquess of Hartington Carrington had been his political colleague for many years. After Devonshire's death he wrote in his diary that he was, 'universally regarded as an honourable, upright man of the highest character – he married the woman he loved and leaves no children'.[19] The woman was Louise, previously Duchess of Manchester, with whom Hartington enjoyed a close liaison for many years. Her second marriage earned her the title of 'the Double-Duchess'. The death of her husband in 1890 was followed in 1891 by the death of his father. The announcement, in August 1892, of their intention to marry, elicited the most tactful of letters from the then Prince of Wales. 'My Dear Hartington, after you left yesterday the Duchess imparted your information to me which I heard with the greatest interest and pleasure – most sincerely do I congratulate you on the important step you are about to make – and after so many years of firm friendship I feel sure you will be very happy.'[20]

In 1908 political swords were again drawn over the Licensing Bill, which proposed to reform and control the issue of licences for public houses. It gained the support of the temperance movement, but aroused fierce opposition from Tories who – bishops included – set themselves up as patrician defenders of the people and their drinking rights. After being passed in the Commons it was clear that the bill would be rejected in the Lords. Among the leading Tory peers there was a feeling that full confrontation between the Houses was not only inevitable but to a degree desirable. With added pressure that the grandees of the brewing trade might withdraw their financial support from the party, outright rejection was advocated. Asquith welcomed the King's suggestion in October 1908 that he should directly approach Lord Lansdowne and urge him to reconsider. The King's line of argument was sensible: 'If the attitude of the Peers was such as to suggest that idea that they were obstructing an attempt to deal with the evils of intemperance, the House of Lords would suffer seriously in popularity.'[21] But Lansdowne and his party had already decided on their course of action and a month after the meeting, the bill was thrown out by the Lords.

Among the few Liberal successes was the Old Age Pensions Act which was introduced in 1908 by Asquith's new Chancellor, Lloyd George and passed through both houses to become law on 1 August – although not without attracting comments from some members of the House of Lords which dismayed the liberal Lord Carrington. He recorded in his diary that Lord Wemyss had argued: 'If from sentimental motives parliament pass this Bill, a system of demoralisation would be established among the working class, thrift would be done away with, families would cease to regard it as an obligation to maintain those of their members whose working days are past, and self-reliance would be diminished.'[22]

The act gave a pension of five shillings a week to those aged seventy and over who had no more than £21 per annum or eight shillings a week of their own – roughly half-a-million people – and lesser amounts to others on a sliding scale. Rather than agreeing with Lord Weymss' objections, the majority of peers' opposition to the act was prompted by their concerns over its costs. In a sense they were proved right; at one stage during the bill's progress Lloyd George had replied to a colleague's concern at the paucity of potential revenue: 'I have no nest eggs. I am looking for someone's hen roost to rob next year.'[23]

In this confrontational frame to mind, and under pressure from the cost of the naval programme as well as the new pensions, the Chancellor drew up his 'Peoples Budget' of 1909, constitutionally the most significant piece of legislation of the twentieth century. In broad terms the Budget – presented by Lloyd George in the House of Commons on 29 April 1909 – contained an increase in death duties, a new supertax and allowances for children. Most pernicious to the Tories was the proposed revision of land taxes. This was an assault on 'unearned increment' and to the Tories land values formed the basis of economic and social stability. A duty of twenty per cent of land values at a set date would be levied in tax on the sale of land, or its transfer by inheritance or death. The budget did not compare with the efforts of past or future chancellors for financial skill or imagination and, ironically, the land taxes were to be repealed by Lloyd George's post-war coalition government, due to their minimal revenue. Lord Rosebery, however, considered the Budget 'a social and political revolution of the first magnitude.'[24] It was perceived to be sowing the seeds of class warfare.

While the Budget or Finance Bill was amended in the House of Commons fierce argument was carried on outside, although politicians on both sides were surprised at the level of public apathy. As with the previous contentious measures, Edward was as concerned with the conflict the Budget promoted as with its content. In March, he had told Esher that he 'liked Lloyd George and was not much frightened by what the latter told him of the budget.'[25] For the King, the nadir of the public argument came with Lloyd George's Limehouse Address of 30 July. During the preceding weeks the Chancellor had been the main target of the furious opposition to his Budget and now he got into his stride with a vengeance, taunting in particular: 'the Dukes' with the topical joke that 'A fully equipped duke costs as much to keep up as two dreadnoughts and is more difficult to scrap'.²⁶ It was too much for the King, who complained vigorously to Asquith. The situation was calmed by a civil letter to Edward from Lloyd George which maintained that he had been unduly provoked by the attacks of his opponents. The King's reply, while stressing that his principal concern was the dignity of ministerial office, illustrated the blend of courtesy, tact and generosity which smoothed his relations with ministers.

> As regards the budget itself, the King expresses no opinion, but he was very glad to see the Chancellor of the Exchequer on two occasions concerning it, and to have had some interesting conversations with him on various details connected with the Bill . . . The King readily admits that the Chancellor of the Exchequer has been attacked by some Members of the Opposition with much violence, and he regrets it, but he must remind him that though those gentlemen may have passed the fair limits of attack, they are private members and do not hold a high office in the Government, as is the case with Mr Lloyd George.
>
> If therefore the Chancellor of the Exchequer had been a private member, it certainly would not have been within the King's province to offer any official criticism on his speech; but it is owing to the fact that he holds one of the most important offices under the Crown and is an influential member of the cabinet, which made him feel it his duty, with much regret, to remonstrate with the Prime Minister against the tone of the Chancellor of the Exchequer's speech, and to express to him his fear that Mr Lloyd George was departing from the best traditions of his high office, traditions that had always been invariably observed by his distinguished predecessors.
>
> The King in conclusion, must give the Chancellor of the Exchequer every credit for the patience, and perfect temper which he has shown, under considerable provocation, during the debates on the Budget.²⁷

A few weeks later, during what proved to be their last meeting, while promoting alterations which might reduce the Budget's contentious nature, the King said quietly: 'I am an old man, and I am giving you my advice.'²⁸

By the time the Budget had completed its slow passage through the House of Commons in November, it was clear that the House of Lords were likely to reject it – something that had not occurred since the seventeenth century. More than its disagreeable contents, grounds for rejection were that the bill was not strictly financial, but social legislation in disguise. The peers were in combative mood, but as Balfour, Lansdowne and their supporters prepared to act, the Liberals discussed suitable responses to such constitutional outrage. Reform of the House of Lords by restricting its power of veto and possibly redefining its membership was their goal.

Edward VII was faced with a constitutional crisis that weighed heavily on him and the monarchy. On 18 September Esher wrote to his son Maurice:

> Asquith made a good speech. Obviously they are determined to fight. This being the case, I am sure that it is safest *not* to throw out the Budget. Entre nous – the King agrees with that view. The P of W [Prince of Wales] took the opposite stand which was a *dangerous* one. He is a good family man like Charles I.[29]

Whatever his own view, the King demonstrated admirable impartiality and constitutional correctness. At Balmoral after returning from Marienbad he saw Haldane and McKenna who put the Liberal side that rejection would be utterly unconstitutional. They were followed by Lord Cawdor who argued that the Lords had no option but to vote against, thereby forcing a general election at which the public would decide. Asquith recalled after his audience with the King, that Edward inquired:

> Whether I thought he was well within constitutional lines in taking on himself to give advice to, and if necessary put pressure upon, the Tory leaders at this juncture.
>
> I replied that I thought what he was doing and proposed to do, perfectly correct, from the constitutional point of view . . . He said that in that case he would not hesitate to see both Balfour and Lansdowne on his return to London. He went on to say that they might naturally ask what, if they persuaded the Lords to pass the

Budget, they were to get in return. It had occurred to him that the best answer would be: 'an appeal to the country – such as you say you want: only *after* and not before the final decision on the Budget'; in other words a dissolution and a general election in January.[30]

It says much for the King's reserves that the situation did not entirely dampen his spirit. Two days after Asquith's arrival at Balmoral Esher – an annual guest – sat next to the King at both lunch and dinner.

He was in excellent form. His memory so remarkable for anecdotes, which (unlike most) are almost always apposite . . . The King tells some rather risqué stories. One of his nieces when married was given for her nuit de noché a great four poster bed with a gold eagle central on the canopy baldaquine. When she came down next morning she said, 'A dreadful thing happened in the night, the gold eagle fell down and poor Ernest is hurt.' 'Where is he hurt?' someone asked. 'In the back!' was the reply.[31]

The King saw Balfour and Lansdowne four days later in London. They suggested that they had not finally decided on their course of action, but the King held out little hope that his intervention would sway them. Having travelled to Newmarket for the Cesarewitch meeting, he wrote to Esher from his rooms at the Jockey Club that he doubted: 'Whether any result of importance will accrue from my conversation with them'.[32] They now had no chance of halting the momentum that had built up among peers to turn out the Budget. On 30 November it was rejected by 350 votes against 75.

Throughout the latter weeks of 1909 the King's private secretary Francis Knollys became increasingly agitated about the damaging effect the crisis would have on Edward and his constitutional position. Knollys threatened to vote in the budget debate in the House of Lords, but the King was alert to the danger of his secretary officially taking sides in the dispute and Knollys was dissuaded.

Contrary to Knollys' fears, the crisis proved the stability that Edward VII's monarchy enjoyed and the non-political foundations it had acquired. Lloyd George's assertion three years earlier that the King ruled with his peers and not the people could have ranged the monarchy alongside the House of Lords in opposition to the forces of democracy. Far from such a possibility ever materializing, leading politicians on both sides were aware of the independent strength the monarchy had acquired. Balfour was no doubt covering himself for the likely outcome of the Lords rejecting the budget when, earlier in November, he confidently asserted to Esher that there was no danger to the position of the King, whatever course he may adopt. But when they discussed the last similar situation, the 1832 Great Reform Act, he went on to say:

> You forget the changed circumstances since 1832. During the latter half of Queen Victoria's reign and more than ever now, Great Britain means the British Empire. Our people overseas do not care a hat for Asquith or me. They hardly know our names. For them the symbol of Empire and union between the different parts of the Empire is the King. Hands laid on the Sovereign would mean the disruption of the Empire.[33]

Rejection of the budget meant the government was without funds and therefore powerless. On 3 December the King dissolved parliament and a general election was set for 14 January 1910. At Sandringham for Queen Alexandra's birthday the King deplored the course events were taking and declared that he 'had never spent a more miserable day'.[34] Ironically, at this stage Lansdowne guaranteed that if the Liberals won the election, his party would accept the people's mandate and pass the budget. It was too late. Asquith launched the Liberals' campaign at a rally at the Albert Hall, with a pledge that his party would not accept office unless they were assured of limitations on the powers of the upper house. To put these ambitions into effect he and his ministers began to formulate what became the Parliament Bill. This now replaced the budget as the item of legislative contention.

The proposed bill raised the issue of the King being asked to create peers to boost their Liberal ranks. Far more than any of the previous developments, it shed fierce light on the monarchy, to the grave concern of royal advisers. The day after the Lords' vote Esher wrote to his son:

> The political atmosphere is very charged with storm. The government proposes to ask the King for authority to use his prerogative

to create peers in the event of their obtaining a majority at the election. But they want him to give this pledge *now*. I most sincerely hope he will refuse. He may have to give way *after* an election. But it is monstrous to ask him to do so now. His action ought to be guided by the state of parties after the appeal to the country. One always knew he would be placed in a great difficulty and probably in a most humiliating position. I cannot believe that the Tories will win. But no one can tell.[35]

The issue at stake was the creation of sufficient peers to enable the Liberals to secure legislation. Prominent amongst their early measures would be a bill giving the House of Commons absolute control over finance, limiting the House of Lords' veto on other bills, and confirming the reforms of its make-up that the mass creation of peers would inevitably involve. The possibility of Asquith asking for an early guarantee from the King carried sinister suggestions of coercion of the monarchy and, if the King agreed, a substantial concession of prerogative. In this light Esher asked Balfour if he would be prepared to form a government if, in the event of the King refusing to give a guarantee after the election, Asquith resigned. Balfour sensibly said it would depend on the make-up of the House of Commons. He also added that whatever his answer, the King would certainly be safer refusing such a request than agreeing to it. Such a charged atmosphere required a response which the King gave Asquith in late December. In a letter from Knollys he told the Prime Minister that the policies Asquith was proposing effectively destroyed the House of Lords in its existing long-established state. This was an issue of sufficient importance to merit a second general election.

The King's demand for a second general election was prompted by his belief that if there was to be an assault on the House of Lords it could only be authorized by an electoral mandate. He also fervently hoped that the extra time would release the intense pressure building up as the January election approached. He held out little hope of an easy settlement, however, and the result of the election confirmed his fears. The Liberals lost over a hundred seats to retain 275, only two more than the Unionists at 273; in addition there were 82 Irish Nationalists and 40 Labour members. Asquith and his government were now not in a position to bully the King over the creation of peers. But the near deadlock increased the likelihood of Edward having to make a firm decision to resolve the crisis, a decision that would inevitably have great political overtones. In addition, the reduced Liberal majority now threatened their ability to steer the budget through the Commons in the face of Irish opposition.

The King was strained and unwell and when Asquith refused a invitation to Windsor after the election, preferring to set off immediately for a holiday in the South of France, his ungraciousness confirmed the King's earlier opinion that he was 'deficient in manners'. Asquith's action infuriated Esher who wrote: 'The King is too good natured, *so* good natured that the commoner type of minister takes liberties. It is criminal for a Prime Minister to refuse the Sovereign, because (unlike a private person) the Sovereign cannot retaliate'.[36]

If the reality of modern-day politics was unedifying, the King was courteous to the last. In reply to Asquith's letter of apology he wrote that the he quite understood the Prime Minister must have been 'completely knocked up by the election'.[37] But while the Prime Minister was tired, the King's health was failing.

His resolve, however, was undiminished. After performing the State Opening of Parliament on 21 February Edward refused to bring forward his planned departure for France and thereby curtail the busy schedule of engagements that he had before leaving England. Of these the most satisfying was the dinner he held at Buckingham Palace the evening before his departure. His guests were a selection of his friends and eminent men from various walks of life. The King had begun the dinners on his own initiative some years before and they reflected his sure feel for popularising the monarchy. On 6 March he travelled to Paris where he saw the play *Chantecler*. His disappointment at the performance – he wrote to the Prince of Wales that he had never seen 'anything so stupid and childish'[38] – was exacerbated by the chill that he caught in the theatre. On arrival in Biarritz it was clear that the holiday needed to be, as far possible, a period of recuperation.

CHAPTER FOURTEEN

A MONARCHY FOR
THE FUTURE

On 26 April 1910 Sir Charles Hardinge wrote from the Foreign Office to Sir Edward Goschen at the British embassy in Berlin in great secrecy.

> The fact is that the Government have not begun to realize that in view of their asking for guarantees, the impression is gradually spreading that the King is about to be coerced. Now, as you know, the King is far more popular than the government . . . I hear that even Cabinet members are saying that if the people can be convinced that pressure has been put upon the King, the Radicals will not stand a chance at the next election. All this is private but it comes from a very good source.[1]

The King may have been in need of rest during his visit to Biarritz but, characteristically, he was not idle. Hardinge recalled receiving on 5 April a letter of five sides in the King's close handwriting, discussing a wide range of foreign affairs. He was greatly looking forward to entertaining the American President Roosevelt in June and outlined his plans for the visit, but was less enthusiastic about the activities of his German nephew. Hardinge recalled that the King wrote:

The way Germany is intriguing against us and Russia is really too bad. They must have 'a finger in every pie' and interfere with us everywhere, at the same time being surprised that we do not like them! It is the old Bismarkian policy which is not yet dead, though I believe the present Chancellor is a most amiable and conciliatory man.[2]

Popular support for the King may have been widespread, but when he returned from Biarritz the political crisis was continuing unabated. This did not, however, prevent him from attending the opera in the evening, as he had done throughout much of his life when arriving in London from abroad. It was not only his personal enjoyment of the opera that prompted these visits. He felt it was important to be visible after a period of absence and this emphasis of the monarchy's public role was one of his surest touches. His friend Lord Redesdale was in the theatre, however, and remembered that it was a poignant appearance.

The King came in and sat down in his usual corner place. I noticed that he was looking very tired and worn. He sat through one act, all alone. Then he got up, and I heard him give a great sigh. He opened the door of the box, lingered for a while in the doorway, with a sad expression on his face – so unlike himself – took a last look at the house, as if to bid farewell, and then went out.[3]

It was not his last attendance; two days later he went again, to Covent Garden, after two crowded days work which included audiences with Asquith and wrestling with the problem of who should succeed Lord Minto as Viceroy of India. The King favoured Lord Kitchener and saw both him and the India Secretary, Lord Morley. Morley's preferred candidate was the King's favourite diplomat, Sir Charles Hardinge. No doubt the prospect of losing Hardinge partly accounted for Edward's opposition to his candidature. At one point he told Asquith that he would not mind Hardinge going as Ambassador to Paris, where he would be able to get hold of him at short notice, but Hardinge's name was not to be suggested again as Viceroy. Later in the year, after the King's death, Hardinge was appointed.

On 28 April a milestone in the constitutional crisis was reached. Having been passed in the Commons, the budget was finally accepted by the House of Lords. In Edward's absence at Biarritz Asquith had, on 14 April, spoken in the House of Commons with the aim of securing Irish support for the budget, which he was clearly unable to 'buy' by acceding to their demands not to increase duties on whisky. The Irish leaders had earlier stated that in order to support the budget they required guarantees that a bill dealing with the House of Lords' veto would be tabled within the year. For them, an end to the House of Lords veto would, at last, open the door to Home Rule.

In his speech, during debate of the draft resolutions for the Parliament Bill, Asquith said: 'If the Lords fail to accept our policy, or decline to consider it when it is formally presented to the House, we shall feel it our duty immediately to tender advice to the Crown as to the steps which will have to be taken if that policy is to receive statutory effect in this Parliament.'[4] Such an assurance satisfied the Irish sufficiently to gain their support. But it avoided specifically upholding the King's demand for a second general election before giving any guarantee to create peers. This hint of political chicanery, albeit justified by expediency, was deplored. For Francis Knollys it threatened 'the greatest outrage on the King which has ever been committed since England became a Constitutional Monarchy.'[5]

Edward VII embarked on the last week of his life travelling to Sandringham for the weekend. As he had done so often during the last fifty years, he spent two days looking round his beloved estate, inspecting his gardens and greenhouses, his racehorses and farm stock, talking to his staff and planning the future. Queen Alexandra had left England for Corfu, to stay with her brother George, King of Greece, at the same time as the King had travelled to France. Her absence from Sandringham meant solitude for Edward, something he found hard to bear throughout his life and which spurred him to be outside more than was prudent.

A letter from Arthur Cavendish-Bentinck to his brother-in-law Willy James at West Dean, written two days after Edward's death, describes in detail events after the King returned to London on Monday. Throughout the time, Alice Keppel and her two daughters stayed with the Cavendish-Bentincks.

That evening he dined with Agnes Keyser, no one there but Mrs Keppel, she returned to Grafton Street early, much upset. The King had one or two bad attacks of colic, and she thought him quite ill again, very like his Biarritz illness. He left soon after dinner and no bridge was played. On Tuesday she went to see him and he did not seem either better or worse and he told her to bring Venetia [Cavendish-Bentinck's wife] with her to dine and play bridge at the Palace. They, of course, went, he was in fairly good spirits and apparently no worse, played two rubbers, and they left before eleven o'clock.

On Wednesday Sidney Greville was to have given him a small dinner, the Maguires and ourselves, but the King arranged that we were all to dine with him at the Palace as he did not expect he would feel equal to going out. On Wednesday morning a message came putting off the dinner and telling Mrs Keppel to bring Venetia for a game of bridge at 9.30 after dinner. They went, he was pleasant and full of talk, very anxious for V. to see all the things in the private room, but not feeling up to bridge, and V. went into another room to play picquet with Fritz [Ponsonby] leaving Mrs K. to talk to him – they did not stay very long and certainly V. when she came away was not alarmed at his state of health – although of course she thought him ill. On Thursday after Mrs K. came back from seeing him she was in a great state of alarm, and said she knew he was dying.[6]

The Wednesday evening that the two women had been summoned to play bridge after dinner, Edward VII closed the diary he had kept since boyhood with the brief – and rare – entry: 'The king dines alone'.[7] It seemed he knew his life was ending when he was in Biarritz. On his last day he looked out to the Mediterranean from the Hotel du Palais and murmured: 'I shall be sorry to leave Biarritz', adding, 'perhaps for ever'.[8]

Alice Keppel's alarm was heightened by the knowledge that the next day, Thursday, Queen Alexandra would return from Corfu, having been summoned by the Prince of Wales. Given the atmosphere of crisis the King would be surrounded by his family and close household. The Prince of Wales had been anxious not to alarm his mother and his message did not fully indicate the seriousness of the King's illness. In the past Edward had invariably been at Victoria Station to greet his wife when she returned from overseas. On this occasion he was not there and only his absence revealed the gravity of the situation to the Queen.

That evening, in the knowledge that people would have noticed the King's absence from Victoria Station a bulletin signed by his doctor Sir Francis Laking was issued to the papers informing them that the King was 'suffering from bronchitis and that his condition was causing some anxiety.'[9] But the King had had attacks of bronchitis throughout his reign and there was no inkling that his life was in danger. Esher was one of the many who knew Edward's strength of spirit and took heart, even at this late stage.

Personally knowing the king's wonderful powers of recuperation, his determination to fight for every inch of life, I never lost hope. He insisted in rising in the morning and showed fastidiousness about his clothes, rejecting what his valet brought him, and asking for others. He saw Davidson [Sir Arthur Davidson one of the private secretaries] early, and went through some papers. He then saw FK [Francis Knollys] and discussed business, but he was feeble in speech. At eleven, just as he'd asked for Probyn, he had one of the violent fits of coughing which had so terrified his attendants on Thursday. But at midday he saw Cassel, who arrived a few days ago bringing home his sick daughter. The King wanted to hear all the details of her illness [tuberculosis], but Cassel was not allowed to stay more than a few minutes. In the afternoon he walked to the window to look at his canaries, whom he always loved. Princess Victoria was with him. He felt faint, and she got him into his chair just in time. It was the first of his alarming fits which made his medical people abandon all hope that he would live.[10]

By late afternoon the King had lapsed into a coma and he was unconscious when Alice Keppel was summoned to the Palace at 4.30p.m. Perhaps this was as well, for according to Esher, her appearance was: 'a painful and rather theatrical performance which ought never to have happened. It never would, only she sent to the Queen an old letter of the king's written in 1901 [sic. 1902] in which he said that if he was dying he felt sure those about him would allow her to come to him. This was written in a moment of weak emotion when he was recovering from appendicitis.' Esher went on that, contrary to Alice Keppel's later claims, 'The Queen did not kiss her, or say that the Royal Family would "look after her". The Queen shook hands and said something to the effect, "I am sure you have always had a good influence over him" and walked to the window.'[11] Alice Keppel was led out of the room by Princess Victoria, repeating hysterically, 'I never did any harm, there was nothing wrong between us'.[12]

Esher's condemnation of Alice Keppel continued in his journal.

> After that scene Mrs K. went home, and told Mrs Arthur James all *her* story and Mrs James repeated it then and there to Mrs Walter Burns (one of those odious Bentincks). *She* rang up her sister, Mrs Ford, who was at the Ritz Hotel in Paris, and this woman walked round the tables at the restaurant *before* the poor King was dead, telling everyone about Mrs Keppel's visit to B. Palace, and what passed at an interview which any decent woman would have considered the most sacred and solemn of her life.[13]

The King was able to grasp the brief message from the Prince of Wales that his filly Witch of the Air had won the 4.15p.m. at Kempton. Only when they knew that the end was near did those around the King move him from the seat where he had insisted on staying and lie him in bed. At 11.45p.m. he died after a series of heart attacks brought on by cardiac asthma.

The announcement to the crowds waiting outside the palace was poignantly brief: 'The King is Dead'. The effect was stunning. Only those close to the events had known the King was dying. As befitted a man of such zest and enjoyment of life, the transition from life to death occurred unnoticed to the public at large. They would never carry an image of him as an invalid, but to the end, the portly smiling figure he had been throughout his reign, lifting his hat with an old-world courtesy and carrying the ever-present cane and cigar.

On 10 May Esher wrote at length in his journal after being asked to the palace by Queen Alexandra,

Today I said goodbye to our dear King. The Queen sent for me, and there she was in a simple black dress, with nothing to mark especially her widowhood. Moving gently about his room as if he were a child asleep and I honestly believe that this is exactly what has been in her mind all these days . . . The Queen . . . talked for half an hour just as she has always talked to me, with only a slight diminution of her natural gaiety, but with tenderness which betrayed all the love in her soul, and the oh! so natural feeling that she had got him there altogether to herself. In a way she seemed, and is, I am convinced, happy – it is the womanly happiness of complete possession of the man who was the love of her youth, and – as I fervently believe – of all her life. She talked much of their ultimate resting place together, and of the pictures which had been taken of him, as he lies there, and of the impending hour when they take him away . . . I left her, moved just at the end to tears, and she sat down in the little chair which had been placed at the King's bedside. Round the room were all the things just as he had last used them, with his hats hanging on the pegs, as he loved them to be.[14]

The Queen's reluctance to part with her husband accounted for the unusual delay before, on 17 May, the King's body was moved to Westminster Hall where it lay in state for three days guarded by the royal gentleman-at-arms; and by Sir Schomberg McDonell, Secretary to the Office of Works, who evicted the new Home Secretary, Winston Churchill, and a small party of his family, for trying to enter the Palace late on the second evening. McDonell also wrote a critical entry in his diary for the same evening describing the appearance of the Prime Minister, Asquith and his daughter. Asquith was learning against one of the lamp standards watching the people pass: 'I thought his attitude and personal demeanour rather offensive. I fear he had dined well and he seemed to regard the occasion as mere show.'[15] McDonell wrote a contrasting entry on the first day of lying-in-state when: 'The doors were thrown open to the public. They streamed in in huge numbers. The first to pass were three women of the seamstress class: very poorly dressed and very reverent.'[16] Certainly the occasion was not mere show for them, or the 250,000 other people who filed silently pass the catafalque during the three days. On 20 May the King was buried at St George's Windsor, after a funeral procession through the streets of London to Paddington Station witnessed by tends of thousands.

His son King George V, followed by eight other crowned heads of Europe, lead the funeral procession to Windsor and the pageantry of uniforms was fitting for a King who so excelled in the ceremonials of life. But for his style of monarchy – which Edward Grey so aptly described as 'a rare, if not uniform power of blending bonhomie with dignity'[17] – the loyalty of the seamstress women told as much as the fulsome praise offered from high quarters; from the Houses of Parliament, and from governments in Europe and beyond.

Edward left England in the throes of constitutional upheaval and Europe in a state of increasing instability which in four years time would lead to the war he had dreaded and worked so hard to prevent. It was this state of insecurity, at home and abroad which sharpened the universal sense of loss described by Esher in his assessment of Edward:

> The loss of the King, at this moment, seems irreparable. He stands for our country, our Empire and all our people, in the eyes of Europe and of the world. So much did his personality count, that many virtues were attributed to him, and many acts, which he was the first to laugh at. No man ever knew more truly his own strength and weakness. Experience, not knowledge, instinct not reflection, made him a statesman.

After writing that jealousy was 'a thing he could not stand in man or woman', Esher continued.

> Of his relations with the Queen, it is difficult to write. Beyond a doubt, she was always deeply *in love* with the King. The great sorrows of her life were separations from him. Perhaps he never quite realized this. Last year, when he asked her to go to Paris with him *alone* her joy was the joy of a girl. She cried it from the housetops. To the Queen's caprices he yielded, but not always with good grace for his nature was not of the yielding sort. No other woman – however much he cared – could move his resolve a hair's breadth.[18]

Neither the political argument at home nor the uncertainty abroad were an indictment of Edward's kingship. On the contrary he ensured the monarchy's security for the future, setting out by example how it would best be conducted within the society of a modern democracy. Without ever stooping to low populism he was by dint of character a truly popular monarch who managed to keep the crown above the rancour of political conflict, while lending its impartial authority and the strength of his personality, to the benefit of the nation as a whole.

This was confirmed by Edward Grey in his assessment of the King:

> He became intensely and increasingly popular, and, when he died, the unprecedented long-drawn-out procession to the bier of state in Westminster Hall, was a manifestation of genuine and personal sorrow as well as of national mourning.
>
> Popularity such as this centred in a constitutional Sovereign was an immense advantage to the State. The position is one that cannot be combined with responsibility for policy . . . His death was felt as a national loss, especially by his Ministers, who were in the exposed position of responsibility for the conduct of the nation's affairs.[19]

The dynastic character of the monarchy which had been perpetuated throughout Queen Victoria's reign effectively disappeared during Edward's. He strongly supported the cause of monarchy, but knew that his was first and foremost a national institution, not part of an international family network. The trappings of his period died with him, but he set a pattern of sovereignty: the annual routine; the strange mixture of symbolic ceremonial and public accessibility; and the championing of his people abroad, which has been followed by his successors.

'Not a reading man, but full of natural ability, with a sound head and a warm heart'.[20] The verdict of the ninety-year-old Sir Theodore Martin recorded two years before the King's death confirmed how Edward's best characteristics remained constant from his childhood. Beneath the pomp of his position and the way of life to which he became accustomed Edward was essentially a simple man whose faults and qualities were endearingly human.

This was a man for whom people could feel affection, a King whom Balfour would describe after Edward's death as: 'A great constitutional monarch' who, by virtue of his personality, achieved things 'which no amount of "cleverness" would have enabled a smaller man to do.'[21]

Source Notes

CHAPTER ONE: A STIFLING CHILDHOOD.

[Note: Full details of author's names and titles are given in the bibliography]

1. James. *Albert, Prince Consort.* p127.
2. *Dearest Child: Letters between Queen Victoria and the Princess Royal 1858–1861.* (ed Fulford). p115.
3. James. p120.
4. Spencer Sarah, Lady Lyttelton. (correspondence; ed: Wyndham). pp320–321.
5. Greville diary vol II. p214.
6. Magnus. *King Edward VII.* p1.
7. James. pp126–127.
8. Ibid. p127.
9. Ibid. p128.
10. Spencer correspondence. p325.
11. Greville diary vol II. p216.
12. Spencer correspondence. p324.
13. James. p228.
14. Ibid. p229.
15. Ibid. p232.
16. St Aubyn. *Edward VII.* pp16–17.
17. *Beloved Mama: Private Correspondence of Queen Victoria and the Crown Princess 1878–1885.* (ed Fulford). p85.
18. James. p245.
19. Greville vol II. p455.
20. Esher papers.
21. Diary of Lady Frederick Cavendish (vol I). p26.
22. Spencer correspondence. p326.
23. Ibid. p371.
24. James. p236.
25. Ibid. p238.
26. Lee. *King Edward VII* vol I. p30.
27. Magnus. p8.
28. James. p239.
29. *Dearest Child.* p144.
30. Magnus. p12.
31. Ibid. p10.
32. Lee. (vol I). pp30–31.
33. James. p244.
34. A. Ponsonby. *Henry Ponsonby.* p90.

35. Greville diary vol II. p456.
36. Spencer correspondence. p397.
37. James. p246.

**CHAPTER TWO: A NEW WORLD,
FRIENDS AND PLACES**

1. Magnus. p8.
2. Lincolnshire papers.
3. Ibid.
4. Ibid.
5. Ibid.
6. Ibid.
7. Cadogan papers.
8. Magnus. pp8–9.
9. James. p257.
10. Broadley. *Boyhood of a Great King.* p313.
11. Ibid. p314.
12. Lee. (vol I). p41.
13. Ibid. p44.
14. Magnus. p22.
15. Cadogan papers.
16. Lincolnshire papers.
17. Lee. (vol I). p54.
18. Ibid. p57.
19. Ibid. p60.
20. St Aubyn. p43.
21. Lee. (vol I). p63.
22. Ibid. p63.
23. Hibbert. *Edward VII.* p29.
24. Lee (vol I). p69.
25. Magnus. p28.
26. *Dearest Child.* pp173–174.
27. Cavendish diary. (vol I). p95.
28. Lee. (vol I). p76.
29. Esher papers.
30. Lee (vol I). p83.
31. Ibid. p89.
32. Ibid. p90.
33. Ibid. p90.
34. Ibid. p108.
35. *Illustrated London News,* 10 August 1960. Quoted in Roby. *The King, The Press and the People.* p65.

36. Lee. (vol I). p101.
37. Ibid. p102.
38. Ibid. p103.
39. Corti. *The English Empress.* p59.
40. Kennedy. *My Dear Duchess.* pp143–144.
41. Lincolnshire papers.
42. Ibid.
43. James. p268.
44. Lincolnshire papers.
45. *Dearest Mama.* p30.

**CHAPTER THREE: MARRIAGE AND THE
PUBLIC GAZE**

1. James. p251.
2. Battiscombe. *Queen Alexandra.* pp23–24.
3. Magnus. p45.
4. *Dearest Child.* p354.
5. Magnus. p49.
6. Battiscombe. p19.
7. Ibid. p20.
8. *Dearest Child.* pp337–338.
9. Ibid. p350.
10. Magnus. p49.
11. *Dearest Child.* pp357.
12. Ibid. p353.
13. Ibid. p350.
14. Ibid. p356.
15. Magnus. p53.
16. *My Dear Duchess.* pp180–181.
17. Lincolnshire papers.
18. Stanley. (vol II). p64.
19. Ibid. p69.
20. Ibid. p87.
21. Ibid. p76.
22. Ibid. p68.
23. Ibid. p69.
24. *Darling Loosy.* Longford (ed). p89.
25. *My Dear Duchess.* p214.
26. Downe papers.
27. Stanley (vol II). p126.
28. Ibid. p127.
29. Hibbert. p80.

30. Rose. *King George V.* pp1–2.
31. Cavendish diary (vol II). p69.
32. Lincolnshire papers.
33. Magnus. p108.
34. Hibbert. pp107–108.
35. *Darling Loosy.* p94.
36. James papers.
37. Ibid.
38. Lincolnshire papers.
39. Battiscombe. p118.
40. Lincolnshire papers.

CHAPTER FOUR: IRELAND AND INDIA

 1. Hibbert. p109.
 2. Lincolnshire papers.
 3. Ponsonby. p102.
 4. Ibid. p103.
 5. Hibbert. p108.
 6. Ponsonby. p101.
 7. Magnus. p116.
 8. Lee (vol I). p222.
 9. Magnus. pp116–117.
10. Ibid. p118.
11. Ibid. p119.
12. Ibid. p120.
13. Devonshire papers.
14. Ibid.
15. Ibid.
16. Ponsonby. p103.
17. Esher papers.
18. Northbrook papers (India Office Records).
19. Ibid.
20. *Darling Loosy.* p101.
21. Magnus. p134.
22. Blake. *Disraeli.* p560.
23. Northbrook papers.
24. Ibid.
25. Ibid.
26. Bradford. *Disraeli.* p323.
27. Northbrook papers.
28. Bradford. p324.
29. Ibid. p325.
30. Magnus. p134.

31. Ponsonby. p272.
32. Lyall papers (India Office Records).
33. Downe papers.
34. *Darling Loosy.* p203.
35. Lincolnshire papers.
36. Hibbert. p129.
37. Lincolnshire papers.
38. Ibid.
39. Ibid.
40. Wodehouse papers (India Office Records).
41. Lee (Vol I). p384.
42. Wodehouse papers.
43. Magnus. p138.
44. Wonnacott papers (India Office Records).
45. Strachey papers (India Office Records).
46. Lincolnshire papers.
47. Lee. p399.
48. Ibid. p399.
49. Ibid. p399.
50. Ibid. p399.
51. Lincolnshire papers.
52. Ibid.
53. Lee. p394.
54. Lutyens. *The Lyttons in India.* p87.
55. Magnus. pp144–145.
56. Ibid. p147.
57. Ibid. p150.

CHAPTER FIVE: SANDRINGHAM

 1. Lincolnshire papers.
 2. Ibid.
 3. Arrowsmith and Hill. *I Zingari.* p29.
 4. *Darling Loosy.* p99.
 5. Lincolnshire papers.
 6. Magnus. p89.
 7. Lincolnshire papers.
 8. Bradford. p324.
 9. Battiscombe. p153.
10. Edward Hamilton diary. (Add MSS 48635).

11. James papers.
12. Ibid.
13. Lincolnshire papers.
14. Ibid.
15. Ibid.
16. Van der Kiste. *Edward VII's Children.* p108.
17. Lincolnshire papers.
18. Ibid.
19. Esher papers.
20. Van der Kiste. p31.
21. Ibid. p35.
22. Lincolnshire papers.
23. Ibid.
24. Hamilton diary. (Add MSS 48635).
25. Magnus. p240.

CHAPTER SIX: POLITICS, WOMEN AND HORSES

1. Lincolnshire papers.
2. Hobhouse. *Inside Asquith's Cabinet.* p101.
3. Ponsonby. pp391-392.
4. Ibid. pp390-391.
5. Lincolnshire papers.
6. Boyle. *A Servant of the Empire.* p58.
7. Magnus. p216.
8. Cadogan papers.
9. Magnus. p161.
10. Booth. *Old Pink 'Un Days.* p127.
11. Hibbert. p152.
12. Hamilton diary. (Add MSS 48632).
13. Magnus. p172.
14. Hamilton diary. (Add MSS 48632).
15. Esher papers.
16. Plumptre. *The Fast Set.* p102.
17. Hamilton diary. (Add MSS 48635).
18. Ibid.
19. Magnus. p217
20. Ibid. p188.
21. Ibid. p189.
22. Lincolnshire papers.
23. Lee. p550.

24. Broadhurst. *Life.* p149.
25. Ibid. pp149-150.
26. Ibid. pp151-153.
27. Hamilton diary. (Add MSS 48632).
28. Magnus. p169.
29. Hamilton diary. (Add MSS 48631).
30. Ibid. (Add MSS 48632).
31. Esher papers.
32. Lincolnshire papers.
33. Warwick. *Afterthoughts.* p37.
34. Magnus. p224.
35. Plumptre. p86.
36. Magnus. p227.
37. Ibid. p228.
38. Devonshire papers.
39. Magnus. p231.
40. Lincolnshire papers.
41. Magnus. pp227-228
42. Ibid. p227.
43. Lincolnshire papers.

CHAPTER SEVEN: TOWARDS THE THRONE

1. Battiscombe. p194.
2. Ibid. p194.
3. Lincolnshire papers.
4. Esher papers.
5. Lincolnshire papers.
6. Ibid.
7. Lee (vol I). p691.
8. Midleton (St John Brodrick). *Record and Reactions.* pp295-296.
9. Magnus. p211.
10. Ibid. p214.
11. Hough. *Edward and Alexandra.* p230.
12. Plumptre. p49.
13. Lincolnshire papers.
14. Ibid.
15. Ibid.
16. Lambton. *Men and Horses I Have Known.* p228.
17. *Darling Loosy.* p65.
18. Lincolnshire papers.

19. Esher papers.
20. Lincolnshire papers.
21. Esher papers.
22. Ibid.
23. Lincolnshire papers.
24. Lee (vol I). p801.
25. Edward Hamilton diary. (ed. D.W.R. Bahlman). p395.
26. Lee (vol I). p802.

CHAPTER EIGHT: THE NEW MONARCHY
1. Devonshire papers.
2. Esher papers.
3. Hamilton diary. (ed. Bahlman). p395.
4. Lee (vol II). p22.
5. Ibid. p25.
6. Magnus. pp274-275.
7. Esher papers.
8. Lees-Milne. *The Enigmatic Edwardian*. p156.
9. Esher papers.
10. Ibid.
11. Lincolnshire papers.
12. Esher papers.
13. Ibid.
14. Ibid.
15. Ibid.
16. Ibid.
17. Midleton. p128.
18. Ibid. pp161-162.
19. Ibid. p149.
20. Esher papers.
21. Midleton. p150.
22. Esher papers.
23. Midleton. p162.
24. Ibid. p167.
25. Ibid. p163.
26. Magnus. p295.
27. Midleton. p171.
28. Lincolnshire papers.
29. Lee (vol II). p26.
30. Ibid. p26.

31. Ziegler. *Edward VIII*. p247.
32. Hamilton diary. (ed. Bahlman). p398.
33. Ibid. p399.
34. Ibid. p400.
35. Ibid. p400.
36. Ibid. p402.
37. Lincolnshire papers.
38. Ibid.
39. Esher papers.
40. F. Ponsonby. *Recollections of Three Reigns*. p102.
41. Ibid. p103.
42. Ibid. p103.
43. Hamilton diary. (ed. Bahlman). p401.
44. Esher papers.
45. *Darling Loosy*. p266.
46. Esher papers.
47. Ibid.
48. Ibid.
49. Ibid.
50. Ibid.
51. Ibid.
52. Ibid.
53. Lee (vol II). p96.
54. Ibid. p98.
55. Esher papers.
56. Lincolnshire papers.
57. Esher papers.
58. Ibid.
59. Lincolnshire papers.
60. Ibid.

CHAPTER NINE: ALICE KEPPEL
1. Lincolnshire papers.
2. Ibid.
3. Esher papers.
4. Sermoneta. *Things Past*. p140.
5. Cassel papers.
6. Ibid.
7. Ibid.
8. Ibid.
9. Lincolnshire papers.

10. Hamilton diary. (ed. Balhman). p409.
11. Cassel papers.
12. Ibid.
13. Ibid.
14. Esher papers.
15. Ibid.
16. Lincolnshire papers.
17. Ibid.
18. Ibid.
19. Brook-Shepherd. *Uncle of Europe.* p140.
20. Ibid. p140.
21. Esher papers.
22. Ibid.
23. Ibid.
24. Brook-Shepherd. p142.
25. Battiscombe. p209.
26. Lincolnshire papers.
27. Ibid.
28. Ibid.
29. Magnus. p260.
30. Esher papers.
31. Lincolnshire papers.
32. Ibid.
33. Ibid.

CHAPTER TEN: THE KING AND HIS MINISTERS

1. Lincolnshire papers.
2. Ibid.
3. Ibid.
4. Eshers papers.
5. Ibid.
6. Ibid.
7. Ibid.
8. Ibid.
9. Magnus. p322.
10. Fitzroy. *Memoirs* (vol I). pp161–162.
11. Wilson. *Sir Henry Campbell-Bannerman.* p625.
12. Lincolnshire papers.
13. Egrement. *Balfour.* p148.
14. Esher papers.

15. Balfour papers. (Add MSS 49683).
16. Esher papers.
17. Lansdowne papers.
18. Ibid.
19. Ibid.
20. St Aubyn. p299.
21. Lansdowne papers.
22. Ibid.
23. Ibid.
24. Ibid.
25. Ibid.
26. Ibid.
27. Ibid.
28. Ibid.
29. Ibid.
30. Lincolnshire papers.
31. Ibid.
32. Esher papers.
33. Ibid.
34. Egremont. p159.
35. Balfour papers. (Add MSS 49718).
36. Ibid.
37. Esher papers.
38. Wilson. pp428–429.
39. Magnus. p347.
40. Wilson. p429.
41. Ibid. p429.
42. Ibid. p435.
43. Ibid. p432.
44. Ibid. p444.
45. Ibid. p445.
46. Ibid. p453.
47. F. Ponsonby. p234.
48. Wilson. p145.
49. Magnus. p348.
50. Wilson. p465.
51. Esher papers.
52. Wilson. p506.
53. Esher papers.
54. Wilson. p511.
55. Ibid. p556.
56. Ibid. p556.
57. Ibid. p486.
58. Hibbert. p211.

CHAPTER ELEVEN: ROYAL DIPLOMAT
1. Balfour papers. (Add MSS 49683).
2. Lansdowne papers.
3. Lincolnshire papers.
4. Lansdowne papers.
5. Hardinge papers.
6. Magnus. p307.
7. F. Ponsonby. p155.
8. Magnus. p308.
9. F. Ponsonby. p156.
10. Ibid. p159.
11. Magnus. p310.
12. F. Ponsonby. p161.
13. Lansdowne papers.
14. Ibid.
15. Lee (vol II). p236.
16. Ibid. p237.
17. Magnus. p312.
18. Brook-Shepherd. p197.
19. F. Ponsonby. p171.
20. Ibid. p172.
21. Magnus. p314.
22. Ibid. p337.
23. Esher papers.
24. Lee (vol II). p169.
25. Ibid. p169.
26. Esher papers.
27. Ibid.
28. Magnus. p339.
29. Lansdowne papers.
30. Magnus. p368.
31. Wilson. p145.
32. Magnus. p395.
33. Wilson. p143.
34. F. Ponsonby. p228.
35. Wilson. p144.
36. Esher papers.
37. Lincolnshire papers.
38. Magnus. p395.
39. Barker. *Eminent Edwardians*. p75.
40. Magnus. p409.

CHAPTER TWELVE: PEACE AND UNREST
1. Esher papers.
2. *Darling Loosy*. p74.
3. Balfour papers.
4. Esher papers.
5. Ibid.
6. Lincolnshire papers.
7. Battiscombe. p199.
8. Esher papers.
9. Lincolnshire papers.
10. Esher papers.
11. Ibid.
12. Ibid.
13. Van der Kiste. p93.
14. Esher papers.
15. Ibid.
16. Lincolnshire papers.
17. Ibid.
18. Esher papers.
19. Ibid.
20 Ibid.
21. Ibid.
22. Ibid.
23. RA King Edward VII's Diary. 25 June–1 July 1906.
24. Lincolnshire papers.
25. Lee (vol II). p468.
26. Esher papers.
27. Ibid.
28. Ibid.
29. Ibid.
30. Ibid.
31. Semon. *Autobiography*. p267.
32. Lee (vol II). p633.
33. Ibid. p633.
34. Ibid. p634.
35. Esher papers.
36. Lee (vol II). p642.
37. Magnus. p417.

CHAPTER THIRTEEN: MONARCHY IN DEMOCRACY
1. Esher papers.
2. Ibid.
3. Magnus. p306.
4. Esher papers.

5. Esher papers.
6. Hardinge. *Old Diplomacy*. p158.
7. Hardinge papers.
8. Lloyd George papers.
9. Magnus. p389.
10. Esher papers.
11. Lee (vol II). p468.
12. Ibid. p404.
13. Lincolnshire papers.
14. Lee (vol II). p400.
15. Ibid. p402.
16. Lincolnshire papers.
17. Wilson. p560.
18. Hibbert. p210.
19. Lincolnshire papers.
20. Devonshire papers.
21. Lincolnshire papers.
22. Ibid.
23. F. Owen. *Lloyd George*. p162.
24. Lees–Milne. p200.
25. Esher papers.
26. Magnus. p430.
27. Lloyd George papers.
28. Owen. p182.
29. Esher papers.
30. Spender and Asquith. *Asquith*. p257.
31. Esher papers.
32. Magnus. p437.
33. Esher papers.
34. Magnus. p438.
35. Esher papers.
36. Ibid.
37. Spender and Asquith. p270.
38. Magnus. p450.

CHAPTER FOURTEEN: A MONARCHY FOR THE FUTURE

1. Hardinge papers.
2. Hardinge. p186.
3. Redesdale memoirs (vol I). p182.
4. Spender and Asquith. p279.
5. Esher papers.
6. James papers.
7. Magnus. p455.
8. Lee (vol II). p709.
9. Ibid. p716.
10. Esher papers.
11. Ibid.
12. Ibid.
13. Ibid.
14. Ibid.
15. Schomberg McDonell diary.
16. Ibid.
17. Grey. *Twenty Five Years*. (vol I). p206.
18. Esher papers.
19. Grey. (vol I). pp207-208.
20. Esher papers.
21. Lansdowne papers.

BIBLIOGRAPHY

[Place of Publication: London unless otherwise stated.]

Adams, W. W. S. *Edwardian Portraits*. (Secker and Warburg 1957).
Airlie, Mabell, Countess of. *Thatched with Gold: Memoirs*. (Hutchinson 1962).
Allfrey, Alfred. *Edward VII and his Jewish Court*. (Weidenfeld and Nicolson 1991).
Antrim, Lady Louisa. *Recollections*. (King's Stone Press 1937).
Aronson, Theo. *The King in Love*. (John Murray 1988).
Arrowsmith, R. L. and Hill, B. J. W. *The History of I Zingari*. (Stanley Paul and Co 1991).
Asquith, Margot. *Autobiography*. (Eyre and Spottiswoode 1962).

Bahlman, Dudley W. R. (ed). *The Diary of Sir Edward Hamilton*. (University of Hull Press 1993).
Bailey, John. (ed.). *The Diary of Lady Frederick Cavendish* (2 vols). (John Murray 1927).
Barker, Dudley. *Prominent Edwardians*. (George Allen and Unwin 1969).
Barnes, John and Nicholson, David. (eds). *The Leo Amery Diaries, (Vol I 1896-1929)*. (Hutchinson 1980).
Battiscombe, Georgina. *Queen Alexandra*. (Constable 1969).
Blake, Robert. *Disraeli*. (Eyre and Spottiswoode 1966).
Bennett, Daphne. *Vicky Princess Royal of England and German Empress*. (Collins and Harvill Press 1971).
Bennett, Geoffrey. *Charlie B: A Biography of Admiral Lord Charles Beresford*. (Daunay 1968).
Benson, E. F. *As We Were: A Victorian Peep-Show*. (Longmans, Green and Co 1930).

Benson, E. F. *King Edward VII: An Appreciation*. (Longmans, Green and Co 1933).

Benson, E. F. *The Kaiser and the English Relations*. (Longmans, Green and Co 1936).

Bentley-Cranch, Dana. *Edward VII. Image of an Era*. (London HMSO and National Portrait Gallery 1992).

Beresford, Lord Charles. *The Memoirs of Admiral Lord Charles Beresford*. (Metheun 1914).

Black, Gerry. *Lender to the Lords. Giver to the Poor. (A Biography of Samuel Lewis)*. (Vallentine Mitchell 1992).

Blake, Robert. *Disraeli*. (Eyre and Spottiswoode 1966).

Blunden, Margaret. *The Countess of Warwick*. (Cassell 1967).

Bolitho, Hector. *Victoria: The Widow and Her Son*. (Cobden–Sanderson 1934).

Booth, J. B. *Old Pink 'Un Days*. (Grant Richards Ltd 1924).

Booth, J. B. *Pink Parade*. (Thornton Butterworth 1933).

Booth, J. B. *Sporting Times*. (T. Werner Laurie 1938).

Booth, J. B. *The Days We Knew*. (T. Werner Laurie 1943).

Booth, J. B. *Palmy Days*. (Richards Press 1957).

Boyle, Clara. *A Servant of the Empire*. (Methuen and Co 1938).

Bradford, Sarah. *Disraeli*. (Weidenfeld and Nicolson 1982).

Bridge, F. R. *Great Britain and Austria-Hungary 1906-1914. A Diplomatic History*. (London School of Economics and Weidenfeld and Nicolson 1972).

Broadhurst, H. *A Life*. (Hutchinson and Co 1901).

Broadley, A. M. *The Boyhood of a Great Kind 1841–1858*. (Harper and Brothers 1906).

Brock Michael and Eleanor. (eds). *H. H. Asquith: Letters to Venetia Stanley*. (Oxford University Press 1982).

Brook-Shepherd, Gordon. *Uncle of Europe*. (Collins 1975).

Brough, J. *The Prince and the Lily*. (Hodder and Stoughton 1975).

Bruce, H. J. *Silken Dalliance*. (Constable 1946).

Bryant, Sir Arthur. *A History of Britain the British People. Vol III: The Search for Justice*. (Collins 1990).

Camplin, James. *Rise of the Plutocrats: Wealth and Power in Edwardian England*. (Constable 1970).

Cannadine, David. *Lord and Landlords: The Aristocracy and the Towns 1774–1967*. (Leicester 1980).

Cecil, Lady Gwendolin. *Life of Robert, Marquis of Salisbury*. (Hodder and Stoughton 1932).

Churchill, Winston S. *Lord Randolf Churchill*. (Macmillan 1906).

Churchill, Winston S. *My Early Life: A Roving Commission*. (Butterworth 1930).

Cornwallis-West. *Edward Hey-Days*. (Putnam 1930).

Corti. *The English Empress: A Study in the Relations Between Queen Victoria and her Eldest Daughter*. (Cassell 1957).

Cowles, V. *Edward VII and His Circle*. (Hamish Hamilton 1956).

Cresswell, Mrs Louise. *Eighteen Years on the Sandringham Estate*. (Temple 1888).

Crewe, 1st Marquis of. *Lord Rosebery*. (John Murray 1931).

Cust, Sir Lionel. *King Edward VII and his Court*. (John Murray 1930).

Dangerfield, George. *The Strange Death of Liberal England*. (MacGibbon and Kee 1966).

Dangerfield, George. *Victoria's Heir: The Education of a Prince*. (Constable 1941).

David, Edward. (ed). *Inside Asquith's Cabinet. From the Diaries of Charles Hobhouse*. (John Murray 1977).

Donaldson, Frances. *Edward VIII*. (Weidenfeld and Nicolson 1974).

Eckardstein, Baron von. *Ten Years at the Court of St James's 1895-1905*. (Thornton Butterworth 1921).

Edwards, H. *The Tragedy of King Edward VII: A Psychological Study*. (Victor Gollancz 1928).

Egremont, Max. *Balfour. A Life of A. J. Balfour*. (Collins 1980).

Ensor, Robert. *England 1870-1914*. (Oxford University Press 1936).

Fisher, Admiral of the Fleet, Lord. *Memories*. (Hodder and Stoughton 1919).

Fitzroy, Sir Almeric. *Memoirs* (2 vols). (Hutchinson and Co 1925).

Fraser, Peter. *Lord Esher: A Political Biography*. (Hart-Davis MacGibbon 1973).

Fulford, Roger. *The Prince Consort*. (Macmillan 1949).

Fulford, Roger. *Queen Victoria*. (Collins 1951).

Fulford, Roger. (ed). *Dearest Child: Letters between Queen Victoria and the Princess Royal 1858-1861*. (Evans 1964).

Fulford, Roger. (ed). *Dearest Mama: Letters between Queen Victoria and the Crown Princess of Prussia 1861–1864*. (Evans 1968).

Fulford, Roger. (ed). *Your Dear Letter: Private Correspondence of Queen Victoria and the Crown Princess of Prussia 1865–1870*. (Evans 1971).

Fulford, Roger (ed). *Darling Child: Letters between Queen Victorian and the Crown Princess of Prussia 1871–1878*. (Evans 1976).

Fulford, Roger (ed). *Beloved Mama: Private Correspondence of Queen Victoria and the Crown Princess of Prussia 1878–1885*. (Evans 1981).

Gavin, Catherine. *Edward the Seventh*. (Jonathan Cape 1941).

Gernsheim, Alison and Helmut. *Edward VII and Queen Alexandra: A Biography in Word and Picture*. (Muller 1962).

Gore, John. *King George V: A Personal Memoir*. (John Murray 1941).

Grey, Sir Edward, 1st Viscount Grey of Falloden. *Twenty-five Years 1892–1916*. (2 vols). (Hodder and Stoughton 1925).

Gwyn, Stephen and Tuckwell, Gertrude. *The Life of Sir Charles Dilke*. (2 vols). (John Murray 1917).

Haldane, Richard Burdon, 1st Viscount Haldane. *An Autobiography*. (Hodder and Stoughton 1929).

Hall, Richard. *Lovers on the Nile*. (Quartet Books 1981).

———— ∾ ————

Hardinge of Penshurst, Lord. *Old Diplomacy*. (John Murray 1947).

Havers, Sir Michael (and others). *The Royal Baccarat Scandal*. (William Kimber 1977).

Hough, Richard. *Edward and Alexandra. Their Private and Public Lives*. (Hodder and Stoughton 1992).

James, Robert Rhodes. *The Prince Consort*. (Hamish Hamilton 1982).

Jenkins, Roy. *Asquith*. (Collins 1965).

Jenkins, Roy. *Sir Charles Dilke: A Victorian Tragedy*. (Collins 1958).

Jones, L. E. *An Edwardian Youth*. (Macmillan 1956).

Judd, Denis. *Edward VII: A Pictorial Biography*. (Macdonald and Jane's 1975).

Julian, Philippe. *Edward and the Edwardians*. (Sidgwick and Jackson 1967).

Kennedy, A. L. *My Dear Duchess*. (John Murray 1956).

Keppel, Sonia. *Edwardian Daughter*. (Hamish Hamilton 1958).

Kinley, Roby. *The King, The Press, And The People*. (Barrie and Jenkins 1975).

Lambton, The Hon G. *Men and Horses I Have Known*. (Thornton Butterworth Ltd 1924).

Lang, T. *My Darling Daisy*. (Michael Joseph 1966).

Langtry, Lillie. *The Days I Knew*. (Hutchinson 1925).

Lee, Sir Sidney. *King Edward VII. A Biography*. (2 vols). (Macmillan Co 1927).

Lees-Milne, James. *The Enigmatic Edwardian. The Life of Reginald, 2nd Viscount Esher*. (Sidgwick and Jackson 1986).

Leslie, Anita. *Edwardians in Love*. (Hutchinson 1972).

Longford, Elizabeth. *Victoria R.I.* (Weidenfeld and Nicolson 1964).

Longford, Elizabeth. (ed). *Darling Loosy. Letters to Princess Louise 1856–1939*. (Weidenfeld and Nicolson 1991).

Lutyens, Mary. *The Lyttons in India*. (John Murray 1979).

Lyttelton, Lady (Sarah Spencer). *Correspondence*. (ed: great-granddaughter, The Hon Mrs Hugh Wyndham). (John Murray 1912).

Magnus, Philip. *King Edward the Seventh*. (John Murray 1964).

Magnus, Philip. *Gladstone*. (John Murray 1960).

Marder, A. J. (ed). *Fear God and Dread Nought: Correspondence of Admiral of the Fleet Lord Fisher of Kilverstone*. (3 vols). (Jonathan Cape 1952).

Marie, Queen of Roumania. *The Story of My Life*. (Cassell and Co 1934).

Marsh, R. *Trainer to Two Kings*. (Cassell and Co 1925).

Martin, Ralph G. *Lady Randolf Churchill. A Biography*. (2 vols). (Cassell and Co 1969).

Martin Theodore. *The Life of H.R.H. the Prince Consort*. (5 vols). (Smith, Elder and Co 1875–80).

Maurios, Andre. *King Edward and His Times*. (Cassell and Co 1933).

Middlemas, Keith. *The Life and Times of King Edward VII*. (Weidenfeld and Nicolson 1972).

Midleton, Earl of (St John Brodrick). *Records and Reactions.* (John Murray 1939).
Morley, John (1st Viscount Morley). *Recollections.* (Macmillan and Co 1918).
Munz, Sigmund. *King Edward VII at Marienbad.* (Hutchinson and Co 1934).

Nevill, R. *The Sport of Kings.* (Methuen and Co 1926).
Newton, Lord. *Lord Lansdowne, A Biography.* (Macmillan and Co 1929).
Newton, Lord. *Lord Lyons: A Record of British Diplomacy.* (E. Arnold 1913).
Nicolson, Harold. *King George V.* (Constable 1952).
Nicolson, Harold. *Sir Arthur Nicolson, 1st Lord Carnock.* (Constable and Co 1930).
Nowell-Smith, Simon (ed). *Edward England 1901–1914.* (Oxford University Press 1964).

Onslow, Richard. *The Squire: A Biography of George Abington Baird.* (Harrap 1980).
Owen, Frank. *Tempestuous Journey: Lloyd George, His Life and Times.* (Hutchinson and Co 1937).

Paget, Lady Walpurga. *Embassies of Other Days.* (Hutchinson and Co 1923).
Pless, Princess Daisy of. *From My Private Diary.* (John Murray 1931).
Pless, Princess Daisy of. *What I Left Unsaid.* (Cassell and Co 1936).
Plumptre, George. *Royal Gardens.* (Collins 1981).
Plumptre, George. *The Fast Set. The World of Edwardian Racing.* (Andre Deutsch 1985).
Ponsonby, Arthur. *Henry Ponsonby: Queen Victoria's Private Secretary. His Life from his Letters.* (Macmillan and Co 1942).
Ponsonby, Sir Frederick. (1st Lord Sysonby). *Recollections of Three Reigns.* (Eyre and Spottiswoode 1951).
Pope-Hennessey, James. *Lord Crewe: The Likeness of a Liberal.* (Constable and Co 1955).
Pope-Hennessey, James. *Queen Mary.* (Allen and Unwin 1959).
Prothero, Rowland E. and Bradley, Very Rev G. G. (eds). *The Life and Correspondence of Arthur Penrhyn Stanley.* (2 vols). (John Murray 1893).

Redesdale, Lord. *King Edward VII: A Memory* (Hutchinson and Co 1915).
Redesdale, Lord. *Memories.* (2 vols). (Hutchinson and Co 1915, 1916).
Redesdale, Lord. *Further Memories.* (Hutchinson and Co 1917).
Roby, Kinley. *The King, The Press and the People. A Study of Edward VII.* (Barrie and Jenkins 1975).
Rose, Kenneth. *King George V.* (Weidenfeld and Nicolson 1983).
Rossmore, Lord. *Things I Can Tell.* (Eveleigh Nash 1912).
Russell, William Howard. *The Prince of Wales Tour: A Diary in India.* (London 1877).

St Aubyn, Giles. *Edward VII. Prince and King.* (Atheneum, New York 1979).
Semon, Sir Felix. *Autobiography.* (Jarrolds 1926).

———— ❧ ————

Sermoneta, Duchess of. *Things Past*. (Hutchinson and Co 1929).

Seth-Smith, Michael. *Bred for the Purple*. (Leslie Frewin 1969).

Sewell, J. P. C. *Personal Letters of King Edward VII*. (Hutchinson and Co 1931).

Simpson, Colin. *Artful Partners. Bernard Berenson and Joseph Duveen*. (Macmillan and Co 1986).

Sitwell, Osbert. *Left Hand! Right Hand!* (4 vols). (Macmillan and Co. 1945-50)

Spender, J. A. and Asquith, Cyril. *Life of Herbert Henry Asquith, Lord Oxford and Asquith*. (2 vols). (Hutchinson and Co 1932).

Steiner, Z. S. *The Foreign Office and Foreign Policy 1898-1914*. (Cambridge University Press 1970).

Suffield, Lord. *My Memoirs*. (Herbert Jenkins Ltd 1913).

Sunderland, D. *The Yellow Earl*. (Cassell and Co 1965).

Sykes, Christopher. *Four Studies in Loyalty*. (Collins 1946).

Trevelyan, G. M. *Grey of Falloden: The Life of Sir Edward Grey, Afterwards Viscount Grey of Falloden*. (Longmans 1937).

Tuchman, Barbara. *The Proud Tower*. (Macmillan 1966).

Van der Kiste, John. *Edward VII's Children*. (Alan Sutton 1989).

Vansittart, Lord. *The Mist Progression: The Autobiography of Lord Vansittart*. (Hutchinson and Co 1958).

Warwick, Countess of. *Afterthoughts*. (Cassell and Co 1931).

Warwick, Countess of. *Life's Ebb and Flow*. (Cassell and Co 1929).

Watson, A. E. T. *Edward VII as a Sportsman*. (Longmans Green and Co 1911).

Whitwell-Wilson, Philip, ed. *The Greville Diary*. (2 vols). (William Heinemann Ltd 1927).

Wilson, John C. B. *A Life of Sir Henry Campbell-Bannerman*. (Constable 1973).

Wortham, H. E. *The Delightful Profession: Edward VII, A Study in Kingship*. (Jonathan Cape 1931).

Ziegler, Philip. *Edward VIII. The Official Biography*. (Collins 1990).

ACKNOWLEDGEMENTS

I must acknowledge the gracious permission of Her Majesty The Queen to quote material from the Royal Archives and elsewhere which is subject to Her Majesty's copyright. I would also like to acknowledge the gracious permission of His Majesty the King of Norway for permission to quote extracts from letters written by his grandmother Princess Maud, later Queen of Norway.

The principal manuscript sources for the text are the papers of Reginald Brett, 2nd Viscount Esher, and Charles Wynn-Carrington, 3rd Lord Carrington and later 1st Marquess of Lincolnshire. I would like to particularly thank the present Lord Esher and Lord Lincolnshire's great-grandsons, Julian Llewellen Palmer and William Legge-Bourke, for granting me unrestricted access to these archives. The Esher papers are deposited at Churchill College, Cambridge. The original Lincolnshire papers that I consulted are held by the family; copies of most of the archive are deposited on microfilm at the Bodleian Library, Oxford.

In addition I would like to thank the following people for allowing me to research and quote from manuscript archives. The Trustees of the Broadland Archives (Cassel Papers deposited at the Library of Southampton University); Earl Cadogan (Cadogan papers deposited at the House of Lords Record Office); the Trustees of the Chatsworth Settlement (Devonshire papers held at Chatsworth); the Trustees of the

Edward James Foundation (James papers held at West Dean Park); the Trustees of the Bowood Manuscript Collection (Lansdowne papers held at Bowood); the British Library Board (Balfour papers deposited at British Library, Edward Hamilton diary deposited at British Library); Oriental and India Office Collections of the British Library (Northbrooke papers, Lyall papers, Wodehouse papers, Strachey papers, Wonnacott papers all deposited at the British Library Oriental and India Office Collections); Clerk of the Record Office, House of Lords acting on behalf of the Beaverbrook Foundation Trustees (Lloyd George papers, deposited at the House of Lords Record Office); Syndics of Cambridge University Library (Hardinge of Penshurst papers, deposited at Cambridge University Library); Lord Downe (Downe papers, deposited at North Yorkshire County Record Office).

I would like to express my thanks to all the publishers of books from which extracts are quoted, and documented in the source notes and bibliography.

For their assistance and advice during my research I must thank the staffs of: the Bodleian Library, the British Library, the Cambridge University Library, the Devonshire Collections, the House of Lords Library, the India Office Library, the London Library, the National Library of Scotland, the North Yorkshire County Record Office, the Staffordshire County Record Office, and the University of Southampton Library.

The following people all helped with advice, answers to queries, or guidance towards sources of information and I am most grateful for their patient assistance: The Earl of Balfour, Mark Bence-Jones, Gerry Black, Lord Brabourne, Viscount Bridgeman, Gwyneth Campling, Lord Carrington, the Earl of Clarendon, Viscount Cobham, Robin Compton, Peter Day, Lady de Bellaigue, Lord Deedes, the Duke of Devonshire, Frances Dimond, Viscount Dunluce, Oliver Everett, Dr Kate Fielden, Lady Mary Findlay, Sir Hamish Forbes, Christopher Gibbs, Stanley Hodgkinson, Sharon Kusunoki, James Lees-Milne, Vicky Llewellen Palmer, Hector McDonell, Hugh Montgomery-Massingberd, Peter Sarginson, Charles Sebag-Montefiore, the Earl of Shelburne, the late Earl of Southesk, Colin Simpson, Norman Stone, the Countess of Sutherland, Hugo Vickers, Dr Christopher Woolgar, and Philip Ziegler.

I owe a great debt of thanks to Kenneth Rose who made many suggestions, and read the manuscript. Hubert Ashton similarly helped

INDEX